CONTEMPORARY COPTIC NUNS

STUDIES IN
COMPARATIVE RELIGION

Frederick M. Denny, General Editor

CONTEMPORARY COPTIC NUNS

Pieternella van Doorn-Harder

UNIVERSITY OF SOUTH CAROLINA PRESS

Published in Columbia, South Carolina, by the
University of South Carolina Press

Manufactured in the United States of America

Library of Congress Cataloging-in-Publication Data

Doorn-Harder, Pieternella van, 1956–
Contemporary Coptic nuns / Pieternella van Doorn-Harder.
p. cm. — (Studies in comparative religion)
Includes bibliographical references and index.
ISBN 1–57003–034–0
1. Monasticism and religious orders for women—Coptic Church—History—20th Century. 2. Monasticism and religious orders for women—Egypt—History—20th century. 3. Egypt—Church history—20th century. I. Title. II. Series: Studies in comparative religion (Columbia, S.C.)
BX137.3.D66 1995
271'.98—dc20 94-18770

CONTENTS

GENERAL EDITOR'S PREFACE

As editor of a scholarly book series in comparative religion, I am always on the alert for unusual projects that have something new and important to say. For a decade I have been looking for a manuscript dealing with Christianity in the context of religious studies, or comparative religion, not along the usual lines of theology or church history. How delighted I was when I learned of this work on Coptic nuns. If books treating Christianity from a comparative religion standpoint are rare as hen's teeth, books in English treating Coptic Christianity from any perspective are far rarer. Now, to have a book that addresses Coptic Christianity, from a religious studies perspective, and with a focus on women's religious lives is a series editor's idea of a triple crown.

Dr. van Doorn-Harder's book fills a huge lacuna by providing a comprehensive study of Coptic nuns within their ecclesiastical, social, spiritual, cultural, and historical contexts. The very ancient Coptic community of Egypt has been undergoing a tremendous revival in recent decades, and at a time when Islamic revival is itself one of the world's major religious stories. The Coptic tradition, from its early history, has often been marked by martyrdom and monasticism, so that a particularly powerful vision of the relationship between the everyday world and transcendent reality has been cultivated. *Contemporary Coptic Nuns* leads us through the special world of Coptic spirituality, which is certainly involved with isolation and secrecy, but which also provides for ordinary Coptic Christians an indispensable connection with the saints and the way of salvation. Although Coptic nuns are not leaders at the level of ordained clergy, they are nonetheless at the highest imaginable level of spiritual authority in the real world where the monastic and lay communities have always been mutually engaged in devotion and sanctification.

Frederick Mathewson Denny

PREFACE

A photograph in *Magallet al-Kirāza,* the periodical of the Coptic Orthodox Patriarchate, shows a group of nuns with the patriarch and three bishops in the middle. The surrounding nuns form the background. Quiet eyes look into the camera, mouths are folded in a faint smile, hands are tucked away inside the habits. It is a special occasion. The patriarch has not visited the convent in many years. This time he has come for the installation of the new abbess. He has personally designed a special rite, and to celebrate the event a picture will accompany the text of the rite in the Coptic Church magazine. The photo conveys a general, prototypical image of Coptic women, perhaps of women in Egypt. Women are present in the picture, yet fade beside the men.

After the patriarch and the rest of the clergymen are gone, the convent's gate closes, and the nuns in the photograph return to their real lives—lives few people ever see or know. Visitors can only peek into the convent from the gate or submit their prayers and intercessions in one of the convent's churches.

This present study of Coptic life is in many ways a photo also. The persons pictured, the angle from which the picture is viewed, and the background matter are all changeable. *Contemporary Coptic Nuns* is an attempt to bring this picture to life. Most of all, the book is an endeavor to understand the reasons that induce these (mostly young) women to lead such demanding lives.

I am neither Coptic nor a nun, only an observer. As life within the convents revealed itself to me, my fascination grew. With the help of many people I tried to make sense of what I heard and saw. I owe thanks to many Coptic officials, clergy, and friends who patiently explained and pointed things out to me. First of all I would like to thank the many nuns: the mother superiors—especially Mother Irīnī, Mother

Aghāpī, Mother Maryam, and Mother Odrosīs—and the many nuns and deaconesses all over Egypt who prefer to remain unnamed. In the active community, the former superior, the late Sister Hannah, and the present superior, Sister Aghāpī, were always generous with their time and hospitality. Sister Martha, Sister Ruth, Sister Basilia, and Sister Maria exerted their patience in trying to answer the myriad questions I had. But in fact, I owe thanks to all the members of the Sisters of St. Mary. Their abbot, Bishop Athanasius from Beni Suef, took many an hour from his busy schedule to show me the Coptic universe. His Holiness Patriarch Shenouda III twice granted me an interview. Bishop Ammonius of Luxor received me several times with the greatest hospitality and let me visit monastic projects in Upper Egypt. I also thank Bishop Bishoy and Bishop Pola for granting me permission to visit the nuns at the Convent of St. Dimyānah.

Jane Emile Farid, Amani Barsoum, and Neveen Ghali I thank for their friendship and help, as well as the wonderful memories I have of the many trips to Coptic sanctuaries. Other people who generously shared their insights with me were Father Christiaan van Nispen tot Sevenaer, S.J., Father Maurice Martin, S.J., Anitra Kolenkow-Bingham, Otto Meinardus, Hans Daiber, André Droogers, Jan Helderman, and Mr. Tharwat. I hope that the anonymous Comboni novice who translated an article for me from Italian will one day read these words of thanks.

My supervisor, Antonie Wessels, patiently read through drafts and provided ideas, suggestions, and advice. I am greatly indebted to Kari Vogt for helping shape the ideas for this study. I thank my husband, Paul Harder, for his support, patience, and help with the written English. Beatrijs Dijkstra helped prepare the final manuscript. Only Klazien van Pelt and Coby Dijkstra know best how many hours they have put to the cause of this work. Furthermore, I thank all those, both far away and close by, who made it possible for me to publish this study.

The translations of Arabic sources are, unless indicated otherwise, my own. I take responsibility for them, as well as for the whole contents of the book.

The research for this study was completed in the four-year term during which I worked in Cairo. Further research and writing were funded by a one-year grant from the Board of Mission of the Dutch Reformed Church. The board also provided a stipend for an extra trip to Egypt in order that I might further research my findings. For the follow-up research I received a scholarship from the Veihusset Legat in Oslo, Norway, and from the Van Coevorden Adriani Stichting at the Free University in Amsterdam, Netherlands.

Finally I express my gratitude to Hans Bootsma for being my "boss" during the term in Egypt. Without his support and interest this study would never have been completed. Before his passing away he was able to see the fruition of my work into a Ph.D. degree. He would surely have been thrilled to see my book published.

NOTE ON TRANSLITERATION

In this study two versions of Arabic language are used; the Modern Standard Arabic (MSA) and the Egyptian dialect. Most Arabic books are written in MSA, but sometimes they use the Egyptian dialect to quote oral sources. The interviews in this book were conducted in the Egyptian dialect or in a European language. Due to these two types of Arabic, some words will occur alternately in MSA and in the Egyptian dialect. For example, the word for monastery will be written as "dair" when it occurs in a title of a book and as "deir" when it is used in daily speech. The basis for the transliteration system of the Arabic words is the system used in the *International Journal of Middle East Studies.* Book titles and official names will be given in MSA. For the Egyptian dialect, I will follow the *Dictionary of Egyptian Arabic* by Hinds and Badawi as far as the meaning and representation of the words are concerned, but I will use the system of the *Journal* for the transliteration.

One of the characteristic pronunciations in the Egyptian dialect is that the "j" is pronounced as "g" (as in "go"), but in Upper Egypt it is pronounced as "j." Most of the time I will use "g," but in a case where my informants pronounced the "j," for example in a name, the "j" will be written. The "th" is pronounced as "t," but will be written as "th." The "q" becomes a short glottal stop in Egyptian dialect. When MSA would use the word "*qahwa*" for coffee, this would become " *'ahwa*" in Egyptian. I find that deleting the "q" and replacing it with an apostrophe is quite confusing since the same sign is used to represent the hamza. I prefer to write a "q," even though it is not pronounced as such in Egypt.

For names that are well known like Cairo or Luxor, their local equivalent will not be used. Sometimes the Arabic version is used for the names of people, and sometimes the Western equivalent is used: Ummina Marthā or Mother Martha.

CONTEMPORARY COPTIC NUNS

INTRODUCTION

This study will describe and analyze the life of contemplative and active Coptic Orthodox nuns over the last three decades.[1] The choice of this time span is based on the fact that before the year 1955, when the Catholic Father Giamberardini visited the convents in Cairo, hardly any written material was available about the lives of Coptic nuns. Another consideration for this choice of time is the current revitalization within the Coptic Church that became visible at the end of the 1940s. At the end of the 1950s the revival affected the monasteries; it influenced the nunneries a decade later.

Concurrent with this revitalization that finds its origins in lay and clerical activities of the nineteenth century, there is a renaissance of the monastic movement in Egypt. In the 1950s young Copts who had been active in the church as Sunday school teachers and youth leaders, many with university degrees, decided to explore the full consequences of their commitment to the Coptic Church. These young Copts joined monasteries to live ascetic lives in the footsteps of their desert fathers. Their thoughts for renewal and change were encouraged by Patriarch Kyrillos VI (1959–1971), a charismatic pope whom the Copts already considered a holy person. Patriarch Kyrillos VI promoted many monks of this new generation to important positions in the Coptic Church; the Coptic monks became bishops and abbots, and one became Patriarch Shenouda III after Kyrillos' death. At present the monasteries have resumed the important role they traditionally played in the spiritual and social life of the Coptic Church. Monasteries always played a role in the life of the church. For example, the patriarch and the bishops were chosen from among the monks, but due to several circumstances the importance of the monasteries had drastically diminished over the centuries.

On the whole, very few historical accounts are available about women who lead a monastic life in the Coptic Church. Yet from the earliest days of monasticism there were female monastics. Pachomius (290–346), the founder of the communal monasteries, had a sister, Mary, who followed her brother's example and started a convent opposite Pachomius' community in Tabennesi, on the other side of the river.[2] The present nuns consider Mary their direct forerunner and, with the monks, the nuns strive to copy the early models of desert fathers such as Antony (251–356) and Macarius (300–390).[3]

The fact that information about monasteries and nunneries before the revival is scant also reflects the deplorable states of these institutions. A firsthand account of the backwardness and laziness of the monks at the beginning of the twentieth century is given by Labīb Ḥabashī and Zākī Tāwūḍrūs. Apparently these men were the first Egyptians who, in 1927, ventured a trip to the eastern desert to visit the Monasteries of St. Antony and St. Paul. This extraordinary journey resulted in their publishing an account of the trip.[4] The two travelers were clearly appalled by the ignorance and ennui of the monks.[5] I find their observations confirmed by other sources who speak about the monasteries of those days as havens for social dropouts, scorned by the Coptic laypeople.[6] The traditionally contemplative convents seem to have been inhabited at that time by "retiring, old and disabled maidens or widows."[7] Conventional wisdom holds that the state of a church is reflected in the state of its monasteries. This seemed to be true for the Coptic Church at the beginning of the century; an uneducated, uninspiring, and backward clergy led the Coptic Church.[8]

I mentioned the year 1955 because of Father Giamberardini's visit to the convents. His article "Le Suore Copte Orthodosse"[9] gives a quite detailed description of the state of the Cairene Nunneries and his encounters with the nuns. Father Giamberardini's account gives the impression of fairly organized convents where the nuns were engaged in devotions and handicrafts. Although I will never be sure—since other sources on the subject are lacking—I will regard Father Giamberardini's visit as a witness to the beginnings of a reorganization among the nunneries. His visit was made in the days when most Copts themselves were hardly aware of the existence of Coptic nuns. The visit is furthermore a relative indicator of the nunneries' development because his accounts mention the abbess, Umminā Marthā (1900–1988). Mother Martha later became known for her building activities, spiritual guidance, and encouragement to Coptic laypeople, but at the time of Father Giamberardini's visit she had just been installed as abbess. Her fame was widespread during her life, and many people started to recognize her importance as model for other abbesses and monastics.

Since 1955 the convents have undergone sweeping changes. Nowadays they are populated by well-educated and highly motivated women who want to pursue a religious vocation and are deeply respected by laypeople. A new contemplative convent, Saint Dimyānah, was founded and the existing ones enlarged. For women who did not feel attracted to the contemplative life, a community of active nuns started in the 1960s. In the 1980s the office of deaconess was reintroduced. As was the case with monks, all these different types of nuns serve as examples; and they participated in teachings and publications that strengthen the spiritual life of the Coptic Church.

This new monastic landscape is still in transition. Contemplative nuns are in the process of defining and adapting their newly developed modes of life. The alternatives for active vocations have not quite settled yet. There are experiments and questions concerning consecration rites, rules, types of work, how and where to live, and who should supervise.

INFORMATION ABOUT THE CONVENTS

Very little contemporary material has been published about nuns themselves, contemplative or active, either in Arabic or in any other language.[10] From the seventeenth, eighteenth, and nineteenth centuries, there have been a few travel accounts that mention the convents.[11] Some of the accounts give vivid descriptions, both negative and positive. In 1678 Vansleb wrote about Deir Māri Girgis in Old Cairo: "I went to see the monasteries of the nuns, among the Copties caller Der el banat, . . . but it is a place too filthy and stinky that I could not stay there at any time."[12] In 1884 Butler stated about Deir Abū Saifein that it was "one of the most out of world and picturesque places imaginable, . . . like a walled oasis in the desert of dust and potsherds which stretches for miles south of Cairo: no wheeled thing ever enters there, and its peace is unbroken by any stir and clamour of life or noise of the world."[13] Most writers were not interested in the nuns, rather, it was the architecture and history of the building that aroused their attention.[14] Some Catholic fathers toured the monasteries for men to assess the state of the Coptic Church and to find opportunities for discussions about the Christian faith. Some of them also took a look at the women's convents. Unfortunately these visits did not result in prolific descriptions of the convents. Father Giamberardini's account remains the only one that stands out in this respect. If the convents were mentioned at all, it was in the context of Father Jullien, who describes the nuns of Deir Māri Girgis in Old Cairo as a bunch of oriental women sitting around all day, smoking their waterpipes.[15]

Furthermore, few Arabic sources even mention the convents.[16] There are no works available that deal with female monasticism as a specific topic. For information on monasticism in general, I have consulted books about the monks.[17] General information about the Coptic Church is available in an abundance of material that was published by the Copts during the last three decades. Both in Arabic and in other languages, manifold topics are represented in Coptic publishing such as the liturgy; Coptic faith; theology, pastoral, and educational topics; lives of the saints; and the speeches and Bible studies by Patriarch Shenouda III.

The larger part of the material for this study, however, is information that was gathered by fieldwork which included observations, participation, and interviews.

THE FIELDWORK

I had originally intended to gather mainly historical evidence about the women's convents. I had learned that there were still a number of inhabited nunneries in Egypt and assumed that material could be found in their archives and libraries. The first visit I paid was to the active community of the Banāt Maryam (Daughters of St. Mary) in Beni Suef. Their bishop, Anbā Athanasius, invited me to stay in the mother house of the sisters, and in the spring of 1987 I went to the house for the first time. Their reception was warm and open. I was allotted my own room, and the sisters invited me to join them in their worship services, in their work, their projects, and whatever other activities they were engaged in doing. The written sources I was looking for, however, were not available since the community was still fairly new. The literature the sisters themselves read, on the other hand, seldom went beyond the sixth century sayings and stories of the lives of desert fathers and mothers and of martyrs. To me this time gap of nearly fifteen centuries was puzzling, more so because it was not limited to the passive reading of literature, but was an active presence in the daily conversations of the sisters. For the sisters the early days of monasticism seemed no further away than the year that had just passed. They felt they were part of a spiritual heritage of the early fathers and mothers that had been the same then as it was now. For example, one time I was discussing a problem with them that in my eyes was modern and bureaucratic. The sisters advised the reading of the story of Moses the Black, a saint from the fifth century. Not only did I have no clue about who he was, I also failed to see what he had to do with twentieth-century questions. At that time I did not realize how strongly the sisters, like many lay Copts and all monastics, felt directly connected to their early heritage by the chain of Coptic clergy that had served the church since the apostle Mark had supposedly founded it. The sisters were proud of the stability of their faith and considered the adaptation of modern forms of worship and the developments going on in churches in the West as anathemas. I assumed that the sisters' attachment to their monastic past might be due to the newness of their community and the lack of recent tradition. So, I decided to return to the convents of the contemplatives, hoping to find an explanation of their attitude.

My first visits to the Convent of St. Abū Saifein were in the autumn of 1987.[18] The convent had been recommended by Coptic friends who regarded St. Abū Saifein's most highly. These visits were uninspiring and even discouraging. The nuns served me a cup of tea while smiling but refused even to chat with me. I thought this was because they were not allowed to socialize with visitors. In spite of the negative advice of my friends, I decided to give it another try at another convent—the Convent of St. Māri Girgis in Ḥārat Zuweilah. My colleagues predicted I would not get any information from the nuns at this convent because it was believed that the women there "were not really nuns." The nuns of St. Māri Girgis received me in a most friendly way. Their superior, Mother Aghāpī, invited me to have lunch with her. She was very interested in hearing everything about my home, country, church, and work. During our meeting, nuns streamed in and out of the room to converse and, before I left they all came to bid me farewell and urged me to visit them again soon.

Like the active sisters, these nuns also constantly referred to the desert fathers and mothers, the saints, and the martyrs of times long past, but there was little written material about the nuns' own history and way of life. Moreover it seemed nearly impossible to get a straight answer to what I considered to be straightforward questions such as: "How many nuns are living in the convent?" and "How old are you?" Numbers were invariably given in round figures like, "forty," "eighty." Age was referred to in cryptic ways: "I was already old when I became a nun," or "I have been a nun for a long time." At that time I did not realize that these figures of speech were used in order to present a respectable Coptic image. One mother superior, for example, insisted that "there were 40 nuns with her"; she still arrived at this number after several new novices had entered the convent. The number of forty hearkens back to the monastic community of the popular Coptic saint, St. Dimyānah. According to the legend, she and the forty virgins who shared the celibate life together in the fourth century were all martyred on the same day.

My only consolation in those early visits to the convents was the knowledge that other visitors, for example Alfred Butler in 1884, had had similar experiences: "No one would believe how many fruitless journeys under a scorching sun can go to a scanty handful of Coptic notes. And if one searches for oral information, trouble multiplies a hundredfold."[19] I also tried to meet nuns at the other four convents but somehow they were busy, or their superior was not present, or their convent was closed during one of the frequent Coptic fasting periods. Slowly I realized why the information about Coptic convents was so scant. Apart from the nuns of Mother Aghāpī it seemed too difficult and time-consuming to get to know Coptic contemplative nuns.

Another obstacle in Cairo was the inaccessibility of general books about Coptic monasticism, archaeology, and Patristic studies. Books were either obtainable in libraries that were only open three times a week for two hours (borrowing was impossible), or books were stowed away in the private collections of the convents. It was sheer luck that one day, at the end of 1987, a Western scholar who had donated several books to the library of St. Abū Saifein's Convent, introduced me to the nun who was the librarian there. I asked her if there was any way I could read a certain book. She said she would discuss the matter with her superior, Mother Irīnī, and invited me to come back a week later. To my great surprise the superior had suggested that I come on Saturdays during nonfasting periods in order to use the convent's library. This meant that the number of Saturdays would be limited as their fasting periods cover two hundred days a year. Nevertheless, these regular visits resulted in an ongoing dialogue with the convent during which I could lay a basis for my study. I then developed better relations with the other convents, which eventually resulted in my meeting with the superiors of all the convents.

Although I knew that the nuns (like cloistered nuns everywhere) needed the approval of their superior before they could speak with visitors, the impact of this rule only became clear to me in August 1988 in the Convent of St. Abū Saifein. Until then I had not met the convent's superior, Mother Irīnī; however, she knew about me and had allowed me to visit the convent frequently. That day the librarian and I were sitting in one of the convent's guest rooms sipping fruit juice, eating cookies, and discussing St. Abū Saifein. (St. Abū Saifein is very popular among the Copts and thousands of people attend the feasts that the church celebrates on the occasions of his martyrdom and the bringing of his relics to the convent.) Unannounced, a middle-aged nun stepped into the room with her hand stretched out, holding a small copper cross. After she gave me the cross she sat down with us and we continued our conversation. She explained to me the Coptic veneration of the saints and expressed her regrets that the people of my church, the Protestants, did not venerate the saints. She then got up and while leaving the room said that "anā baḥibb rūḥik" (she liked my spirit). After she had disappeared several excited nuns rushed into the room; umminā ra'īsa, the mother superior, had spoken to me and in spite of my Protestant background had approved of me. I realized that I might have been wrong in my assumption that the nuns' attitude toward me only sprung from the urge to act and behave decently in order not to bring any kind of discredit to the convent. It seemed only natural to me that the nuns did not want to be known as chatting and gossiping women; rather they wanted their image to be that of serious monastics. After meeting with Mother Irīnī, I realized that the nuns also must have had some suspicion toward Protestants, whose missionaries in Egypt had created a new church by converting Orthodox Copts.[20] After the superior had given her approval the nuns were noticeably relieved.

The majority of the material for this study was collected in the Convent of St. Abū Saifein and the Convent of St. Māri Girgis in Ḥārat Zuweilah. Each of these convents represents a different lifestyle of the modern nun: the Convent of St. Abū Saifein is progressive and instrumental in the present renaissance of the Coptic Church, while that of St. Māri Girgis is perceived as representing a more traditional idea of monasticism. At St. Māri Girgis the atmosphere is more relaxed, and somehow life in the convent seems to blend naturally with the life of the surrounding Egyptian society. When one visits St. Abū Saifein, one steps into a different world. Although the chaotic, noisy atmosphere of Cairo is just outside the convent's walls, life in the Convent of St. Abū Saifein is disciplined and well organized. Copts who knew of both convents tended to speak highly about the more modern convent (Mother Irīnī's convent), and while most of them were aware of the traditional convent (Mother Aghāpī's convent), they tended not to know as much about it. I visited all the other convents, the annexes or detached sites of most of the convents, the newly inhabited monastic sites in Upper Egypt and interviewed all the superiors. I attended feasts, special occasions, gatherings, and worship services. As the nuns and I got to know each other better, my visits became more pleasant and relaxed. That each visit still was quite energy-sapping for me had more to do with the Egyptian climate than with the nuns. Somehow, in Egypt, it rarely seems possible to have discussions or meetings in a concentrated way. Focusing on a specific topic for any time longer than a few minutes becomes difficult since meetings are often interrupted by visitors, laborers, or nuns who move in and out with questions or requests. It sometimes happened that the nun I was talking to was suddenly called elsewhere and totally forgot about my presence.

Most of the time interviews and discussions were conducted in an unstructured way. Several times I tried to ask questions on the basis of a systematic list, but the nuns were often not interested in this dry and direct questioning. They preferred to choose their own topics such as the latest visit of a bishop to the convent, the new altar curtains, or what they had been reading lately. However, as seems to happen in field research, several pieces of key information were revealed in the most unexpected moments. (For example, while waiting with a nun for the bus or while holding the waterhose in the garden.)[21]

A certain imbalance in the material was inevitable since I was not allowed to spend the night at the contemplative convents, although I was welcome to stay with the active sisters for any length of time. The superiors of the active community knew from the outset of my visits that it was my intention to do a study on contemporary female monasticism. I did not really inform the contemplative nuns until my last year in Egypt. Few of the people I interviewed or who volunteered information in the contemplative convents knew why I was so interested in them. The fact that I was not clear about my aims for a study until 1990 can mainly be ascribed to my own uncertainty. I had no idea whether a complete study of the topic would ever prove feasible.

In January 1992 I went back to Egypt and discussed the manuscript with some of the nuns and one of the bishops. Their comments were often very illuminating and several are incorporated in the text of this study. This visit again showed how quickly the monastic situation in Egypt changes. In the one year of my absence, two important figures in present monasticism had died (Tāsūnī Ḥannah, Sister Hannah, the superior of the active community, and Mother Aghāpī, the second in charge at the Convent of St. Abū Saifein), and both Mother Irīnī and Mother Aghāpī of St. Māri Girgis were seriously ill.

THE QUESTIONS

One cannot help but ask several questions about Coptic nuns, such as "Who are these women who replaced the 'old and disabled maidens' "? Apparently the nuns had little to start with—dilapidated convents and few models to imitate. Apart from these obvious questions, one wonders what happens within the convents. Are the nuns governed by a certain rule? What is the role of their superiors? And to what extent is the monastic tradition a part of their daily life?

In view of the Egyptian culture where the celibate life is not a current ideal, I would like to know why and how a young woman opts for leaving her family to become "dead to the world." And what types of work do these women do? Are they allowed to play an active role in the revitalization process of the Coptic Church? Did their foremothers (who were for the most part society's misfits or people who practiced isolation from society) leave them adequate spiritual examples? Who are the nuns' role models and can the nuns themselves serve as models for laypeople? And finally, how are the nuns perceived by the laypeople?

This study primarily focuses on Coptic religious women, but one of my questions has to do with the significance that the convents might have for Muslims. The nuns are members of a religious minority, which means that conclusions about life within cloisters are inadvertently affected by cultural and social Muslim influences. Among others, these influences include: Muslim visitors to the convents, the region in which a convent is geographically located, and the general atmosphere of relations between Copts and Muslims.

Nowadays there are three types of religious women in the Coptic Church: the traditional contemplative nuns, the newly developed community of active nuns, and the so-called consecrated women, a type of deaconesses. The main focus of this study will be on the contemplative and active nuns. They are considered "dead to the world" because they were initiated into monasticism by a special rite. Of the contemplative nuns, I will deal mainly with the communities that have, more or less, taken shape. This means that I will not discuss in depth the projects to reinhabit old monastic sites that are currently going on in Upper Egypt. The consecrated women are a brand new phenomenon in the Coptic Church. The process of redefining rules and regulations for their communities was only recently finalized, in 1992. While this study was in preparation, the consecrated women were still lacking an official status. In the course of this study, consecrated women will be referred to frequently; however, an extensive description of their lives would require separate research.

The monks and their monasteries will be regularly introduced because for directions, inspiration, and information about the monastic life, the nuns necessarily turn to religious publications that are mainly produced by and about men (monks, priests, and bishops). Thus I will draw the monks into the discussion whenever it is necessary for comparative or explanatory reasons.

THE HIERARCHIC STRUCTURES

Before I can spell out the aims of this study, I have to consider certain questions concerning hierarchy, authority, and power. The topic of monasticism in itself inevitably leads to such questions. In the Coptic context, I am interested in the nuns' position with regard to the Coptic hierarchic structures. Looking at the nuns' positions in the church and in society, one can discern three different hierarchic systems: the ecclesiastical, the social, and the spiritual hierarchy.

The ecclesiastical hierarchy is defined as "a definitely ordered group of men endowed with sacred power, or that power itself precisely as exercised within a framework in which the lower ministries are subordinate to the higher."[22]

The social hierarchy is governed by the cultural environment which prevails in the surrounding society where the Copts and Muslims interact. This is reflected within the Coptic Church.

The spiritual hierarchy is the metaphysical system or cosmology that transcends the human level, but it is a hierarchy in which humans can participate as well.

Studies about women in the Muslim world have shown that women of different social strata deal with the hierarchic system in which they find themselves by developing their own activities, discourse, and strategies to evade, avoid, or ignore the system. These women have developed strategies to support their position and to exercise indirect influence, especially in the field of religion and the supernatural. In this process they form their own extrahierarchic or counterhierarchic systems.[23]

Louis Dumont argued in his book *Homo Hierarchicus* that Westerners cannot grasp the notion of hierarchy adequately because they are no longer able to "even conceptualize a notion of hierarchy that is not intrinsically unfair."[24] For example, a concurrent phenomenon of hierarchic situations is meditation; someone who is on the low side of the ladder can obtain the cherished favor or job by asking a person who has a slightly higher position to put in a good word with the authority in charge. This way of advancement, normal in present-day Egypt, is often considered unfair in the West—an allegedly egalitarian society. Louis Dumont has argued that "hierarchy need not be oppressive if it allows for communication across the boundaries it assumes."[25] For Coptic nuns, as for other women in Egyptian society, the key to success in any of their activities apparently lies in the way they manage to manipulate the hierarchy. In this process these women will be crossing and testing the boundaries of the system. This implies, among other things, that the more skillful they are in using intermediary agents, or in becoming mediators themselves, the more successful they will be in reaching their goals.

In order to understand the nuns' place in the three hierarchic systems better, I must first outline these systems more clearly.

The Ecclesiastical Hierarchy

The ecclesiastical hierarchy in fact consists of two levels: 1) ordained clergy who can administer the church's sacraments (this group can include married priests and ordained monks); 2) monks who are not ordained.

Women are excluded from the first level. They can never be ordained into any of the seven Holy Orders.[26] The statement of Patriarch Shenouda III that "We [the Coptic Church] do not use the word hierarchy for women"[27] clearly illustrates this point. But, in a sense, Coptic nuns do belong to the same level of hierarchy as unordained monks. All are monastics, initiated by a rite that is quite similar for men and women. Their purely monastic state reaches back to the origins of monasticism as a movement outside the ecclesiastical institution. In fact, nuns are granted an unofficial ecclesiastical status on the basis of their monastic position.

Ordained ministry excludes women in most churches. Neither the Roman Catholic nor the Orthodox churches allow women to administer the sacraments. For this study it is relevant to know the official position of Coptic women in general. One can discern three major arguments against official positions of women in the church: the arguments in the Pauline epistles, the religious anthropological argument of Eve's original sin, and the argument of ritual uncleanness caused by a women's monthly cycle.

First I will discuss the Pauline argument. St. Paul said that women should keep silence in the churches (1 Cor. 14:34–36). Paul also stated that it is forbidden for a woman to teach men or have authority over a man (1 Tim. 2:12). About this topic, Mattā al-Meskīn, the present spiritual father of the Monastery of St. Macarius and one of the leading Coptic authorities on monastic and spiritual life, explains that "the Apostle Paul here forbids women to teach men not because they are forbidden to teach or because they do not have the gift, for they share in all gifts, but because for women to teach men in the church would put them in a position of leadership and give them authority over men which the apostle sees as not permissible."[28] Father Mattā al-Meskīn argues that the fact that women are not allowed to teach in church is the source of the ban on women entering any degree of ordination.[29]

Father Mattā al-Meskīn then links the Pauline argument with Eve's original sin by quoting St. Paul that "Adam was created first," and that "it was not Adam who was deceived; it was the woman who, yielding to deception, fell into sin."[30] According to Mattā al-Meskīn, it was Eve "who offered sin to her husband," and so "it is fitting and right that she should be offered counsel, then reconciliation and forgiveness (in the sacrifice of the eucharist) by men."[31]

According to church belief, the third factor that prevents women from attaining ecclesiastical positions is their monthly menses. In the Coptic Church, a menstruating women is not allowed to take communion, and it is forbidden for a woman who has not reached menopause to enter the altar. The basis for these restrictions is according to the Copts, found in the Old Testament codes of purity (Lev. 15:19–25).[32]

In the surrounding Muslim world these last two arguments of Eve's sin and of the female pollution strongly work to exclude women from certain religious practices. Eve's sin is used as an unspoken argument to subdue women in general though, as among others Riffat Hassan has argued, "There is no Fall in the Qurʾan, hence there is no Original Sin."[33] In Islam a menstruating woman is not allowed to enter a mosque, to touch the holy objects (the Koran in particular), or to pray.[34] This practice is not applicable to Christian women, who are never prohibited to pray or touch the Bible or other holy objects.[35] One can only conclude that in both Muslim and Coptic communities a woman in her reproductive years is considered unclean.[36]

The Social Hierarchy

From the preceding description, it has become obvious that the nonbiblical arguments against official positions for women in the church are influenced by the second type of hierarchy—social. A woman in Egypt, due to her gender, always has an inferior position to a man. The situation is twofold for a Coptic laywoman. On the one hand she is a woman in a Muslim society, which causes her to share in the general attitudes toward and opinions about women. On the other hand the Coptic woman is partly subject to a different juridical and theological system. Muslim laws, for example, concerning divorce, polygamy, and the right to take care of the children, are not applicable to a Coptic woman.

The Spiritual or Divine Hierarchy

In Egyptian society, where religion plays a crucial role in daily life, the third type of hierarchy (the spiritual cosmology) plays an important role. This cosmology that descends from God is conceptualized by Copts by reference to the Trinity. For a Copt, it is a daily reality that her/his life is regulated and preordained by God and that she/he is in the constant company of God and all the saints in heaven (who intercede on behalf of the believer). The spiritual cosmology includes the following: St. Mary, the angels, the apostles, the prophets, martyrs, and all other saints. Human beings can preemptively obtain a place in the divine realm as well, for example, by an ascetic or devout lifestyle. The spiritual hierarchic system supersedes all human inventions and follows its own rules regarding how one can participate. Human beings can strive to reach a place in the spiritual hierarchy by having a high ascetic commitment or by developing relations with intercessors (saints) that are part of the cosmology. As intercession or mediation plays an important role in dealing with authorities in a social hierarchy, so too do they play important roles in dealing with the supernatural in a spiritual hierarchy.[37]

Eickelman, though speaking in a different context, observed that: "human relations with the supernatural work in almost the same way as do relations among persons themselves."[38] Through their ascetic activity, prayers, and interactions with the members of the spiritual hierarchy in heaven, nuns can become mediators and intercessors for other people. If a nun is successful, healings or miracles may occur through her. During this study there will be frequent mentioning of saints and how the most respected mother superiors have reached a higher spiritual status by following the saint's ascetic/spiritual model. Through lengthy prayers and imploring the intercession of their convent's patron saints, two mother superiors in particular became instrumental in healing. Reaching a degree of what Copts perceive to be as holiness lends the holy nun a power that can be used in creative ways to help the community of nuns redefine its position in the hierarchic structures.[39] Strategies that are developed to exercise power and authority, to maintain a position, or to obtain favors, operate on several different levels. As Droogers has pointed out, reciprocal interactions not only take place between people or between people and the society they are part of, but also between people and the supernatural.[40]

This occurrence can create unexpected situations that sometimes reverse the general accepted structures. For example, what happens when a priest who is endowed with the power to administer the sacraments has no visions or apparitions from the saints, while a nun without sacramental power, has such revelations? Obviously both appear to have been given a measure of charisma, or revelatory blessing, albeit in a different way. Coming back to Dumont's remarks on hierarchy, one sees that certain events can reverse the order of hierarchy.[41] Furthermore, there is a subtle interaction between the different levels of the spiritual hierarchy.

In order to tie the previous description in more concretely, I will give an example of the many stories from Coptic oral tradition about how the saints sometimes interfere to advance someone's spiritual position. One story tells about a monastic candidate who found herself rejected by the mother superior. The candidate withdrew into the convent's chapel and fervently prayed to God and asked the convent's patron saint for intercession in order to secure a place in the convent. The mother superior's decision was reversed because, as the story goes, the patron saint intervened on behalf of the future novice. The aforementioned young woman now has been an integral member of the convent's community for many years.

AIM OF THE STUDY

This study aims at describing and highlighting how the contemporary contemplative and active Coptic nuns have developed their place within the framework of the Coptic Church. In this process, I show how the nuns can draw from their rich tradition which they manage to redefine in order to justify a place and role for religious women in their church and community. Furthermore, the nuns can make use of higher levels of education and the increasing opportunities for Egyptian women to pursue a profession.

This study also shows how the nuns turn to the Coptic cosmology in order to find help and encouragement in reaching their spiritual goals.

DIVISION OF CHAPTERS

In the first chapter I will discuss the position of the Copts in Egyptian society. A brief historical description will then lead to the roots of the church's revival; then I will try to indicate the theological, liturgical, and traditional characteristics that give the Coptic Church its own identity, followed by an excursus about Copts and Islam. The chapter will end with some aspects of the monastic history and tradition. Who the nuns are, how they live, and in what way their convents are directed are dealt with in the second and third chapters. Once I have described the living conditions of the nuns, I will investigate in the fourth chapter how a young woman becomes a nun. I shall discuss what it takes to leave the world and to prepare for the monastic life. In chapter five, I will described how a novice enters the monastic state. The initiation rites of the contemplatives, the active sisters, and some aspects of the monks' rites will be dealt with.

In chapter six, I will look at the nuns' activities and their work, especially the role of the active community in the revitalization. The core of nuns' existence—the spiritual life—will be discussed in the seventh chapter. Through spiritual direction, the Coptic monastic life is lived out and its goals are shaped. This spiritual direction is combined with a life of regular devotions, prayer, and fasting. Because of their ascetic vigor, some nuns become models for laypeople and as such are instrumental in providing spiritual advice.

While chapter seven only mentions the significance of Coptic saints briefly, chapter eight is entirely devoted to the role of the saints in the lives of the nuns. In the relationships with the saints, one touches upon aspects of the unofficial or popular religion. The saints represent another layer of the popular hierarchic system.

And finally, in chapter nine, the secular world outside will enter into the convent. The interactions between the nuns and laypeople and their possible roles as examples, or religious advisers, for laywomen, form the core of the ninth chapter. A conclusion closes the study.

CHAPTER 1

The Copts in Egyptian Society

Faith is taught. It is not only intellectual, it is in our whole nature. We have to teach our children. We sing the hymns with them, show them how to pray, help their hands make the sign of the cross. We show them the icons and ask "Where is Our Lord? Where is St. Mary?" They will imitate us and grow into it. It is all a process of growth.

Bishop Athanasius on church revival

Religious revival does not arise from a vacuum, but as Wallace says, it is a "deliberate, organized, conscious effort by members of a society to construct a more satisfying culture."[1] In order to understand the parameters of the Coptic revival and the position of the Copts in Egyptian society, I will start this chapter with a historical sketch of Egypt and the Copts. Then I will discuss the specifics of the Coptic revival, identity, and the church. The chapter will close with a historical outline of Coptic monasticism.

A SHORT HISTORY OF THE COPTIC CHURCH BEFORE THE NINETEENTH CENTURY

According to the Copts, their church has existed since the year 61 when the apostle Mark set foot in Alexandria. St. Mark is considered the first patriarch and the present Patriarch Shenouda III (patriarch since 12 November 1971) his 117th successor in an unbroken line of succession.[2] Popular belief holds that the Egyptian population readily accepted the Christian faith because the Holy Family's flight was an event that was still present in the minds of the people by the time St. Mark arrived.[3]

During the Roman period (30 B.C.–641), Egyptian Christians suffered waves of persecutions, including a particularly brutal period under Emperor Diocletian. To commemorate the martyrs who died for their faith under Diocletian, the Coptic calendar was invented. (The Coptic calendar counts time from the so-called Era of the Martyrs that began in 284, the year of Diocletian's accession to the throne.)[4] Even today the Coptic Church practices a highly developed martyr cult.

Along with the Syrian, Ethiopian, and Armenian Orthodox churches, the Coptic Church belongs to the group of Oriental Orthodox churches. These churches are called "Monophysites" although they prefer to be referred to as "non-Chalcedonians." The term non-Chalcedonians refers to the Council of Chalcedon (451) where one of the main points of debate was the nature of Christ. The Copts hold the belief that the nature of Christ consists of "two-natures—divine and human—mystically united in one, without confusion, corruption, or change."[5] The Monophysite doctrine is based on the Christological Tenet of Cyril I, the bishop of Alexandria (412–444).[6] The Eucharist lay at the heart of this Christology and guaranteed the believer salvation. "The body of life received in the Eucharist united the Christian with the Word to make him immortal and incorruptible."[7] Loyalty to their patriarchs induced the Egyptian monks to accept Cyril's Christology.[8] After all, the monks characterize Chalcedon as a rejection of the faith of Nicea as expounded by Athanasius and the Council of Ephesus, and as an acceptance of Nestorianism.[9] The crucial question whether Christ existed "in two natures," or "out of two natures" gave rise to heated debates in the Roman Empire and eventually led to a break between churches.[10] The process preceding the schism is highly complicated and runs along cultural, geographical, and political lines. W. H. C. Frend observes that in the end, "the empire had been forced into the position of permanent opposition towards the Monophysites. There was no place for two organized churches. Its political philosophy could never have envisaged the emperor being head of two separate and rival groups of Christians."[11] Subsequent emperors had tried to achieve reconciliation between adverse parties.[12] But in spite of reconciliatory moves, none of them gave in to the request of the Monophysite leaders that in order for the churches to reconcile, the emperor should repudiate the Council of Chalcedon.[13]

In Alexandria, there existed an anti- and a pro-Chalcedonian party. The latter formed the origin of the Melkite, or Imperial, Church.[14] Parties were scattered all over the country. Tolerance or suppression of Monophysitism depended on many factors that played in the empire. One of them was the christological view of the emperor. The memories of this period that still linger in the Coptic mind today are tainted by the memory of Cyrus the Caucasian, the last Chalcedonian patriarch before the Arab invasion. While the Monophysite Patriarch Benjamin was in hiding, Cyrus terrorized the anti-Chalcedonians in Alexandria from 635–641 and "whatever loyalty had been felt towards Heraclius and the Roman Empire ebbed away."[15]

In 641 the Arabs, under the command of ʿAmr ibn al-ʿĀṣ, captured the Fortress of Babylon after a one-year siege. Constantinople never sent help to ward off the Arabs in Babylon, and after handing over the city of Alexandria in 642 the imperial forces sailed away.[16] The Copts greeted the invasion with mixed sentiments. On one hand this marked the end of Roman suppression—a relief; however, on the other hand they now had to deal with revolts and resistance from the local population against the Arabs.[17] From the time of the Arab Conquest, a long sequence of Muslim regimes followed. The policy of the Muslim rulers toward the Egyptian Christians was not necessarily based on religion, but was often dictated by economic conditions, political turmoil, and the wealth of the Christians. In many respects the fate of the Copts was closely connected to the general fate Egypt suffered under its alternating rulers.

From the time of the Arab Conquest, until its abolition in 1856, the Copts (with other Christians in Egypt and the Jews) acquired the discriminatory status of *Ahl al-Dhimmah,* or protected "people of the covenant," who in return for paying a special taxation (the poll tax, *jizyah*) enjoyed protection, security of personal property, and a limited freedom to practice their religion.[18] *Ahl al-Dhimmah* were not allowed to carry arms and often had to wear distinctive clothing. They faced restrictions on repairing churches and building new ones, but their situation mainly depended on the bigotry or tolerance of the rulers. For example, during most of the Fatimid Reign, the Copts enjoyed a fair degree of freedom and were able to hold high offices. But the third Fatimid, Al-Ḥākim (996–1021) turned into a cruel persecutor of Christians. During his reign "distinctive marks on clothing, the carrying of heavy crosses on the person, the destruction of churches and their use for the Islamic *adhān,* or call to prayer, and other humiliations belonged grievously to this period."[19]

After the eighth century, the Coptic language (Bohairic) was gradually replaced by Arabic and died out as a spoken and literary language.[20] Nowadays Bohairic is still used in the Coptic liturgy.[21] As the Coptic community shrank to the present-day minority, it turned inward, clinging to its identity by stressing its tradition, piety, liturgy, and family life. With regard to Christians of other creeds, the Copts became "self-centered in their own religious nationalism."[22]

THE NINETEENTH CENTURY AND THE COPTIC REVIVAL

The nineteenth century started with the brief French expedition by Napoleon into Egypt (1798–1801). This event proved momentous for Egypt because it was the first contact with a European country since the Crusades.[23] In the year 1801, Muhammed ʿAli had arrived in Egypt to join the army that defeated the French. In 1805 (until 1849), he established a modern nation that aimed at the development of Egypt based on the European model, which included army discipline, modern techniques, and science. Muhammed ʿAli was generally favorable toward the Copts and ready to employ their skills. The nation of Egypt benefitted from the free market economy of the times, and several Coptic families rose to considerable wealth and influence. According to sources from the census of 1918, Copts held about 25 percent of the total wealth of Egypt and controlled 60 percent of all Egyptian commerce, serving as bankers and financiers.[24] After the abolition of the status of *Ahl al-Dhimmah,* political assimilation of the Copts began. A side effect of Muhammad ʿAli's military campaigns was an increase of non-Coptic Christian elements within Egypt, in particular Greek Orthodoxy, a Chalcedonian variety of Orthodoxy.[25] Kenneth Cragg analyses these influences on the Coptic community as follows: "Through these factors—the stimulus of Muhammad ʿAli's regime and the sense of a rivalry, whether benign or sinister, from the Greek Orthodox presence—came a challenge to the Coptic leadership and a sense of an incubus to be cast off and inertia to be overcome."[26] This challenge seems to have been taken seriously already by the Coptic Patriarch Peter VII (1809–1852), who was aware of the needs of the church and supported the steps undertaken by missionaries of the Church Missionary Society directed to "raising the educational level of a generally ignorant Coptic clergy."[27]

His successor, Patriarch Kyrillos IV (1854–1861), is considered to be the *abū al-iṣlāḥ* (father of reform). During Kyrillos' short reign he initiated ecclesiastical training for priests and deacons. He also enforced church discipline, repaired old churches and built new ones, and constructed schools where a wide range of subjects were taught by qualified teachers for students from all faiths. Furthermore, Kyrillos introduced the first private printing press in Egypt.[28] Under his successor, Demetrius II (1862–1870), these reforms stagnated.

In subsequent years, this stagnation continued and eventually led to the Coptic laity severely criticizing their clergy. Under the long rule of the conservative Patriarch Kyrillos V (1874–1929) the tense relationship between Coptic laity and clergy became increasingly aggravated. Through other developments that had been set in motion (such as the conversion of some Orthodox Copts to Protestantism) and the opening of schools by American Presbyterian missionaries, the reform activities were gradually transferred into the hands of the laity.[29] Furthermore, there was a growing Catholic community in Egypt that had its own Coptic Catholic patriarch appointed in 1895. Copts who had grown tired of the backwardness of their own church converted to a Protestant or Catholic church.[30] The leading lay Copts started to form a *majlis millī* (lay council), that would "press for communal reform" and "assist the clergy in furthering reform in the Coptic community."[31] The results of the manifold efforts of this lay council and other Coptic associations that were formed afterward were fruitful in supporting schools, charities, and matters outside the *awqāf* (religious endowments). But the majority of the clergy, led by Patriarch Kyrillos V and his successors, was bent on thwarting all schemes for reform in the clerical field.

The patriarch had and has traditionally been the Coptic representative to the government and has fulfilled the role of a powerful symbol within the Coptic community. Never in Coptic history had a patriarch been forced to share his authority with a lay council whose members actually constituted a threat to the church and its doctrines—since their deeds seemed inspired by the foreign Protestants.[32] The patriarch represented the monastic tradition and upheld traditional church policy, which included a "discreet existence in safe obscurity opposite a potential hostile environment."[33] With the powerful weapon of excommunication in his hands, the patriarch had the final say, regardless of the sincere need for reform advocated by the laity.[34]

THE TWENTIETH CENTURY

Besides their internal struggle to reform the Coptic Church, in the beginning of this century the Coptic community faced strained relationships with the Muslims. The British occupation of Egypt in 1881 had aroused feelings of nationalism that were pan-Arabic and largely Islamic.[35] Provoked by the assassination of the Coptic Prime Minister Butrus Ghali, the Coptic community called for a conference to discuss Coptic demands in Assiyut in March 1911.[36] Butrus Ghali's appointment in November 1908 had "aggravated a then tense situation between Copts and Muslims."[37] The Coptic Conference resulted in a Muslim countercongress in Heliopolis, in May 1911, where all the Coptic demands were rejected and statements were made such as: "The religion of the Egyptian people is Islam."[38]

After World War I, the intellectual climate became more liberal. Secular and Coptic hopes were raised by the *Wafd* Party that, under the leadership of Saʿd Zaghlul, had led the 1919 revolution against the British. The *Wafd* stressed unity and equality of all Egyptians, Muslims, or Christians, and several Copts played important roles in the party, alongside Muslims, in trying to obtain independence for Egypt after the war. Two Copts were selected for the cabinet of ten ministers.[39] The belief on a secular basis that a full political and social integration was possible for the Copts diminished by the 1940s when intercommunal relations had deteriorated again.[40] By the 1940s the activities of the fundamentalist Muslims like the Ikhwān al-Muslimīn, the Muslim Brotherhood, had lead to a polarization between Muslims and Christians. There was even a tiny group of young Copts who reacted by forming a militant organization called Al-Umma al-Qibṭīya (the Coptic nation). Both the Coptic and the Muslim organizations were dissolved by Gamal Abdal Nasser in 1954.[41]

The 1952 revolution of Gamal Abdal Nasser had a more secular than Islamic ideology. Consequently the interreligious strife halted. Due to land reform, prominent Coptic families lost their property and influence and as a result, there was no political role for the Copts in the new revolutionary government. In this period many wealthy and/or well-educated Copts emigrated and subsequently a considerable number of Coptic communities came into existence in Europe, Canada, the United States, and Australia.[42]

Nasser's regime coincided with the reign of Patriarch Kyrillos VI and was a period of relative religious peace (most likely due to the fact that Kyrillos basically avoided involvement in national politics). The main discordant between Nasser and the Copts was in 1955 when Nasser abolished the Christian and Muslim religious courts and changed the personal status law.[43]

In 1971, Anwar Sadat allowed Islam to be reintroduced as state religion and gradually gave the Muslim Brotherhood more freedom after their activities had been curtailed under Nasser. During Sadat's reign, religious strife was common in Egypt and regular clashes occurred between Muslims and Christians.[44] Social, political, economic, demographic, cultural, and religious reasons have been mentioned for these clashes. One reason was the religious revival in both the Muslim and Coptic communities.[45] The Muslim revival is interpreted as a reaction to Western influences and secular modernization during the time of Nasser,[46] and dissatisfaction with the regime of Sadat.[47]

The movement of both Coptic and Muslim workers from the country to the cities resulted in masses of unemployed moving to the suburbs. Outside their nuclear community, the workers' only means of social integration were religious fraternities that emerged on both the Coptic and Muslim sides. The fraternities also mushroomed among university students.[48] Some indices of the Muslim revival that were noticeable in the personal lives of the Muslims are: increased religious observance, more emphasis upon Islamic dress and values, proliferation of religious programming and publications, the revitalization of Islamic mysticism (Sufism), all in combination with a greater emphasis on identity, language, values, and community.[49]

The Coptic revival is partly an interior reaction to developments within the Coptic community itself, and partly a reaction to the surrounding Muslim revival. In certain aspects the Coptic revival carries the same indices and symbols as the Islamic revival.

An observation concerning the interreligious disturbances during the Sadat period, is that Patriarch Shenouda III had a different leadership style than his more reserved predecessor. Shenouda's view was that the church should vigorously defend the rights of the Coptic community.[50] This belief eventually led to a head-on collision with Sadat who accused Shenouda of magnifying the interreligious incidents and thus generating reactions from the Islamic groups and Muslim extremists.[51] At the same time when many Muslim extremists were rounded up, the patriarch was sent into internal exile in one of the monasteries in September 1981. One month after this, on 6 October, Sadat was assassinated by Islamic fundamentalists.[52]

Presently, under President Mubarak, intercommunal clashes are increasing again after a decade of relative peace. Although the violence of extremist groups against government officials, Copts, and Western tourists garners the most attention, the predominant part of Islamic revivalism consists of what John Esposito calls "the quiet revolution represented by the proliferation of organizations engaged in religio-social and moral reform."[53]

THE COPTIC REVIVAL

The roots of the present-day Coptic revival can be found at the end of the nineteenth century. Patriarch Kyrillos IV had carried out church reforms, while the Coptic laity had started several social projects to strengthen the Coptic community. These social projects were successful, but the laypeople failed to stimulate reforms that directly affected the church.

One exception was the Sunday School Movement that was officially launched in 1918 by a layperson, Ḥabīb Girgis, the director of the Coptic Seminary. Probably inspired by Protestant examples, he introduced Sunday schools in the churches of Cairo and other cities, developed educational material, and pointed out the importance of Christian education. This autonomous and extra church movement had the backing of the patriarchs. The Sunday school magazine (*Magallet Madāris al-Aḥad*) was started in 1946 and became an important platform for the dissemination of new ideas concerning the life of the church. Several of the present leaders of the Coptic Church, including Patriarch Shenouda III, were active Sunday school leaders and exchanged ideas by means of the magazine. The Sunday School Movement featured "an aggressive puritanism and assiduous study of the Bible."[54]

An important task of the Sunday School Movement was to provide young Copts with Christian religious instruction that is nearly nonexistent in the public schools. As such, it became an instrument in shaping the identity of young Copts, especially from the middle class.[55] The ideals of integration and full participation in the Egyptian nation that certain Copts had at one point, were gradually replaced by a formula of social separation.[56] Church and family life became the central points for Copts and induced them to be more closed off to the Muslim environment.

A crucial event in this process was a genuine spiritual renewal at the time of Patriarch Kyrillos VI. Kyrillos himself was inspired greatly by the example of the Ethiopian hermit ʿAbd al-Masīḥ al-Ḥabashī who lived in a cave near Wādī al-Natrūn.[57] Through his ascetic lifestyle as a monk, hermit, and patriarch, Kyrillos VI conformed to the monastic ideal, regaining the monasteries a central place in the church. Kyrillos' position on monasticism had a far greater appeal to the Copts (whose rallying point was the patriarch and who traditionally had regarded their church leaders with far more deference) than any lay reform movements.[58] Abūnā ʿAbd al-Masīḥ al-Ḥabashī's rigorous variety of monasticism inspired both Patriarch Shenouda III and Father Mattā al-Meskīn among others. Shenouda led an anchoritic life in a cave in the Wādī al-Natrūn (from about 1957 until 1962). Mattā al-Meskīn was the spiritual leader of a small group of monks who lived as hermits from 1960–1969 in the Wādī Rayān (some 35 kilometers southwest of the Oasis of Fayoum).[59] After his installation as patriarch, Kyrillos kept urging the young hermits to give up their lifestyles and enter active church service. However, his requests were virtually disobeyed. In 1962 Shenouda was ordained bishop for Christian education and in 1969 Mattā al-Meskīn and his group complied with Kyrillos' request and moved into the dilapidated Monastery of St. Macarius in order to start its transformation into the model monastery it is today. These reclusive hermits who lived as, what Victor Turner has called liminars, nowadays are the main agents of Coptic Church reform.[60] All of the hermits of the formative period of contemporary Coptic monasticism eventually left their liminal state (and the glowing example of Al-Habashī) behind in order to move into powerful positions within the church.

The fact that Kyrillos was identified as a strong spiritual guide and a holy person during his lifetime, served the Copts as proof that he was the true renewer of their church. Kyrillos' example attracted many of the university graduates who had been active as Sunday school teachers to enter the monasteries. The graduates realized that joining the church from within was the only way to be instrumental in reforming the church. As Sunday school leaders many of them had been writers in the Sunday school bulletin. In the monastery they continued this activity by publishing educational and spiritual works that called for a return to the spiritual ideals of Christianity as it was in the days of the apostles and early fathers.[61] This parallels the Muslim return to the Arab-Muslim heritage.[62]

Kyrillos VI also put an end to educational deficiencies among the married priests by issuing his 1960 decree that all priests must be graduates of the Clerical College. The patriarch furthered the monastic revival by initiating the building and renovation of new monasteries—one such monastery being Deir Mār Mīnā, the Monastery of St. Menas that was founded in 1959.

The clergy had caught up with the educated laity and continued to develop to the extent that many observers of the Coptic Church now refer to a "clericalization" of Coptic Church workers. This term was first introduced by Fadel Sidarouss in his dissertation *Église Copte et Monde Moderne*.[63] The author used the term to describe the increasing involvement of clergy, mainly priests, in nonliturgical activities such as clubs and trips organized by the church. The priest became more and more responsible for making the church not only a spiritual place, but also a communal place where Copts could feel safe and confirm their identity. All the layworkers in a church looked to their priests for guidance and left the ultimate responsibility for the programs up to the individual priests.[64] Nowadays the term clericalization has developed into an idea that incorporates layworkers into the official church system by consecrating them as deacons, or, in case of the women, "consecrated women." By consecrating the layworkers, the Coptic Church has acquired direct responsibility for its social and charitable activities. To supervise the different nonliturgical activities, in 1962 Patriarch Kyrillos VI appointed, for the first time, bishops without territorial dioceses.

The clericalization process was accelerated by Patriarch Shenouda III who from the beginning of his reign tirelessly worked at restructuring the Coptic Church. More than fifty new bishops were consecrated, dioceses were divided into smaller (more easily managed) regions and the workforce of priests in Cairo alone was expanded by 310. Thus every Copt was provided access to a church, a bishop and Coptic social activities.[65] Restructuring also encompassed the building of new monasteries, the renovation of old ones, and the expansion of the Coptic Seminary to include seven new branches throughout Egypt and three abroad.

In this dual capacity as patriarch and bishop for Christian education (a Coptic bishop is appointed for life and does not retire or leave his assignment), Shenouda holds the powerful position of the head, manager, and editor of virtually every Coptic institution, from the Sunday schools, to *Al-Kirāza* (the church magazine), and all of the convents and monasteries. In fact, the patriarch reigns as a shrewd effective autocrat.

The major characteristic of the Coptic revival is a renewed emphasis on monastic and ecclesial traditions. This idea is realized by more frequent celebrations of the Eucharist, stress on the church's identity as an apostolic church, renewed emphasis on the study of Coptic language, commemoration of a glorious past, emphasis on the fathers of monasticism and the church fathers, and the upholding of the ideal of martyrdom.[66] Furthermore, the Coptic Church stresses family life and strives to draw groups of people from different social strata, age, and educational background into the church system. Hence there are a variety of groups for all ages and for both females and males. Service to the church and a social life that centers around the church have become important aspects in the lives of most Copts.

THE COPTIC POPULATION

It has always been difficult to establish the exact number of Copts. Some sources estimate the number to be around four million, while some Copts themselves maintain that they are at least seven to eight million.[67] According to the census of 1986, the Copts were slightly more than 6.3 percent of the Egyptian population; however the most recent estimates shows Copts at 5.7 percent of the population.[68] The reasons given for the decline of the Coptic population are: a lower birthrate and a tendency to marry later than Muslims, emigration, and conversions from Christianity to Islam.[69]

In spite of their minority status, the Copts have always been numerous enough to be important to the Muslim state because of the functions they perform in Egyptian society. Due to a greater motivation to acquire good education for their children, and in part due to willingness and ability to pay for education, Copts traditionally have had an educational advantage over Muslims.[70] Copts hold this educational advantage in spite of restrictions they face, such as limited admissions to graduate schools, military, and police academies, and difficulties obtaining fellowships.[71] At present, the largest occupational group among the Copts are farmers. In the cities, the poorest Copts often work as *zabbalīn* (garbage collectors), while more wealthy Copts are pharmacists, doctors, lawyers, accountants, bankers, and engineers.[72]

COMMONALITIES AND DIFFERENCES WITH MUSLIMS

Egyptian Christians and Muslims have many common customs and similar patterns of speech and thought. They both share popular beliefs, an interest in the supernatural, the celebration of festivals for saints and funerals, and in some cases they even share the reverence for the same saints.[73] Many Copts have good relationships with Muslim friends, colleagues, and neighbors. On feast days members from both communities visit each other with holiday wishes and national attention is even paid to some Coptic feasts. (For example, every year on 7 January the Coptic Christmas celebrations are broadcast on television.) When faced with external challenges like the Six-Day War of June 1967, or events like the apparition of St. Mary in Zeitun, Cairo, in April 1968, Copts and Muslims show similar reactions and their social relations and actions are also similar.[74]

In spite of many cultural patterns that Copts and Muslims have in common, Copts remain an enigma to the Muslims—a stubborn people who refuse to accept the manifest truth of Islam. Popular articles have been written in the international press about interreligious strife between Copts and Muslims, but it is hard to find scientific research done on this sensitive topic. This problem is probably due to the fact that, in trying to unearth information on these tensions, the researcher is likely to tread on highly emotional ground. Members from one religion feel threatened by members from the other. For example, Kenneth Cragg observed that Copts "for all their exposure to power not their own, are seen as a threat to the dominant community—an imagined threat, to be sure, yet significant nevertheless. . . . They are suspected or accused of possessing hidden resources, of exercising a power beyond their numbers . . . , of conspiratorial capacities."[75] Muslims often fear Copts because of their alleged secret knowledge of magic.[76] Copts are haunted by the fear (both real and imagined) of physical violence from Muslims.[77] The reality is that Copts have to deal with recurring clashes—initiated by extremists—between themselves and Muslims.

COPTIC IDENTITY AND THE COPTIC CHURCH

In spite of the many similarities to the Muslim Egyptians, a distinct Coptic identity is shaped by cultural patterns and Coptic spiritual life. The Copts consider themselves to be the true descendants of the pharaohs. Coptic Christians can be identified by a tattoo of a cross on their right wrist. According to the Coptic belief, the cross is such a powerful symbol that it makes evil spirits feel uncomfortable, so that when a Copt is in danger she/he makes the sign of the cross, or says "*Bi-ism aṣ-ṣalīb*" (in the name of the cross). The Bible is also recited in such instances since certain Psalms are recited during exorcism.[78] Icons are symbols of the protection of the saints, and some icons are considered miraculous—meaning that one or more divine events took place in connection with them. Monasteries, convents, and even certain people like the patriarch or the bishops could be considered as symbols of Coptic faith.[79] Furthermore, Copts are separated from Muslims through their fasting, their devotional habits, and the different religious calendar they use.[80]

The center of Coptic Church life is the seven sacraments: Eucharist, baptism, confirmation (with holy chrism), confession and absolution, unction of the sick, matrimony, and consecration into one of the holy orders.[81] In order to participate in the Eucharist, one has to be a full member of the Coptic Church, which means that one has to be baptized and confirmed (confirmation takes place immediately after baptism, by means of anointment with holy chrism). It is also impossible to receive Communion without having received absolution after the confession of sins. In addition to this, a Copt is not allowed to take food after midnight and must have fasted for at least nine hours prior to the Eucharist.[82] Through these conditions, a tightly knit community of people (who hold the same belief and confess the same creed) is formed. Children can take Communion from the moment they are baptized and much attention is given to their upbringing in the church community. The family is brought together through Sunday school programs and religious guidance and a closed community life is guaranteed by a tradition of strict rules that are applied by the sacrament of matrimony. These rules state that when a person of another denomination intends to marry a Copt (according to the Coptic Church rite) she/he must convert to Coptic Orthodoxy and be rebaptized into the Coptic Church.

In the Coptic faith, God is the omniscient and omnipotent while humans are essentially poor sinners who would be destined to eternal damnation were it not for God's grace and infinite love.[83] The profound Coptic faith in God is characterized by spirituality, asceticism, humility, repentance and redemption, and prayers. At the same time, the Copt feels the closeness of saints, angels, and the early and recent models of monasticism.[84] A close link with tradition is essential in Coptic faith. This link is connected with emphasis on "living in the Holy Spirit." The Copts reason that since the Bible does not mention everything Jesus said and did, the believer has to be continuously aware of the guidance of the Holy Spirit. The Spirit inspired the leaders and guides of the church including the church fathers, the hermits in the desert, and the patriarchs. That is why the Copts stress the importance of the writings and sayings of these leaders. For example, the Liturgy of St. Basil (330–379) that is used during the Eucharist is considered a direct product of this guidance. The liturgy is recited in the Coptic language in its supposedly unaltered, original form.[85]

A noteworthy aspect of the Coptic faith is its optimism; one seldom sees pictures representing hell. Although, in popular piety much attention is given to devils and demons, according to Coptic clergy these religious images are best ignored.[86] During times of interreligious riots, this attitude is maintained. For example, young Copts, even when they live in a violent area, say that they try to avoid mentioning these events in Bible studies or youth clubs for fear that the students will end up thinking that unpleasant happenings is all life is about. One university student explained, "we insist on focusing on the good side of life." During interreligious riots, priests will try to encourage the afflicted community by preaching about the solace and support of the saints, the virtue of Christian forgiveness, and the powerful weapon of prayer.

COPTIC MONASTICISM: A SHORT HISTORY

The Desert Fathers and the Monks

Orthodox monasticism is not divided into specialized orders and congregations as, for example, is Catholic monasticism. In Egyptian monasticism the basic model is derived from the earliest desert fathers: St. Antony (251–356) and St. Pachomius (292–346).

As a wealthy young man, St. Antony sold his possessions and withdrew from the world after hearing the Gospel words: "If you would be perfect, go, sell what you possess and give to the poor, and you will have treasure in heaven; come, follow me."[87] At first, Antony lived in "the pigsty or cowshed at the bottom of the garden of his old home."[88] As Derwas Chitty observed, Antony "was not the first in the field." There was an old hermit in the neighborhood, and there were others further off, to whom Antony could look to for advice. But "there was not yet in Egypt this continuous chain of monasteries: and, indeed, none knew the distant desert."[89] After the place in the garden, Antony lived for several years in a tomb outside his village. From there he moved to a deserted fort on the confines of the desert, and after twenty years he went into the inner desert. There he stayed in the vicinity of where today the eponymous monastery can be found. Each of Antony's moves away from the inhabited world marked a development in his spiritual growth toward Christian perfection. During his lifetime he became well known and sought after by others who asked for spiritual guidance and who wanted to imitate his anchoritic life. After his death his fame was spread by Athanasius the Great of Alexandria (d. 373), who wrote Antony's hagiography. This account was disseminated in the East and the West and inspired Christians to live the monastic life. Although other hermits are known to have existed before Antony became an anchorite, the most famous being Paul the Hermit, Antony is considered as "*the* father of monasticism, *the* ideal of *the* real Christian way of life."[90]

Pachomius, another early desert father, converted to Christianity after a career as a soldier in the Roman army. When Pachomius felt called to a life of Christ, he started out under the guidance of another old anchorite, Palamon.[91] After Palamon's death, Pachomius started to organize groups of monks, and later nuns, in a communal or cenobitic way of life. This means that Pachomius' monks and nuns lived a communal life of sharing and mutual service.[92]

Already during the lifetime of St. Antony, several semianchoritic monastic settlements were formed in Nitria, Kellia, and Scetis. Nitria was founded by Amoun (d. 356) around 325 or 330. A dozen years later, the monks in Nitria had become so numerous that, on the advice of Antony, Amoun founded Kellia for the monks who wished to live in greater solitude.

Probably inspired by Antony as well, Macarius the Egyptian (300–390) set up a cell near the site of the present Deir al-Baramūs in 330. He was quickly surrounded by monastic followers who wanted him as their guide to the monastic life. The semianchoritic life in these settlements meant that during the week the monk stayed alone in his cell where he prayed, ate, and worked on his handicrafts. On Saturday and Sunday the monks gathered to celebrate the Eucharist, followed by a communal meal.[93] Thus, in the fourth century the development of three monastic lifestyles was under way—the anchoritic, the semianchoritic, and the communal.

In 370, as a boy, Shenute of Atripe (d. 466) entered the monastery and around 440 he constructed the White Monastery. Shenute became important as a religious leader of many monks and nuns, and was a prolific writer in the Coptic language.[94]

The sources for what one knows about the first monks and nuns (apart from *The Life of Antony*), are from accounts made sometime during the fourth century by a few travelers and hermits who visited the monastic communities. Three such accounts are as follows: *The Lausiac History* of Palladius, the *Historia Monachorum in Aegypto*, the *Institutes* and *Conferences* written between 420 and 430 by John Cassian. Another important source for information on the early monks is the *Apophthegmata Patrum* (The Sayings of the Fathers). All these works, written in Latin or Greek and disseminated to the West, spread the fame of Egyptian monasticism and are still among the main sources of inspiration for Egyptian monastics today.[95]

The Desert Mothers and the Nuns

At the time St. Antony gave up his worldly life, there must have been groups of women living a monastic type of life together, since Antony "entrusted his sister to a community of virgins."[96] Pachomius, himself started a community for women that was headed by his sister Mary. The group was led according to the principles Pachomius designed for his own community.[97] Through Palladius' writings (*Lausiac History*) and the *Apophthegmata* some of the women who lived monastic lives are made known. Among others, Palladius mentions virgins who lived the ascetic life in their own homes or in a cloister near their own city. He also mentions the convent where Ammā Talis was the superior, and he describes deaconesses such as Olympias.[98] In the *Apophthegmata* one can find the words of the spiritual Mother Sarah and Mother Syncletica.[99] Other sources mention women who lived in the desert alone (Mary of Egypt) or in man's disguise—Hilaria (known as Hilarion the Eunuch) and Theodora.[100] The Coptic tradition has its own "woman-monk," St. Marina.[101] Furthermore there are female martyrs who lived the monastic life, such as St. Dimyānah and her forty virgins.[102] In spite of these examples, few women are known to have lived the anchoritic life in the desert, the preeminent place for male anchorites. The desert was perceived as too dangerous a place for a solitary female. The fact that the Council of Gangra (340) forbade women to disguise themselves as monks, might indicate that women tried to imitate male anchorites by going into the desert.[103] An alternative for some women who wanted to live a monastic life can be seen in the fifth century, where some eighteen hundred nuns were living under the guidance of Shenute in the White Monastery.[104]

The heritage left by these early monks and nuns is still avidly studied by the contemporary monastics. By constant study of the hagiographies, monastics strive to imitate the spiritual and ascetic practices of their forebears as far as the modern world will allow them. The example set by St. Antony is still seen as the supreme form of monasticism and every monk tries to come as close as possible to St. Antony's anchoritic life. Because, "St. Antony formed the monk from inside with love for the solitary life and quiet, . . . away from everything, . . . he busied his mind and heart only with God in a life of quiet."[105] The beginnings of Egyptian monasticism are still generally veiled in obscurity so one's knowledge is shaped by the hagiographic literature.

After the Arab invasion in 641, few stories were heard about solitary hermits, and the surviving monasteries became important fortresses of Coptic heritage. The monasteries assured their importance in Coptic life after the invasion by securing the role of custodians of the memory and hagiography of early monasticism. The monasteries became ethnic symbols and models of holy living in the world.[106] During the Arab medieval period, the monasteries' influence gradually declined. Again, little is known about the period from the fourteenth century to the end of the eighteenth. The main source of information is *The History of the Patriarchs of Alexandria,* ascribed to Sāwīrus ibn al-Muqaffaʿ. This text gives the official history of the Coptic Church and should be considered as a "tradition of historical writings" from the first to the thirteenth century, with fragments from the fourteenth to the early twentieth century.[107] At times, monasticism in Egypt was "reduced to poverty and stripped of ecclesiastical dominance," but it did not expire.[108] The convents for women also survived, but even less is known about them. From the time of Shenute's convent for women (fifth century) until the second half of the twentieth century there is not one document available that deals solely with the convents. However, a footnote in *The History of the Patriarchs of Alexandria* does mention a rich Lady Tarfa who donated money to the convents in the twelfth century.[109]

Throughout the history of the church, the patriarch remained the focus of Coptic life. This is shown by the fact that the Copts have produced a complete list of all the reigning patriarchs beginning with St. Mark and including the present patriarch, Shenouda III. The patriarch and the incidental holy man or woman secured the hagiographic tradition and kept the memory of the early church alive. Thus one can explain why at the beginning of this century, the Coptic majority backed their clergy in hampering the reformation of the laity. And why Bishop Athanasius, the Metropolitan of Beni Suef and Bahnasa, commented that it is wrong to draw the simple conclusion that the Coptic Church was in decline. According to Bishop Athanasius, "the renaissance of the church did not come out of a vacuum." He pointed to "outstanding monks and patriarchs such as Patriarch Kyrillos IV and Kyrillos V, saintly Bishop Sarabamun (exact date unknown, sometime during the end of the eighteenth century), and Bishop Abraam (1829–1914)."[110] These remarks bring one back to the conclusion that only persons, considered holy on the basis of position, lifestyle, or both, qualified to initiate a lasting church reform.

SUMMARY

The role the Egyptian Christians played in the Roman Empire ended abruptly with the Arab invasion. The centuries which followed saw the Copts turning inward, stressing the apostolic character of their church, and clinging to its tradition. Coptic Church life became strictly separated from the Muslim environment and from other Christian traditions. Nowadays, this Coptic attitude might be interpreted as a reaction to the Islamic environment which equally stresses its traditions and unaltered religious texts and rules.

The Coptic revival started as a reaction to religious, social, and economic challenges from outside the church. The revival materialized from the end of the 1940s onward, when well-trained clergy became available to guide it. Eventually, this revival took place by means of education and social projects and became visible in the increase of religious and ascetic practices. Many Copts indicate Kyrillos VI as the person who united these different efforts for reform. At the end of the nineteenth century, the Coptic community's goal was to equip itself to face the influences brought about by increasing contacts with the West and to keep pace with the rest of the Egyptian society. During the 1950s this goal shifted to strengthening the community in the face of Islamic revivalism.

In spite of many similarities between Copts and Muslims, their respective religions will remain incompatible based on their self-understandings. Copts do not understand the Muslim insistence in denying the sonship of Christ, while the official tenet of the Coptic religion that "Christ is God" is blasphemy to Muslim ears.[111]

The monastic heritage of desert fathers and mothers still plays an important role in the present. This heritage is more or less confined to the centuries prior to the Arab invasion. What came after the invasion remains rather opaque.

The role of the monasteries for men was crucial for the revival. Apart from generating leaders and models, from the 1950s onward they produced literature to equip the Copts for realizing and discovering their own identity and faith in the present.

These developments prepared the setting in which women could also have active roles in the life of the church. Women often had already participated as volunteers in social projects and in the Sunday School Movement. An increasing clericalization contributed to the incorporation of laywomen into social church activities. At the same time, contemplative nuns resumed and reshaped the traditional monastic life for women.

CHAPTER 2

The Monastic Landscape

There are a variety of groups of women and men living a celibate life in a contemplative or active monastic community who are helping to shape the present Coptic landscape. I will first look at the largest and most influential groups, but because of their diversity and the rapid changes in Coptic society, this picture is descriptive only and necessarily condensed. After this introduction, I will then discuss how and where these groups live—the buildings and the environment of monastic life. Because the patron saints are closely connected with the convents, I will discuss some aspects of this relationship between the two in this chapter.

THE VARIOUS MONASTIC VOCATIONS

Within the present female monastic movement one can discern three groups: the contemplative nuns, the active nuns, and the consecrated women.

The Contemplative Nuns

The contemplative nuns live a completely cloistered life and claim to follow the authentic monastic ideal as it was initiated in the fourth and fifth century by Antony and Pachomius. To date, there are six nunneries in Egypt that are recognized by the Holy Synod, the supreme ecclesiastical authority of the Coptic Church. The Holy Synod is the highest legislative body in the church, with the patriarch as its head and all the metropolitans, bishops, abbots, chorepiscopi, and patriarchal deputies as its members. At present the Holy Synod has seventy members and is the

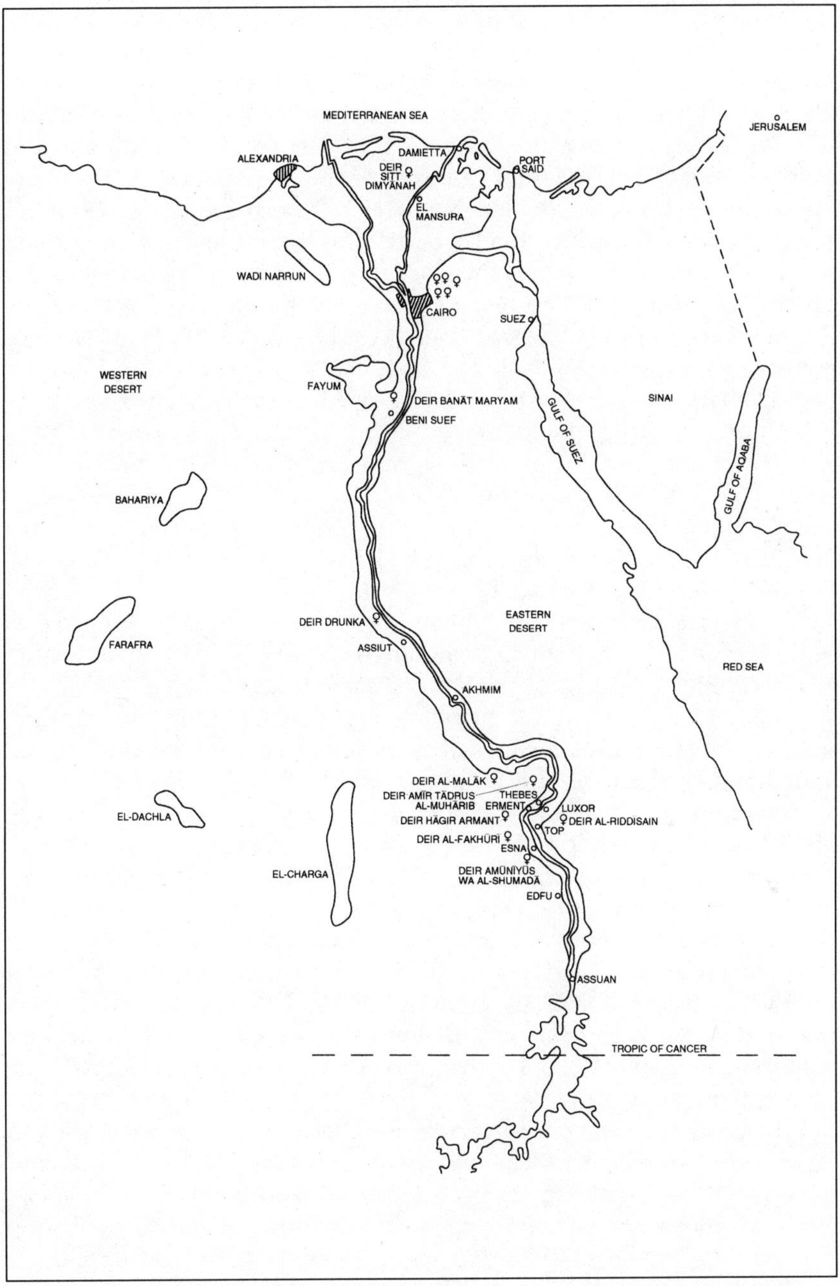

Coptic convents, women's monastic projects, and active groups in Egypt

sole body that can ratify the founding of a new convent or monastery.[1] There are five convents in Cairo: Deir Abū Saifein, or the Convent of St. Mercurius, and Deir Māri Girgis, or the Convent of St. George, both in Old Cairo; Deir al-ʿAdhrāʾ, or the Convent of the Virgin or of St. Mary, and Deir Māri Girgis, or the Convent of St. George, both in the heart of Cairo; and, finally, Deir Amīr Tādrus, or the Convent of St. Theodore Stratelates.[2] The sixth convent is in the Northern Delta about 6 miles north of Bilqās. It is called the Deir Sitt Dimyānah, the Convent of Lady or St. Dimyānah, and was officially recognized in 24 September 1978. The present convent is the result of a reinhabitation project around the Shrine of St. Dimyānah where annually a big *maulid* (the feast to commemorate the day a saint died or was martyred) takes place from the fifth to the twentieth of May.[3] Before the present convent was established, two monks of the Monastery of St. Antony used to live near the shrine in order to serve potential pilgrims.[4] Apart from the officially recognized convents, in Upper Egypt several abandoned monastic sites are being reinhabited by female monastics. For these projects, nuns have been recruited either from established convents or were initiated by Bishop Ammonius, the local bishop.[5]

The precise number of nuns involved in these reinhabitation projects cannot be given since both contemplative nuns and consecrated women are involved. Novices in Upper Egypt do not decide which monastic lifestyle they will choose until after they have finished their novitiate period. Hence one finds a mixture of contemplatives, consecrated women, and novices living together in these convents.

Contemplative nuns are dressed in long black garb that symbolizes their death to the world. The nun's head is covered by a long black veil over a tight black skullcap. A contemplative nun is called *umminā* (our mother) and the mother superior is called *umminā raʾīsa* (our mother superior). Contemplative nuns are also addressed by the Coptic equivalent for "our mother," *tamauf*. The Arabic word for nun is *rāhiba*. The word for their convent is *dair* in modern standard Arabic (which is pronounced as *deir* in the Egyptian dialect). Few ever make the distinction between contemplative and active communities; rather, that knowledge is already presumed.[6]

When one tries to count the total number of contemplative nuns in Egypt, one is inevitably faced by an enormous discrepancy of opinion. Superiors are often reluctant to volunteer the exact number, or they may give a fictitious number. Relying on the information given by Bishop Athanasius, I came to an approximate estimate of 485 contemplative nuns and novices for all Egypt. The majority of these nuns and novices are found in Deir Abū Saifein that has a population of around 100 nuns.

Other convents in Cairo have a total of 245 inhabitants, which brings the number of nuns in Cairo to around 345. The rest of the contemplative nuns live in Deir Sitt Dimyānah, the projects around Luxor, and other places scattered all over Egypt. In an article of 1973 Bishop Athanasius counted 150 nuns for the whole of Egypt. This means that the number of nuns has more than doubled in the last twenty years.[7]

Apart from the contemplative nuns who live in convents there are a few female hermits living in Egypt. Since I am not aware of all of them, I can only acknowledge that they exist. These anchorites may live in small apartments in Cairo, or on a monastic site.

The Active Community in Beni Suef

This active community of nuns was established on the feast of the Holy Cross, 19 March 1965. On 1 January 1969 the first two women of this community took their vows, and on 30 January 1970, the Feast of St. Antony, they were officially initiated.[8] This active community has the blessing of Patriarch Kyrillos VI (1959–1971) but has not yet been officially recognized by the Holy Synod. The active community was a new phenomenon in the Coptic Church and was established as an alternative to the existing contemplative convents. One of the aims of active communities is "to practice the monastic tradition of the early church fathers in accordance with the instructions of contemporary church and monastic leadership."[9] This wording indicates that the community intends to follow the pattern of the early fathers just as the traditional contemplative monastics do. The active community derives its name from St. Mary (the Mother of Christ) and is called Deir Banāt Maryam (the Daughters of St. Mary); Mary is their patron saint. The sisters are dressed in grey ankle-length dresses with short grey veils on their heads. According to the nuns, they chose this design after consultation with Patriarch Kyrillos VI, who stipulated that they wear a dress different from that of the contemplatives. He wanted the dress to be comfortable and suitable for the sisters' active work.[10] The patriarch also stipulated that, although the Arabic word for the active nun is *rāhiba*, as it is for the contemplative, the active nuns would be addressed as *tāsūnī* instead of *umminā*. *Tāsūnī* is the Coptic word for "my sister" (in Arabic, *ukhtī*). When I speak in this study about the active nuns I will use the word sister, or *tāsūnī*.

The community of active sisters started in Beni Suef under the guidance of Bishop Athanasius. The bishop had guided the first two sisters of this community since 1962 when they approached him with the idea of living a monastic life. The two women had been actively involved in social and church work before they contacted the bishop. Since they were not attracted to the contemplative convents, they hoped that the bishop could help them find an alternative.

The newly built mother house for the active community is in Beni Suef. The house provides room for all the members of the community, even members who live in Cairo or in other places where the convent runs social service projects. Away from the convent, the nuns live near the social projects, in retreat centers, orphanages, and in other such places. In January 1992, the community had eighty members, including initiated sisters and novices.

The Consecrated Women

During the 1980s, the Coptic Church started to experiment with the consecration of young women to a type of deaconess position.[11] The term *consecrated* is actually not accurate because the young women do not belong to the body of consecrated officials such as deacons or priests. *Dedicated* is perhaps a more appropriate word. The word *mukarrasa* that is used to designate these young women is derived from the verb *karrasa,* which means to "consecrate" or to "dedicate oneself."[12] At present, *mukarrasāt* (the consecrated or dedicated women) are living in small groups, under the jurisdiction of a local bishop whom they assist in social, medical, and educational activities.[13]

All the *mukarassāt* work with women, the elderly, and children. The *mukarrasāt* are not allowed to perform any tasks pertaining to the holy sacraments, such as carrying "the Holy Communion from the church to the homes of sick women" or helping the priest "to baptize or to chrismate"; nor can they read from the Bible during the liturgy or a public meeting.[14] Sometimes the consecrated women are sent abroad to assist a bishop or a priest (in, for example, Nairobi or Kenya or in Coptic communities in the United States).

The *mukarrasāt* are initiated or dedicated during a special ceremony for which a new rite has been recently introduced.[15] The system in which they work is still under design. Patriarch Shenouda III expressed the intention to develop a system with three steps of consecration: (1) consecrated or dedicated woman, (2) consecration as sub-deaconess, and (3) consecration as *shammāsa* (deaconess).[16]

Like the active nuns, members of the *mukarrasāt* are called *tāsūnī* (sister). Some of these young women are dressed in distinctive grey ankle-length dresses with small grey veils on their heads, while others wear secular clothes with a headscarf. Although most of these young women have taken a vow of celibacy before their official dedication, there are cases in which a young woman is free to marry after a few years of church service.[17]

Because these women are scattered all over Egypt, trying to estimate the number of *mukarrasāt* is as difficult as it is to find out the number of contemplative nuns.[18] The rough estimate is that there are about six hundred *mukarrasāt* scattered over the different dioceses in Egypt.[19]

The Female Hermits

The handful of female hermits in Egypt, or nuns who live as recluses with one or two other women, follow the example of the earliest desert mothers like St. Mary (of Egypt), St. Alexandra, St. Syncletica, and St. Sarah. There must have been many other female recluses; we do have accounts of nuns who lived alone during the 1950s.

The Monks

There are twelve monasteries for monks in Egypt that have been recognized by the Holy Synod. As is the case with the contemplative nunneries, all monasteries are located on historical monastic sites. A monk is called *abūnā* (our father), the same title by which one addresses a priest, and usually dresses in a black floor-length garment.

Recent estimates are that there are at least a thousand Coptic monks. Because many monks hold clerical positions outside the monastery, counting them is difficult due to the fact that one can seldom find all the monks actually present in any one place.[20] At present several reinhabitation projects are also taking place among the monasteries for men.

This description of the traditional and modern monastic groups operating within the present Coptic Church cannot claim to be more than a rough sketch of the monastic lifestyle. The modern monks, nuns, and consecrated women are experimenting today with new tasks and roles and finding modern modes of life. At the same time, the Holy Synod of the Coptic Church is studying issues concerning the liturgies for consecration, division of responsibilities, and other matters. The perception changes at any time with events such as the death of an inspirational leader, new decisions by the Holy Synod, and external social factors. For example, higher levels of education and economic considerations induce many young people to postpone marriage and find fulfillment in church activities. Since, in Egyptian society it is not accepted

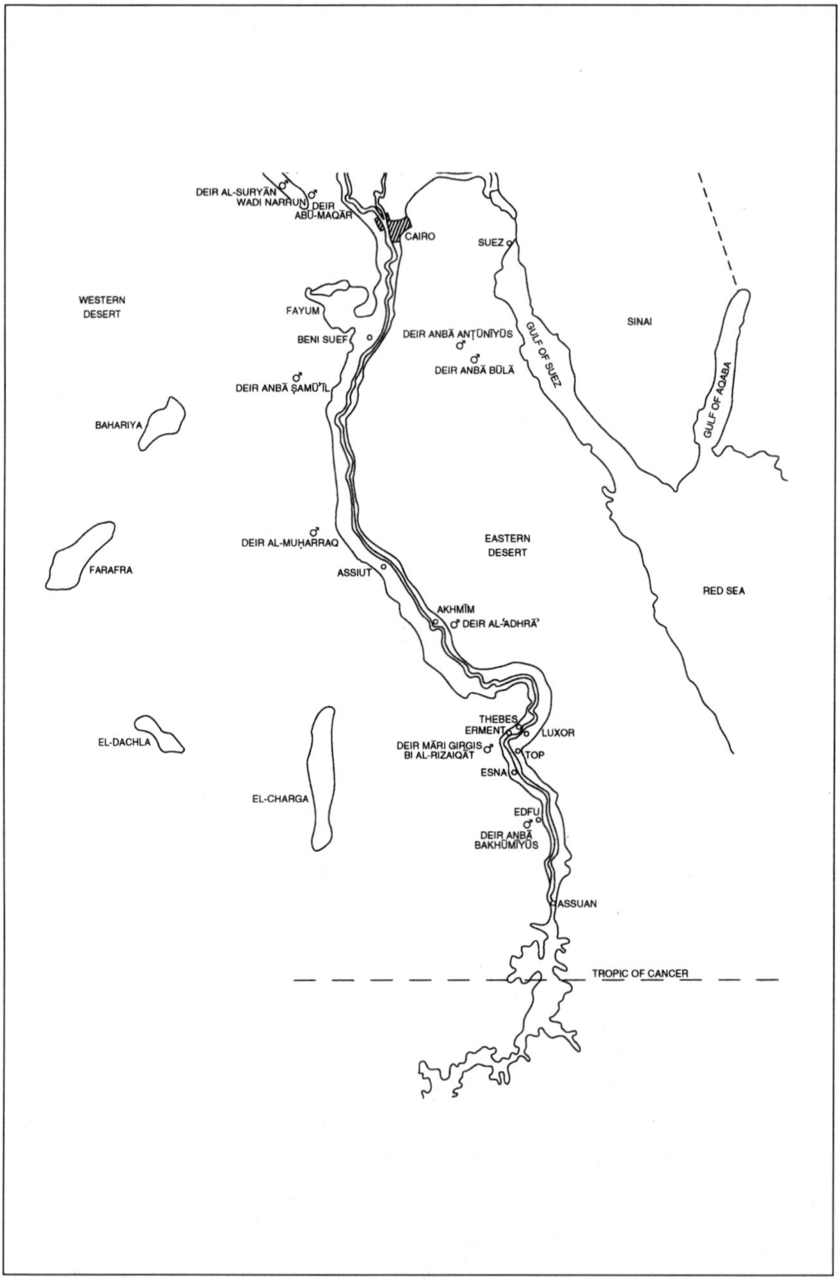

Coptic Monasteries in Egypt

that a young woman remain single without intending ever to marry, women might opt for a monastic career in order to avoid marriage. But the contemplative convents are overcrowded and do not have room to accept considerable numbers of novices; and there is a good chance that young women will not find a place in a convent. Nevertheless, they might decide to pursue a career in lay-church activities, to become a *mukarrasa,* or active sister. It is difficult to predict what the impact of an increasing number of celibate young women will be, for example, on the social life of the Coptic community.

PHYSICAL ENVIRONMENTS

The Contemplative Nuns

All convents are situated on historical Coptic sites and four of them have been (at certain times) connected to the residency of the patriarch. From around 1061, the patriarchal residence was in Old Cairo; from 1300–1660, the patriarch lived at Ḥārat Zuweilah from where the residence was moved to Ḥārat al-Rūm. Here the patriarch resided until 1799, when the residence moved to Claude Bey.

The Convent of Abū Saifein was part of a walled complex that included three churches, various houses and gardens. The convent used to be called Deir al-Banāt (the Convent of the Maidens), while the whole complex had the name of Deir Abū Saifein, named after the principal church within it.

Deir Māri Girgis, in Old Cairo, was part of what used to be the ancient Roman Fortress of Babylon, now called Qaṣr al-Shamaʿah. The fortress contained six churches, one of them being the chapel of Māri Girgis that adjoins the present-day convent.

According to legend, the Holy Family stayed at the sites where later the convents in Old Cairo and Ḥārat Zuweilah, were built. Legend has it that the Holy Family moved from North Cairo (the old Heliopolis now known as Mataria and Mostorod), to Ḥārat Zuweilah, from where they proceeded to Babylon. South of Babylon they crossed the Nile and, via Memphis, continued their way southwards to Upper Egypt.[21]

Religious life in Deir Sitt Dimyānah has been rekindled recently; in 1969 several nuns were recruited from other convents in order to reinhabit the ancient monastic site. This reinhabitation project reaches back to the days of Patriarch Kyrillos V (1874–1929), who encouraged the restoration of many churches, monasteries, and nunneries. In the case of the complex where the modern convent is situated, it was Bishop Butrus of Daqhaliyyah (d. 1920) who started building a new church to provide for the needs of the numerous pilgrims who attend the annual feasts in honor of St. Dimyānah.[22]

While the monks' monasteries are built in the desert, all the recognized convents are situated in a city or inhabited district. According to the Coptic Church this is so because "due to their weak nature" women cannot cope with life in the desert.[23] This official explanation for city-based convents results from the attitude that "women need protection, they cannot live on their own, especially not in this Muslim environment."[24] This argument is also used to explain why convents often adjoined the patriarchal residence. The patriarch gave the best protection possible, while at the same time the nuns could see to the patriarch's needs. They cooked and cleaned for him and did other services. The traditional argument against women going into the desert used to be that they could be a temptation for the monks. Nowadays neither the written nor the oral sources express this argument.

The present convents in Cairo are situated in old, populous quarters. The precise word used to describe the areas hosting the convents is the Egyptian Arabic word *baladī*. *Baladī* stands for "traditional Egyptian style"; the people who are considered to be "baladī" belong to the conservative lower class, opposed to what is modern and effected by external influence.[25] The baladī districts are old districts where one can still find the oriental style of towns with narrow streets and towerlike structures. Nowadays they are hosted by poor people, living in relatively uncomfortable conditions. Going into the area means leaving the modern world behind and stepping back in time. The ever-present television sets and radios—products of modern technology—do not change physical and psychological removal from the modern world. Men, clad in the traditional long dress with wide sleeves, the *gallābīya*, with a shawl around the neck and one around the head in the shape of a turban, sit on chairs in front of the coffeehouses. They watch the passers-by while inside the male customers discuss life's problems, play backgammon, and watch television. Further on the way to the convent, the visitor has to evade the shopkeepers hawking their wares, barefoot children, and the occasional car plowing through the masses of people making their way along the narrow, confined streets, little more than oversized sidewalks. Young men, bicycling with ungainly trays of bread balanced on their heads, zigzag through the crowds. A maze of narrow alleyways leads up to the convent.

Female Hermits

Today these women live in apartments that are often part of a church compound with other buildings that are used for retreats and meetings. This means that during long stretches of time the area is quiet and deserted. Often the co-users of the premises are the doorkeeper and his family who assist the recluses with running errands and buying food. These hermits rarely leave their cell. Only for medical reasons, to attend church services from behind a screen in the church, and to celebrate Christmas or Easter with other nuns do these women come out of their cells.

The living conditions of the modern hermits resemble what Father Giamberardini saw in 1952 when he visited some solitary nuns in Old Cairo. He met a nun called Mother Angela who was living in "a cave with traces of ancient Christian pictures." Giamberardini continues that the cave "is inside Deir Malāk Mīkhā'īl, Old Cairo, that is now converted into houses for Coptic families. Mother Angela still lives there, prays there, eats and sleeps there."[26] On one floor of the same building lived two nuns who had previously belonged to a convent that they left "because of health reasons."[27]

Architecture of the Contemplative Convents

None of the convents is built identically to any others. Upon scrutiny, however, a general pattern emerges in the architecture of the buildings and premises. From the outside, the convent almost reminds one of a prison. It often has a high wall around the garden, and the buildings that meet this garden wall all have barred windows. The windows are high up so that a pedestrian cannot cast a glance inside. Outside the walls is a heavily bolted door with an imposing knocker. One enters into a receiving area that has an open connection with a garden or inner courtyard. Around that garden or courtyard, the living quarters are built.

Inside the nunneries there is a strict division of public and private space by means of differing levels. On the ground floor one finds the reception rooms, a kitchen to cater to guests, chapels, and shrines. One of the rooms serves as a souvenir shop and some of the convents have a tiny clinic. The other floors contain the cells of the nuns, their refectory, meeting rooms, a library, a pharmacy, and in some cases a small chapel. Some convents house small livestock facilities such as chicken coops or barns with sheep. The structure is like that of a traditional oriental house. The area for guests is directly accessible while all the private quarters, including the living quarters of servants, are inaccessible to the guest. This architectural style aims at protecting the privacy of the house's residents in a way reminiscent of upper-class Cairene homes as described by E. W. Lane in 1836: "the principal aim of the architect is to render the house as private as possible, particularly that part of it which is inhabited by the women."[28]

Convents do not have facilities to lodge guests, as male monasteries do. The nuns explain that, due to the structure of their convent, there is no possibility of adding buildings for guests. Since the convents are situated in densely populated areas, they are surrounded by adjacent buildings standing wall to wall. As is the case with most urban people, the nuns find their space constricted. The only possibility for extending their living space is to add floors on top of the existing buildings, a widely practiced solution. The nunneries seem to have endless construction going on.

Because of the increase in the number of monastic candidates, the problem of space has become critical for the convents. Since only so many floors can be added to an existing building, the nuns have had to look elsewhere for space. Three convents, Abū Saifein, Māri Girgis in Ḥārat Zuweilah, and the Convent of Al-ʿAdhrāʾ, have managed to expand their property by purchasing a plot of land where the nuns have built farms. At the outset, the problems involved in obtaining an extra plot of land to build for monastic purposes seem insurmountable. Apart from the fact that contemplative nuns are not allowed to go out, there is the problem of financial backing and the difficulty of obtaining building permission from the government. Nevertheless, the nuns managed to overcome these problems in a skillful and adept way, relying on God, Jesus Christ, and the intercession of the saints to help them.

Only the Convent of St. Dimyānah in the northern Delta has spacious premises that allow for the construction of an adjacent retreat house for young women. Furthermore, the convent holds an apartment in Cairo in a building that belongs to the Coptic Church. One of the elderly nuns lives here almost permanently in order to look after the convent's interests.

The Active Sisters

During the formative years of revitalization, at the end of the 1960s, the first four active nuns in the Coptic Church lived in a rented apartment. With the increase in the number of active nuns, the sisters were allowed to borrow a more spacious house that the Diocese of Beni Suef originally had constructed for a project involving male deacons. The house had become vacant; the majority of the deacons had preferred to join a monastery. As the nuns' community kept on growing, the sisters had to look for a more spacious abbey during the 1970s. Unlike the contemplative communities, this new community was not restricted to a historical convent, which gave the sisters more leeway to purchase or build a place. The present mother house was built in the 1970s. It is a six-story modern apartment building with room for expansion. The house was designed to provide a room for each member of the community, regardless of whether or not the sister worked in a project outside Beni Suef. The mother house is situated in the heart of the city, behind the bishopric. Its premises are shared with buildings that house several of the community's activities: a clinic, a nursery, an old people's home, and a boardinghouse for young women from broken homes. The entire complex is surrounded by walls. A *bawwāb* (male doorkeeper) guards the main gate, which is opened during the day. In the daytime there is a constant flow of visitors, children, patients, sisters, and workers.

The convent's annexes are housed in buildings that vary from a simple apartment to structures that have room for several dozen people. All of these facilities are situated in the middle or next to the projects where the sisters work. There are three community houses in Cairo; other active sisters live in small-scale projects spread throughout Egypt.

Only the interior design of the mother house ensures visitors that they have entered a convent. As was the case with the contemplative nunneries, in the quarters of active sisters there is a strict division between public and private space. Right behind the entrance on the ground floor sits a receptionist with her back to the stairs that lead to the sisters' living quarters. Regular visitors are allowed into the living quarters, for example, to join the communal meal. Inside the convent is a sober and practical environment, with walls painted in light colors. The rooms, or cells, are about 2 x 3 meters each, and each one contains a bed, a desk with a chair, and a wardrobe. Light and sun can enter through windowed doors that open onto a balcony. On each floor there are communal toilets with showers and basins to wash laundry. Both the mother house and the bigger annexes have a chapel for worship services. The mother house contains a library, offices, and workshops for handicrafts.

Where I could observe that the contemplative nunneries were enclosed in crowded areas, I could conclude that the active community voluntarily chose to be in populated places, in order to be closer to the sisters' work. I also observed that the active community's struggle with space is less urgent as far as living quarters are concerned. Most of their problems consisted of finding room to carry out their projects.

The Men's Monasteries

Traditional monasteries are situated in the desert, away from the inhabited world. In earlier days a visit to the monastery required a long journey by camel. Monasteries were built to protect their inhabitants and to provide shelter and provisions for long periods of time. The fortresslike edifice is surrounded by a high, thick wall. In order to prevent unwelcome visitors from entering, some monasteries did not have a door. Everyone entering had to be hoisted up into the monastery by means of a pulley.[29] The standard layout inside used to consist, and often still does, of living quarters, kitchens, a bakery, mills, a refectory, a library, and a guest house. Monasteries typically have several churches within them. Today, apart from the traditional monastic elements, one can find in the modern monasteries a pharmacy, workshops for repairing cars and agricultural machines, a printing press, and a souvenir shop.

As was the case with the contemplative and active convents for women, one finds a strict division between the private and the public life within the enclosed walls of the monastery. This division is hardly noticeable to the ordinary visitor unless one gets a full view of the complex from above the monastery's wall or from the top of a hill nearby. In the private quarters of the complex are the monks's cells, most of the workshops, and certain chapels. This portion of the monastery is inaccessible to visitors in order not to disturb the monks in their spiritual exercises. The father who is in charge of the guests, together with some of the older monks, takes meticulous care so that guests do not enter the wrong door. Now that the monasteries' centuries-long isolation has been broken and women are able to visit, the monks feel that their psychological/spiritual peace is threatened.

The guest houses are built in the public quarters and were not originally intended to house female guests, since the only visitors to the monastery (apart from Coptic priests, bishops, and monks) had been European travelers who were often clergymen themselves.

Most of the monasteries own a farm in the fertile area along the Nile where vegetables are grown and where the older monks can move in the event that life in the desert becomes too harsh. Apart from these farms there are *maqārr* (houses) in Cairo where the monks can stay whenever they have any business to do in the capital.

The Cell

The *al-qallāya* or, in spoken language, *al-qillāya* (cell) is the most important place in the life of a monastic after initiation. In some monasteries the monks consider their cells as holy as a church, and, as they do before entering a church, the monks take off their shoes before they go inside. In the words of one of the fathers: "Go and sit in your cell; the cell will teach you everything."[30] While the monastic stays in the cell (praying, keeping vigil, and doing works of repentance) he or she learns the essence of the monastic life and lives it. When one wants to know whether or not nuns hold an egalitarian position in relationship to the monks in the Coptic Church's hierarchy, an analysis of the condition of their cells can provide some useful information. With E. T. Hall's remark in mind that "space speaks" because it is a "message system," one can look at the various degrees of monasticism in connection with the place of the cell.[31]

In the highest degree of initiation, the male or female hermit lives in a solitary place, in or outside the monastery. The cell can be a cave, a traditional cell, a tomb, or anything that provides a certain degree of shelter. The hermit is self-supporting and only has to leave the abode once in a while to get provisions. The place is hard to reach and most of the time only a few people know where to find it.

For the monks the location of the monastery in the desert is clearly removal from the world itself. And inside the monastery, there is the further division of public space and private space. Until initiation, the novice lives in the public space which he has to share with visitors, workers, and guests. The monks' cells are situated in private space and represent the quintessence of an ascetic life of seclusion. The interior of the cell is designed in such a way that the monk can stay alone for many days, never needing to leave. Not even the need for food can force him out of the cell since he can stock up and prepare what he needs in his own little kitchen. As an alternative to his cell, the monk can take a walk in the desert.[32] A monk can, provided his spiritual father approves, stay in his cell and perform his prayers and daily devotions by himself. This means that his solitary and private devotional life has priority over communal devotions.

Contemplative nuns used to be more or less forced to live in the city. Ideally speaking, the nuns' cells are supposed to have the same purpose as the monks'—solitude. However, the nuns' cells lack the space of the monks' cells, and thus the nuns are forced to leave their solitary rooms in order to get food. Because of the location of convents in the cities, a walk in the desert has been out of the question for a nun. Nevertheless, in the past two decades nuns have begun to catch up with monks in terms of the possibilities to live a semianchoritic life. The nuns of Deir Sitt Dimyānah insist on eating alone in their cells. There is room to walk inside some of the farms the nunneries have built. And the newly inhabited monastic settlements in Upper Egypt are situated on the edge of the desert, allowing the nuns more solitude. Recently contemplative nuns have developed activities that provide them with more options to return to the ideal state of being, apart from the world.

The cell of an active sister merely serves as a place for her to sleep, rest, and perform her private prayers. Once a week the sister has a *khalwa* (day of retreat) that she spends in her cell. The cell is situated in a private part of the convent and is not accessible to outsiders. However, this is not the case with the cell of a *mukarrasa* (consecrated woman). The consecrated women live in the middle of the people they serve, or in the middle of a city in an apartment that is accessible to visitors.

THE PATRON SAINTS OF THE CONVENTS

Each of the officially recognized convents bears the name of its patron saint and possesses the saint's relics and icons or other holy objects connected with the saint. These possessions are especially venerated by the nuns. (For example the Convent of Māri Girgis in Old Cairo guards the chain of Māri Girgis, a chain that is said to have healing power.) In the case of Deir al-ʿAdhrāʾ the nuns venerate a historical icon of St. Mary that is dated 1736. Most convents have special relationships with one or more saints other than their patron saint; of course all of the nuns, both the contemplatives and the actives, insist on a special connection with St. Mary, the Mother of Christ. The Convent of Abū Saifein houses two churches dedicated to St. Dimyānah and St. Mary where, according to the nuns, miracles of healing and apparitions have taken place. Deir Māri Girgis in Ḥārat Zuweilah has an icon of St. Efrūsīnā (1228–1308), a saintly mother superior who, during her life possessed healing power and the gift of clairvoyance.[33] The present nuns say that believers still call upon St. Efrūsīnā to heal them. Apart from icons of St. Dimyānah and St. Mārīnā the convent of Amīr Tādrus has a well with holy water that is associated with St. Onuphrios (Abū Nūfer al-Sāʾiḥ), a hermit from the fourth century.[34] The well was discovered about two centuries ago through the intervention of St. Onuphrios himself. The story of the well's discovery was passed down orally, and because it is illustrative of the relationship between the nuns and their patron saint(s), I will quote it almost in its entirety. The present nuns have recorded this story as it was told to them by Mother Martha, the convent's superior who died in 1988:

> Saint Abū Nūfer al-Sāʿiḥ appeared to mother Malikah, one of the convent's superiors more than two centuries ago . . . and asked her to dig a hole to a certain depth at a place inside the convent that he pointed out to her. The place was where nowadays the well is situated, inside the *al-maqṣūra* [special chapel]. But she did not give attention to carrying out this order because she thought that it was the devil. But the saint appeared again to her three times, saying: "I am not a devil but I am Abū Nūfer al-Sāʿiḥ." . . . Then she ordered a hole to be dug, as he had told her to, and indeed, the well appeared and water came pouring out of it. However, the water was bitter and not fit for human consumption; it was only used for bathing in order to obtain the blessed healing of many diseases. Mother Martha, the former superior of the convent, told us [the nuns] that Saint Abū Nūfer al-Sāʿiḥ appeared to her in a vision during the celebration of the Holy Week. He told her after the Mass of the Holy Saturday that for the water to become sweet she should throw the contents of the *al-shūriyah* [incense chalice], in the well, together with the "Abū Ghalamsīs" oil.[35] So Mother Martha did as she was told in the vision and she threw the contents of the incense chalice into the water, together with a bit of Abū Ghalamsīs oil, and the water of the well was no longer bitter but became potable and still is today for anyone who wants to get its blessings."[36]

It is said that later on the water of the well became instrumental in many healings, a consolation in times of distress and for whatever physical and psychological problems people brought to the attention of Mother Martha.

Finally, the Convent of St. Dimyānah forms part of a complex of churches built around the Shrine of St. Dimyānah and her coterie of forty virgins. St. Dimyānah is an extremely popular saint in Egypt. She is said to have been martyred during the Era of Diocletian (284–305) together with the forty virgins who shared the monastic life with her. One of the churches bearing the saint's name is built over the grave in which all of them are said to be resting, their bodies lying in the shape of a cross with St. Dimyānah in the middle. The shrine was and still is a popular pilgrimage site.[37]

SUMMARY

In summary one might observe that, in the cases of the contemplative nuns and the monks, a link with monastic tradition is maintained by having the convent or monastery situated on a historically monastic site. The site is often connected with the church hierarchy or the tomb of a popular saint, or it was the area of a well-known pilgrimage. More modern forms of monasticism call for more modern housing. This means loosening an important connection with the monastic tradition by locating some of the monastic groups in areas other than the traditional sites.

The contemplatives nuns' location in the cities was justified by the argument that women need protection and are not capable of living alone in the desert—an argument that was already used at the Council of Gangra (340). This argument could be interpreted as a hidden statement concerning women's inability to fight the devil or the demons that are believed to dwell in the desert. Furthermore, there is the underlying argument that women in the desert are potential temptations for the monks. The way that the cell is set up in monastic places reveals that monks still have the advantage over nuns of living close to the eremitic ideal. However, contemporary contemplative nuns are trying to recapture this early monastic ideal themselves by building farms and by reinhabiting settlements in desert land.

CHAPTER 3

The Ruling Mothers and Fathers

Conditions and implications concerning the hierarchy and management of a monastic institution are regulated by "the rule." But just as Orthodox monasticism is not divided into specialized orders, so it never knew a detailed rule as can be found in the Catholic setting. The Coptic Church tends to define the rule in terms of imitating the monastic tradition and finding ad hoc solutions for unprecedented problems. The first part of this chapter will discuss what types of rules are used in the present monastic settings and how these rules were developed. Then I will look at the hierarchic models that are used to manage a monastery or convent and how the balance of power is maintained within the traditional monastic models.

THE RULE IN EARLY COPTIC MONASTICISM

In original anchoritic and semianchoritic monasticism, as it was developed by St. Antony, St. Amoun, and St. Macarius the Egyptian, there was no common written rule. From the days of St. Antony (251–356) the guidelines for the monastic life were transmitted through the example and advice of the elder monks. Apart from the example of the elders, the monk was guided by the Scriptures, and most of all, by the advice of his spiritual guide.[1]

In the communal (or cenobitic) system St. Pachomius (292–346) organized, he guided the community himself: he gave the monks advice, admonished them, and prayed for them. He also stressed the importance of instruction and reading of the Holy Scriptures. Later Pachomius drew up a series of rules that he took from the Scriptures. These rules were used in all subsequent monasteries related to his monasteries. When Pachomius' sister started to live a monastic life with a group of women, he sent the same rules to her convent. These rules were meant to regulate penance, responsibilities, daily schedules, and the tasks and responsibilities of the housemasters—the ones who were in charge of an individual house.[2]

In the *Lausiac History* Palladius recounts the legend according to which Pachomius was given the rules by an angel. When Pachomius objects to the rules because he thinks that they are not strict enough, the angel answers: "I arranged these so that even the little ones might achieve the fulfillment of the rule without grief. As for the perfect, they have no need of legislation, for they have dedicated all their life to the contemplation of God by themselves in their cells."[3] Philip Rousseau argues in his study *Pachomius: The Making of a Community in Fourth-Century Egypt* that many of the rules drawn up by Pachomius are of a general nature and originate from "the admission of human weakness and individual need" at the same time that they leave "an enormous amount unsaid and offer great scope for individual initiative and temperament."[4] Rousseau concludes that "to live under the rule, then, was to acknowledge that a variety of influences governed your life, or rather, provided for your weakness and fostered spiritual growth: the scriptures, the elders of your community, your immediate superior." Another important observation Rousseau makes concerning the Pachomian system is that "it was Pachomius himself who was the 'rule' in the fullest sense."[5] This situation implies that Pachomius, in order to exercise his authority, must have been a charismatic personality—a view Rousseau elaborates in his book *Ascetics, Authority and the Church.* This view is also stressed by James Goehring in an article entitled "New Frontiers in Pachomian Studies."[6] Both Rousseau and Goehring point out the importance of this charismatic authority that at the same time can lead to trauma at the death of the charismatic.[7] This observation is not only valid in Pachomius' case; it applies in any system in which the charismatic Abbā, or spiritual father, exercises his traditional authority. When no suitable guide or leader emerges who is powerful enough to replace the charismatic authority and continue the guidance of the group or community, the group's survival is threatened.

In early times, the role of the spiritual father was crucial in all the varieties of monastic life. He was the one who guided his followers or the members of his community in their spiritual life. The basis of his guidance was the Scriptures and prayer. He was unofficially assisted by the elders whose example was followed by the young monks.

THE PRESENT SITUATION

At present, when asked about the way of life they follow, monks and nuns often answer that they strive to follow one of these traditional models of monastic rule. In the case of the men's monasteries, the monks live according to what is called the idiorhythmic way of life. This means that in an average monastery there is a variety of types of religious life: the hermit, the recluse, a group of cenobitics, and the monk who leads an active life and works as a priest outside the monastery. The Arabic term used for the idiorhythmic system expresses clearly the meaning of this system: according to *al-fardīya al-mutarābiṭa* (or interconnected individualism) the monk lives as a solitary person but at the same time is connected with the monastic community. He celebrates the Eucharist with the other monks, gets his ration of food through the community, and enjoys the community's protection within the walls of the monastery. As in the earliest times, in this system the role of the spiritual father becomes crucial, because he decides on the daily schedule of a monk and on the different spiritual exercises.

In some monasteries, the monks tried to reintroduce what they considered to be the Pachomian system, by which they meant an organized cenobitic system. In the 1950s Anbā Tīʿufīlus, the Abbot of Deir al-Suryān, encouraged the young monks of his monastery to live according to the cenobitic system. At the same time he started to formulate a body of rules for these monks.[8] This seems to have been advanced, since until that time the monks were used to the semianchorite or idiorhythmic system. Unfortunately the project was not carried through, and they went back to the idiorhythmic system. But the idea took hold in these monks, because later, when some of ʾAnbā Tīʿufīlus' monastic pupils came into positions of power, they implemented the ideas of a cenobitic life. The most favored system in the monks' monasteries still is the semianchoritic system. Nevertheless, there are recurring attempts to introduce a more communal way of life, often called "the Pachomian system."

The present patriarch, Shenouda III, is said to have devoted his energy to reintroducing this Pachomian system, both before and after his appointment as patriarch.[9] Patriarch Shenouda himself, however, testifies to the pitfalls of a system that depends on one charismatic figure and the ambivalence of the actual situation when he writes:

> St. Antony founded the true monasticism. The system that he set lasted more than any other, . . . more than the life of cenobitism that depends on a strong, firm superior like St. Pachomius, for example, managing it [the system] with precision and seriousness and penalizing him who breaks its laws; . . . so if this

superiority is not present, monasticism ends consequently . . . and so many of the Pachomian monasteries ended.[10]

THE CONTEMPLATIVE CONVENTS

In the majority of the contemplative convents the nuns try to live according to what is considered to be the Pachomian system. This system takes shape in community life in common meals and prayers, in specific types of work that are assigned to each nun, and in the daily chores that are carried out on a rotating basis. It was Umminā Irīnī (1940), the superior of Deir Abū Saifein, who first introduced this system to her convent; subsequently, any convent that had one of her pupils as their superior also used it. At present, all but one of the convents in Cairo use the Pachomian system.

The nuns of the Convent of St. Dimyānah claim to follow the system of St. Antony. This dictates that they live as semianchorites. The nuns do not have common meals and most of them perform their daily work in seclusion; however, their prayers are still performed communally.[11]

LITERATURE ABOUT THE RULE

In spite of all the developments and projects of the last three decades that aim at reviving the original monastic ideal, there is still much ambiguity concerning the internal management of the convents and monasteries. The monastics claim that they take the rules of Pachomius and some other classic works on monasticism as the basis for their present daily life. But Pachomius left only a limited set of rules, and, as we have seen, he himself guided his community and formed the actual embodiment of the rule.[12] Nowadays, in spite of several attempts to create a general, binding rule for Coptic monastic life, a singular rule still does not exist. This means that young people who are interested in a monastic career have to rely on visits to monasteries or convents and talks with the monks or nuns in order to obtain information about this kind of life as it is lived today. Furthermore, laypeople can investigate only certain spiritual works and works of the early fathers that are recommended by the church authorities.

One of the guidelines that is followed for the monastic life is a book called *Bustān al-Ruhbān* (The Garden of the Monks). It was published in 1968 in a version revised by Bishop Athanasius, the present bishop of Beni Suef and Bahnasa. The *Bustān* is a compilation of the histories and sayings of the desert fathers. The most recent Arabic version is based on Arabic manuscripts from the tenth century, and Coptic, Greek, and Syrian sources that were edited and translated into French or English.[13] This book was first published in the 1940s and about 40 percent more material has been added to that first edition, according to Bishop Athanasius. The *Bustān al-Ruhbān* deals with different topics of the monastic and spiritual life, all based on the lives and teachings of the desert fathers. The topics are arranged in clusters about: (1) directing the will (on poverty, obedience, chastity, work, and solitude); (2) directing the spirit (prayer, repentance, humility, fasting, and silence); (3) directing the mind (contemplation, discernment, controlling one's thoughts, and visions); and (4) the position of the monk (in regard to God, to society, and to the world). The book is meant as a source of inspiration for modern people, both monastic and lay. In the foreword it is stated that since the spirit of strong faith is lacking in the present world, one has to turn to the desert fathers who showed exemplary strength of asceticism and faith with the Bible as their primary guide. At the same time the reader is addressed with a warning: he or she should keep in mind that the stories are about people who lived in a different time and under different circumstances.[14]

Father Mattā al-Meskīn wrote two voluminous works in order to prepare and equip contemporary monks for the monastic life. In 1952 he wrote the first edition of *Ḥayāt al-Ṣalāt al-Urthūdhuksīya* (Orthodox Prayer Life), which deals with several spiritual topics and uses many quotations from the early fathers. And in 1972, Mattā al-Meskīn wrote a book entitled *Al-Rahbana al-Qibṭīya* (Egyptian Monasticism), on the monastic life in the time of St. Macarius. These examples merely illustrate the literature available to Copts that promotes the monastic life, disseminates the tradition that reaches back to the desert fathers, clarifies its rules, and gives monasticism its due place in Coptic heritage.

During the last decade several books and pamphlets have been published that try to give insights to laypeople on the monastic way of life. Two widely read books are *Sumūw al-Rahbana* (The Excellence of Monasticism) by Bishop Matāʾus, and *Al-Rahbana* (Monasticism), written by the priest Yusuf ʿAsʾad. *Sumūw al-Rahbana* was first published in 1984 and has since been reprinted. Bishop Matāʾus' book, as the title shows, stresses the sacred nature of the monastic life. Another popular book, *Al-Rahbana* was published in 1980 and reprinted in 1988. Both of these books give descriptions of the vocation, preparations for the monastic life, daily routine, prayers, consecration rite, and so on.

To provide more information about the monastic life for laypeople, the Monastery of Barāmūs specifically produces a series of booklets called *Qiṣṣaṣ Rūḥīya Qaṣīra wa Hādifa* (Short and Effective Stories). These short stories are written by anonymous contemporary monks who are trying to bring the monastic life to the people.

Most of these works deal with the male monastics. Here and there some attention is given to the female monastics. Father Yusūf ʿAsʾad tries to include nuns in his book. For example, he mentions the specific kinds of work the nuns do and devotes special attention to their initiation rites.

Since there is not one clear rule available for the contemplative nuns and monks, they rely mostly on the works of the early fathers and try to read any related material that happens to be available to them in Arabic. As noted earlier, the main written source for the monastic rules is the *Bustān al-Ruhbān*.

One can observe that, as in the days of old, the spiritual leader forms an important source of information concerning the way of life for monks and nuns. For example, for laypeople and future monastic candidates, during his public Bible studies on Wednesday evenings Patriarch Shenouda regularly answers questions concerning the choice of a monastic life. Questions address topics such as how to prepare before entering a monastery or convent and what to do when the community proves to be a disappointment for the young monk or nun. The patriarch also gives lists of books that young people who want to become monks or nuns should read.

For monastics, the patriarch holds regular sessions in the Monastery of St. Bishoy. According to the information Father Gregory provided, during these sessions the patriarch only makes general statements concerning communal prayers and meals and the respect monks should have for their abbot. These talks are not available in writing, but they are distributed among the monks on cassettes. Father Gregory's impression was that the meetings with the patriarch were a follow-up of the attempts that were made a decade ago to reintroduce the communal system.

Apart from the patriarch, other spiritual leaders provide rules for monastics. Bishop Athanasius clarifies the rules and the monastic way of life in regular spiritual sessions with the sisters of the active community and Father Mattā al-Meskīn guides his monks among others by telling them what books they are allowed to read and which ones not to touch.[15] Other forms of guidance come from the Holy Synod which decides and hands out new regulations by which monastics are to live.

As I have not been able so far to give a precise answer concerning what the Pachomian system exactly stands for and which rules are used to govern the monastic life, one can only draw conclusions on the basis of observations and the information from available material. Bishop

Athanasius' remark that "the Coptic Church is trying to dip up and revive the original classification of the monastic system" indicates that the process of redefining and discovering the original heritage is still going on.[16] And perhaps the situation is described most aptly by Father Gregory when he explains the current situation by saying that there is a rule for monastics, and at the same time there is not. According to him, all the monks follow and apply the basic monastic principles of poverty, chastity, obedience, and seek to live by the sayings of the early fathers. But the way these principles are applied and the literature used to study their implications in daily life differ from one monastery to another.

The fact that there is no fixed rule also grants a certain freedom, both to monastics and to the church. This means that the monastics can draw from the tradition as it best suits their present lives. By renewing and adapting the tradition according to their own needs, the monks and nuns become instrumental in an ongoing process of reinventing tradition. By this constant retrieval they are in perpetual contact with Egyptian monastic tradition through the centuries. It is through the temporary influx of monastic candidates that the need for a firmer framework has become more urgent.

The discussion concerning the Pachomian system and the rule can be identified as a product of the revitalization that in many ways wants to produce the opposite of what the monastic mores have become during the last centuries by imposing exacting rules and regulation. This discussion also shows that reinventing tradition is a difficult process full of contradictions. The moral attitudes of different types of monasticism in a particular environment, combined with the traditional authority of the charismatic Abbā, were derived from an ideal that was set long ago. These mores continue to represent the most current monastic ideal: the semianchoritic way of the desert fathers. Hence it will probably never happen that a smooth transition is made toward a strict system of monastic living that adheres to the rules of Catholic monasticism. On the one hand, this means that monastics have no firm rules by which to live. On the other hand, a more general system leaves monasteries and convents freedom to develop their own identities.

THE RULE OF THE CONTEMPLATIVE NUNS

As we have seen, most of the contemplative convents insist that the nuns follow the rule of Pachomius. Upon further inquiry, however, it appears that neither novices nor nuns ever receive Pachomius' rules in writing. In Deir al-ʿAdhraʾ the mother superior disappeared for a moment when I asked her about the rule and returned with a copy of the three volumes of the *Pachomian Koinonia*. These are the life, chronicles, and rules of St. Pachomius, edited and translated into English by Armand Veilleux (1980, 1981, 1982). Although an Arabic translation by a French scholar, Gerard Viaud, exists, it seems that the nuns do not use this work.[17]

According to the nuns of Deir Abū Saifein, Mother Irīnī has designed a document of her own that replaces the rule. However, this document is never handed out to the nuns because novices are supposed to learn by imitating the example the mother superior (assisted by the rest of the nuns) sets. One of the nuns explained the system by making the comparison with the way a child grows up: "A child imitates the mother's behavior. It does its best to please the mother. For example, when you store a lot of things in your cell while you see the other nuns possess nothing, you feel ashamed by your luxury. So you start to give it away. At the same time you would hate to be rebuked for having so much."

It seems that this testimony again takes one back to the original model of the example of the elders and the guidance of the spiritual father or mother. Furthermore, one of the nuns, Mother Alexandra, made a remark concerning the rule that concurs with Father Gregory's observations. According to her, the rules followed by Catholic orders are based on the writings of the early fathers. To enforce her argument she showed me a copy of the rules for Catholic monks in Lebanon and pointed out that after each rule came a note that revealed the rule was taken from sayings and lives of the early fathers.[18] "This is exactly what we follow in our monastic life," she said; "we just never write it down with so many details."

When I asked Umminā Alexandra why then the nuns insisted on calling their system Pachomian, she answered that "the nuns call it Pachomian because Ummīnā Irīnī uses that term." Although Mother Irīnī herself never wished to elaborate on her reintroduction of the term *Pachomian*, this simple remark by Mother Alexandra provides one with some clues.

First of all, one can associate this reintroduction to the different initiatives in the 1950s when the search for establishing a more coherent monastic system was a priority. The Pachomian system was obviously considered as a tool that could help revive the monastic life. Furthermore, there are social and gender-related issues that should be considered. By striving to achieve the Pachomian system as it is thought to have existed, that is, as an orderly organization, the nuns distinguished themselves from the monks who still follow several types of monastic life within the walls of the same monastery. For the nuns, Pachomian rules stand for a well-organized system in which every member has her role defined and where communal activities take place at fixed times. From the beginning Mother Irīnī has made it her trademark to instill a sense of order, cleanliness, and neatness in the nuns. Consequently her convent always looks immaculate to the extent that visitors comment on this perfect state of cleanliness that is considered unusual for Egyptian circumstances. All things considered, the monks failed to reinstall such a system. So one can observe that *Pachomian* also stands for an alternative traditional system from the earliest days, which provides the nuns with an acknowledged system that ranks in respectability almost as high as the anchoritic ideal.

THE RULE OF THE ACTIVE NUNS

The fact that one speaks about the community of the active sisters already indicates that the members are not supposed to live in a semianchoritic way. The pledge to be dedicated to the communal life forms part of the vows the sisters take upon initiation. The term *Pachomian* is never mentioned, but the system is presupposed since in Egyptian monasticism the concepts of "communal" and "Pachomian" coincide.

There is no difference between the types of literature contemplative and active sisters read; the *Bustān al-Ruhbān* is equally important to both groups of nuns as a monastic guide. When the sisters enter the novitiate they receive a little booklet which is called *Qānūn* (The Rule). The booklet actually is more of a guideline to the goal and intentions of the community than a full rule. In addition to addressing the community's goal, it deals with the community's target groups and the meaning of the seven vows the sisters take, of chastity, poverty, obedience, community life, work (to earn their own living expenses), service (to carry out social projects), and silence (to maintain the monastic spirit of quietness and contemplation). The booklet also explains how these vows should be lived out. The procedure from postulancy until one is a fully initiated sister and the requirements the candidate has to fulfill are also discussed. At the end of the material is an overview of the administrative positions within the convent and their concurrent responsibilities. The importance of the spiritual guide is also stressed through a quotation from St. Antony that says that the monastic person should always seek the advice of the abbā, or spiritual father.[19]

The spiritual guide of the community, Bishop Athanasius, also fulfills the role of abbot. He guides most of the sisters in their spiritual life and in fact has an important voice in all decisions concerning the nuns. To quote the bishop's own words to me in an interview in 1992: "I am forced to have a decisive voice." According to him, he never intended to guide the community in such an autocratic way: "I insisted on having effective committees. Unfortunately, this is not always successful in the Egyptian environment. People want me to give the final word. But, although there are still a lot of problems, at least the sisters now have their own meetings and delegate their work themselves." At present, the situation of the active community seems to be that, although the bishop gives priority to and encourages meetings and democratic ways of decision making, the community still has a lot in common with the communities Pachomius started in the fourth century. Just as Pachomius was the embodiment of the rule with the actual rule in the background, so Bishop Athanasius creates individual rules for different sisters. In this sense the active community is comparable to contemplative convents and monasteries: the spiritual leader has remained the pivot of the system.

For both systems, contemplative and active, the rule is not a binding set of regulations. Rather, in Coptic monasticism it is a presupposed organizational model, a framework. The blueprint for this framework is what is known about the system Pachomius designed for his community. For both the nuns and the monks *Pachomian* has come to mean an organized communal life. At the same time the rule indicates that formation of contemporary monastic life for the Copts is still in process.

HIERARCHY AND ADMINISTRATION

In this system where the rule merely represents a framework, the role of the spiritual leader becomes crucial for the individual members of the monastic community. In fact, the internal organization of a monastery is very much regulated by the guiding principles of the spiritual father or mother, who in most cases holds the position of abbot or mother superior as well.

In spite of the preferred semianchoritic system, the hierarchic and administrative structures of both the monasteries and the nunneries harken back to the system Pachomius followed in his communities. An understanding of how the men's monasteries are set up will provide the information one needs to discern the particulars in the nunneries' structures as well. After all, it will be remembered that Pachomius' sister Mary implemented the monastic system her brother taught her.

Hierarchy and Administration in the Monasteries

The center of the monastery's administration is the *raʾīs al-deir* (abbot), who holds the rank of bishop. The Coptic patriarch is the official head of all the monasteries within Coptic monasticism. The patriarch nominates the bishop who supervises the monastery's administrative, financial, and spiritual management. The patriarch, however, is still informed of irregularities within each monastery; for example, the patriarch is notified when a monk decides to change to another monastery or wants to give up his monastic life.[20]

In some cases the bishops do not live in the monastery, because they also have to attend to other obligations within their dioceses. In such a case a prior, the *rubeitah,* or *amīn al-deir,* is chosen by the bishop and appointed after patriarchal approval to take over the bishop's regular work in the monasteries. The prior has to consult the abbot in every matter, but since the abbot often is engaged in spiritual guidance or absent on retreat, the prior actually enjoys a great amount of freedom in managing the monastery. He oversees the spiritual and educational needs of the monks and sometimes acts as spiritual father. The prior is in charge of the expenditures for food, clothing, and so forth, is custodian of the monastery's possessions, and sets the rules concerning visitors from outside. He keeps the records, especially concerning the monastery's properties. He handles the personal matters of each monk and sees to it that guests and sick or disabled monks are taken care of. Additionally, the prior supervises the care of buildings, machines, tools, livestock, and crops.[21]

Since the abbot is the caretaker of the monastic rule, the monks render him respect and obedience. In fact, of the regulations that are available, many of them are devoted to respect for the abbot. In the case of mismanagement by the abbot or prior, the regulations also state actions that may be undertaken by the monks.[22] Both the abbot and the prior can be removed from office in case of theft, corruption, or well-founded complaints by the monks.[23]

Hierarchy and Administration in the Contemplative Convents

A convent's administration is not entirely identical to the traditional hierarchy in the men's monasteries. The patriarch is, as is the case with monasteries, formally the head of all convents. According to Patriarch Shenouda III, no bishops are appointed to oversee the convents in order to avoid conflicts of authority and interference with the role of the mother superior as spiritual head.[24]

The patriarch is the sole authority for the abbess to consult in matters of direction. The only man, besides the patriarch, who exercises control over the inhabitants of a convent is an elderly monk who takes the nuns' confessions and celebrates the Eucharist in the convent's chapel. This monk, in a special appointment by the patriarch, has a long-term commitment to serve as the priest for all the convents in Cairo. The abbess can discuss certain problems with him, while he can relay to the patriarch urgent matters concerning the nuns or the convent. The position of this monk is comparable to the role that the old monk Peter had in the days of Pachomius. Concerning this topic, the *Pachomian Koinonia* relates: "When our Father Pachomius saw that the number of [these women] was increasing somewhat, he appointed an old man called Apa Peter, whose 'speech was seasoned with salt' [Col. 4:6] to be their father and to preach frequently to them on the Scriptures for their souls' salvation."[25] Nowadays, this old monk's presence in the nunneries mainly has to do with sacramental duties.

There is no officially appointed deputy for the abbess, like the *rubeitah* in the monasteries. In fact, strictly speaking, the abbess' position is the same as that of *rubeitah* since there is no bishop.

The Mother Superior: al-Umm al-Raᶜīsa. In the church's hierarchical order the abbess is given a high degree of authority. Although she is replaced in the case of her absence or sickness, the substitutes are generally only senior nuns with no authority to make independent decisions. The abbess is responsible for all spiritual, physical, social, and material affairs of the convent. She is the nuns' spiritual guide, sees to the nuns' bodily needs (such as food and clothes), receives the visitors to the convent, handles the gifts that come in, and arranges building and renovation activities.[26] She is the "voice" of all her nuns, because of which many nuns refuse to speak their own names. The mother superior speaks for them. The mother superior is *raᶜīsat-al-deir* or *al-umm al-raᶜīsa,* but she is often addressed by the Coptic word *tamauf.*

The reasons for the autocratic nature of the convent stem from the idea that nuns are supposed to live a more enclosed life than monks. Ideally, nuns never leave the cloister. Until about thirty years ago, it was unthinkable that nuns would open agricultural branches outside Cairo. Because the nuns were few in number, and their abbeys were large enough for their needs, and the emancipation of women in general had not yet reached a level where women easily could engage in public activities, the idea of setting up a farm seemed farfetched. While traditionally the abbess did not need a *wakīla* (assistant), nowadays she has assistants who are in charge of the convent's farm, oversee construction and maintenance, and partially fill the role of *rubeitah*, or prioress. In the past nuns were deemed unable to carry out these types of activities because women could not move freely outside the convent. It was always a layperson, usually a wealthy Copt, who would help the mother superior with building activities within the convent. This person would arrange for the purchase of material and the recruitment of laborers and would also assist in supervising the work. Today, with better educated nuns, the situation is changing. Some abbesses have started to move independently outside of the convent in order to administer the convent's affairs more effectively.

The mother superior is the one to whom potential novices come and the one to whom Copts donate money and gifts. Considering the pivotal position of the mother superior and the fact that she is the official leader the convent presents to the outside world, a look at the different types of mother superiors is appropriate.

At present, there are two types of mother superiors, or abbesses. The younger ones who were appointed during the last decade and who are well educated. And the old-style abbesses who entered the convent at a young age (some as young as twelve) during the 1950s with the low-level of education that was usual for the women of their time. One of these traditional abbesses came to the convent as an illiterate and learned how to read and write in the cloister.

The mother superiors of Deir Māri Girgis in Ḥārat Zuweilah and Deir Sitt Dimyānah were chosen by ballot by the convents' nuns while the rest were appointed by the patriarch. In the case of the superior of Deir Abū Saifein, the choice of a new abbess had been revealed in a dream to the then Patriarch Kyrillos VI. The day after his dream, he visited the convent and discussed his choice with the nuns. According to the nuns, the choice that the patriarch made reflected the will of God and they gladly accepted the proposed abbess.

In principle, the mother superior is appointed for life. Whether they belong to the new or to the older generation, all heads of cloisters execute their positions in an autocratic way. An abbess is officially installed during a special ceremony of initiation (the one that used to be the ceremony of initiation into the order of the great-skema bearer).[27]

Although all the nuns are called "mother," the superior is expected to act as a mother in the literal sense of the word and to take care of all the physical and spiritual needs of her nuns. She knows everything about her nuns—their backgrounds, personalities, problems, work, and spiritual exercises. Not even the slightest action in the convent can be carried out without her knowledge. It was said about Mother Martha that she "considered herself fully responsible with respect to God, herself, and all her girls for whom it was her duty to solve all their problems."[28] This responsibility not only includes accepting or rejecting new nuns and sending fully initiated nuns away, but also stretches to include inspection of the nuns' mail. One superior explained this kind of censorship as a necessary tool to safeguard her nuns' peace of mind; "What if the news that one of her relatives has died arrives in the middle of Lent, the most important fasting period in the year? It will disturb the nun so much that it will nullify all her prior devotional efforts and exercises." The same superior's concern for the well-being of her nuns regularly leads her to weigh them in order to insure that obesity does not become an obstacle to the three hundred prostrations a day (*meṭāniyā*).

It is almost impossible to distinguish between the administrative and spiritual work of the superior. For in neither sphere does she have any official deputy. She is the sole arbiter in every affair that concerns the nuns or the convent. For their part, the nuns consider themselves the superior's daughters and treat her with the highest esteem and reverence. When, on visitors' day at the convent, the superior comes down to chat with the guests, one can detect an electric stir moving through the group of nuns. Everytime the mother superior leaves the room the nuns cry out "*Tamauf!*" and jump up and rush toward her in case she might need something. Only after the abbess has disappeared into one of the guest rooms can the nuns relax and continue their work.

Because contemplative nuns follow the community life more often than monks, one can conclude that the system of ruling an abbey is prone to yield the "strong and firm superior" like the one that Patriarch Shenouda described in his meditations on the life of St. Antony.[29] For nuns there is less freedom to design their own schedule and way of life, and the pitfalls of the autocratic system are that the system collapses when a strong superior passes away. Furthermore, the superior hardly has to account for her deeds inside the convent. Although the patriarch is the official head of the convents, he seldom uses his authority unless a matter arises that concerns the Coptic Church at large. This means that for contemplative nuns the ruling system can be oppressive if the abbess lacks natural charisma, and the authority that it holds, and only exercises the power of her office.

Hierarchy and Administration in the Active Community

The abbot and spiritual guide of the active community is Bishop Athanasius. In cooperation with the first sisters, he organized the community from its very beginning and designed an administrative system. According to these active nuns, the system is "identical with monastic systems in the rest of the world."[30] After the bishop, the *majmaᶜ al-deir* (whole community of sisters and novices) is responsible for the organization and well-being of the convent. For example, during general meetings, community members can make recommendations concerning postulants that are ready to enter the novitiate.[31]

Each branch and project is supervised by one of the sisters. For the whole convent a mother superior is chosen: *al-amīna al-ᶜāma* (the general superior). The title of her position is like the one of *al-amīn* (prior) in the men's monasteries, although the nuns call her the mother superior. She is chosen by democratic vote for an unspecified period, though not for life. All the members of the community owe her full obedience. She is responsible for the organizational, material, and legislative affairs of the whole convent and is the convent's representative at official organizations. The superior divides the different types of work and tasks into material, spiritual, and pastoral. She supervises the work and gives pastoral support to the nuns who work in the different branches. She heads the meetings of the sisters who manage the different branches and reports affairs concerning the material, physical, and spiritual well-being of the convent and the sisters to the bishop.[32]

Unofficial Positions in the Hierarchy

Old and Holy Monks in the Monasteries. In many of the monasteries, there is an old and holy monk who receives as much respect and influence as the appointed officials do. This monk is consulted equally by the abbot, the monks, and visitors. The more simple his lifestyle and way of thinking are, the more he is considered saintly. The simple and ascetic behavior of this monk is a source of pride and admiration for the younger monks. One such monk was described by some of his younger colleagues in the Monastery of St. Antony:

"He comes from a village near Qena and entered the monastery about forty years ago. He has never left it since and if ever he talks about the world outside, he talks about things we have never seen because it was so long ago. He always refuses to see a doctor. One day he was afflicted by an eye disease that could easily be operated upon. We took him to a hospital in Cairo, gave him anesthesia and the operation was done. When he woke up and felt the bandage, we told him that his eye had to be cleaned and therefore the doctor had to take it out, whereupon he praised God and was very happy."

This category of monk would be unknown to anyone outside the monastery and might disappear into oblivion were it not that the younger generation draws attention to these elders. Supernatural events (such as a bright light that shines from the cell while the old monk prays) are whispered about among the monks and eventually reach the Coptic community outside.

Old and Holy Nuns in the Convents. Before taking a closer look at one of the more famous old, saintly monks, Abūnā Yusṭus al-Anṭūnī, I will look at some old, saintly nuns. The most famous holy nuns are superiors themselves, like Umminā Marthā (d. 1988), who was the mother superior of Deir Amīr Tādrus in Ḥārat al-Rūm, and Umminā Irīnī, who is still alive. Their holiness has to be compared to the holiness of bishops and the patriarch, because this holiness is partly derived from their position of authority. They do not fit exactly the mold of Abūnā Yusṭus.

This does not mean that old, holy nuns of the type of Abūnā Yusṭus do not exist. Parallel to the observation that the saintly monks would not be known outside the walls of the monastery were it not for the younger monks speaking about them to outsiders is this statement by Father Gregory of St. Antony's: "Of course there were many saintly nuns, but nobody knew them because they were never mentioned. They lived in nunneries that enjoyed very little attention in general, and most of the nuns were illiterate, so after their death no encomium was drawn up through which they could have been remembered." This remark reflects the situation that in general the history of women has seldom been recorded.

Upon further inquiry some contemplative nuns mentioned that they had heard vague stories about a nun called Umminā Raḥma. After more investigation this nun appears to be a fictitious figure, actually a composite of several forgotten saintly nuns. These stories tell of a nun who lived at the turn of the century in Deir Abū Saifein. There she sat all day long in the courtyard, continuously washing clothes without ever uttering a word. The stories have to do with the habit of continuous work, preferably in silence. This is one of the high ideals in monasticism; by tiring out the body and keeping the mind in constant contact with God, the monastic purifies his or her mind and heart and may reach thereby a higher degree of spirituality.

Another story of a saintly nun is that of Umminā Sarah from Deir Amīr Tādrus who also lived at the beginning of this century. The story tells of how she excelled in the ascetic and anchoritic life. Umminā Sarah had the most uncomfortable room in the convent. Her cell had no windows and light only came in through a hole in the roof. She never left this room and ate only once a week. One day, sometime in the 1930s, she left her room and went to downtown Cairo in order to warn a member of her family that a fire would destroy many buildings in his neighborhood and that he should take precautions to protect his shop. This foresight was seen as the major miracle she performed in her life.

One also has some pieces of information about Umminā Safīna (1850–1900), the spiritual guide of Deir Abū Saifein. I will discuss what is known about Umminā Safīna later in the section about spiritual guidance, but it is noteworthy that the scant information about her stresses her tireless hard work. Besides doing the chores assigned to her, she rose in the morning before anyone else in order to prepare the dough for bread, "in those days the heaviest chore in the convent."[33]

Though the number of stories concerning saintly nuns is relatively small, the fact that the stories exist indicates that there must be some truth to them. Old and saintly nuns did exist but were simply forgotten after their deaths because no one told their stories. The present nuns support this view; in their quest for more information about their past, they have to piece together scattered bits of information.

The nuns of Deir Amīr Tādrus report a discovery they made in 1988 in support of their conviction that there has been a tradition of saintly nuns. When the sisters were cleaning and rearranging the corner of the graveyard that is reserved for nuns of their convent, they opened the graves and found several undecayed bodies of nuns that had lived centuries ago. When a body remains intact after death, this is considered a sign of the high degree of the saintliness of the person.

Because there is more written information on holy monks than on holy nuns who became part of the monastery's or convent's hierarchy, I will continue this discussion about the monastic phenomenon of holy people by examining the saintly life of the monk Abūnā Yusṭus al-Anṭūnī.

Abūnā Yusṭus al-Anṭūnī

Abuna Yusṭus al-Anṭūnī (d. 1976) is one of the best-known examples of a saintly monk who has served as a role model for other monks. He hardly slept or ate and realized the ideal of poverty by owning nothing and ignoring his bodily needs. He rarely ever took a bath or accepted medical treatment in case of sickness. Abuna Yusṭus was not ordained a priest, nor did he have an important position in the clerical hierarchy, but he remained in the order of "Reader" his whole life.[34] Abuna Yusṭus impressed everybody who met him by his clairvoyance and the special grace that he seemed to exude. He loved to sit in the company of visitors or other monks without ever speaking a word himself. Apart from the scant advice he sometimes gave, the *abūnā* would often ask: "Es-sāʿa kam delwaqtī?" (What time is it now?). Though he never explained what he meant by this (there are clocks in monasteries), it was understood as a reminder of the temporary nature of life.[35] The younger monks were proud of him because he was the personification of the early desert fathers "who were longing for God with all their hearts and became drunk with the love for their redeemer."[36] He was "a living message," silently reminding people of their origin and destiny.[37] According to the monks, "Yustus just was the monastic way."

The phenomenon of a monk who lives such an austere life in the twentieth century is considered exceptional; it is rare to find people who manage to exercise such a high degree of asceticism and self-mortification.[38] Such a monk is a reminder of the early monks who wore the *Eskīm* (great skema or megaloskema). The great skema represents an advanced degree of monasticism and is proffered after the small skema, or mikroskema. Today the small skema is that equivalent of the *minṭaqa* (belt) which the monk receives during his initiation.[39] The great skema consists of a four-meter-long belt of plaited leather decorated with ten small crosses and two large crosses made of that same material. The belt is worn as a girdle, over the shoulders and around the waist.[40] According to Abūnā Mattā al-Meskīn, originally nobody could be called a monk unless he was wearing the great skema.[41] The bearer of the skema was and is perceived as endowed with an unquestionable spiritual authority. Today this belt can be given as a second initiation, only on rare occasions to senior monks, nuns, or hermits during a special liturgy.[42] There are only a handful of contemporary monks in Egypt who have received the great skema.

The monk or nun who is dressed in the great skema has to follow an extremely austere monastic rule. He or she fasts the entire day, only eating a little at sunset. He or she restricts eating, drinking, and sleeping to only the very necessary; recites almost double the amount of the normal daily devotions; and makes five hundred *meṭānīyāt,* or prostrations, a day. Finally the monk or nun who is dressed in the great skema is not allowed to speak more than seven words a day.[43] This state is one that can only be reached by gradual degrees of stricter and stricter asceticism. The monk or nun starts as a member of a cenobitic community and begins the solitary life within the monastery, observing complete silence while remaining in his or her cell. He or she can leave the cell once a week in order to attend the Eucharist. Only after having become accustomed to the solitary life, and then by the spiritual father's permission, can the monk or nun leave the monastery or convent and live in a cave.[44] The bearer of the great skema is often a hermit who lives in a cave far away from the monastery.

Although there is no documentation that Abūnā Yusṭus was a wearer of the great skema, his biographers insist that he reached a corresponding level of holiness. For example, they state that his utterances hardly ever surpassed seven words: *Mutashakkir* (thanks); *kattur kheerak* (may your good deeds increase); *enta mabsūṭ?* (are you happy?); and *Allah yi'awwaḍak* (may God compensate you).

Abūnā Yusṭus' prayers, vigils, fasting, utter poverty, and silence make him the classic contemporary example of Coptic monasticism because the true ideal of monasticism still is *tawaḥḥud* (absolute eremitism).[45] Even before they enter the monastery or convent, while they are still in the world, the future monks and nuns are inspired by stories of the early fathers and mothers, by the saints and their way of life, and want to follow their examples. The ideal way for this type of spirituality to be fully realized is through a life in seclusion where the monk or nun can be devoted entirely to God and the soul can reach the state where the gifts of the Holy Spirit reign.

In a final remark about the nuns I have to add that, according to an essay about the Coptic Church written in 1930, more nuns than monks wore the great skema.[46] This does not seem to be the case any longer. Theoretically nuns were considered better candidates for the great skema since they never had to leave the cloister. Nowadays, even though nuns are contemplatives, they have to deal more and more with the outside world. This might be the reason for the disappearance of wearers of the great skema among the nuns.

SUMMARY

In spite of all the new developments, opportunities, and possibilities in contemporary Coptic monasticism, the first and foremost ideal remains faithfulness to tradition. The desert fathers and mothers, their ideals, sayings, and way of living have been held up as the first role models for monastics to emulate.

Hence the importance of monastics like Abūnā Yusṭus and the significant amount of attention paid to their behavior. Whether or not these holy people actually existed or lived as the stories claim that they did, what is most important is that their stories have been incorporated into monastic themes of today and provide a powerful link with the tradition. Furthermore, these holy personalities indicate the potential for surpassing the official hierarchy, inside or outside of the convent or monastery. A mother superior or an abbot can always be challenged by the spiritual authority of the saintly man or woman. Charisma is free flowing and can reign equally inside or outside of the ecclesiastical institution. Each nun or monk can reach the spiritual goal for herself or himself.

Because of their idiorhythmic lifestyle, the monks often live as semianchorites or are active in secular vocations. Hence they are confronted less with the problems pertaining to a strong, firm superior than are the contemplative women. Inside their own convents the mother superiors have free rein, which in principle brings them to the same level of power and authority as their male counterparts, the abbots. The mother superior of a contemplative convent gains freedom where her nuns lose it.

In the active community the rule and a strong mother superior are more or less replaced by a democratic system of decision making. The system as such safeguards the personal freedom of each sister. But the bishop, who is the official abbot, still has the final say in many affairs. Both systems of convents in fact reflect the authoritarian structures that can be found in Egyptian sociey and begin with the family. This same kind of situation is reflected in one observer's remark that in Egypt, "Chiefs, bosses, sponsors all are expected to play fatherly roles that go far beyond what is required by the dry routine of office work."[47]

CHAPTER 4

Leaving the World

The Novitiate

In the career of a monastic, the novitiate is a crucial period during which the vocation of a person is tested. The novitiate is especially important, because after the initiation rite a monastic is not allowed to leave the convent or monastery to resume a life in the outside world. In this chapter, I will discuss several issues that determine whether or not a person will become a monastic: How does a person enter the convent or monastery? What are some of the reactions a novice's family might have to the decision to enter a convent? What motives drive candidates to take this step? After discussing recruitment, the type of candidates, and the selection process, I will focus on what happens when the novice's vocation does not materialize or fails altogether. Finally, I will look at how vocational roles of nuns effect laywomen.

PREPARATION AND REQUIREMENTS

Contemplative Nuns and Monks

Young women or men who want to enter the convent or monastery are expected to prepare themselves for this new life while they are still living in the secular world. As a first step these women and men must read the *Bustān al-Ruhbān* (The Garden of the Monks). By reading this book, the aspiring nuns/monks are introduced to the world of the early fathers' way of life, their daily worship, rules, and ideals. At the same time, these young people are advised to memorize as many psalms as possible, to withdraw from family and friends, and to keep themselves away from mundane amusements.[1] A future nun will change her way of dressing slightly: she starts to cover her head by wearing a scarf and, preferably, wears plain, simple clothes and no makeup. Regular visits to the nunnery or monastery of choice are strongly recommended.[2] The aspiring monk is strongly encouraged to have spiritual sessions with the older monks and discuss his reasons why he wishes to become a monk. The aspiring nun has spiritual sessions only with the mother superior or the nun acting on the mother superior's behalf. For a nun, the ultimate choice of the convent depends on several criteria and hardly coincides with the candidate's own choice. The lack of space severely restricts the number of novices a convent can accept each year. The Convent of Abū Saifein, for example, receives between 250 and 300 applicants a year but has a place for two or three novices.

The ultimate decision for accepting or rejecting a candidate lies solely with the abbot or abbess. One abbess said that she uses several techniques in order to make the decision on a candidate's acceptance such as devoting special prayers to the matter, consulting the convent's patron saint, and, when the time for a decision is near, writing the name of the aspiring novice on a small piece of paper that the priest puts on the altar during communion.

Furthermore, before a young woman is admitted, the mother superior inquires about the woman's background or obtains a recommendation from the candidate's confessor. One of the requirements for entering a nunnery is that the future novice is not younger than twenty-two years old and not older than twenty-seven. According to one of the mother superiors, St. Pachomius set the minimum age at twenty-two, and this mother superior herself set the maximum age at twenty-seven, "for if you want to give your life to God, you should not wait too long." Preferably, the candidate has worked in a regular job before she enters the convent. "We want her to have experience in normal society. Moreover, we have to be sure the girl does not want to become a nun because she fails to find a husband. The older they are, the more realistic this possibility is."[3] The average age of the candidates for the monks' monasteries is slightly higher, between twenty-seven and thirty-five years of age.[4]

Although a college education is preferred, some convents will still consider candidates with less education. Nowadays illiterate candidates are no longer accepted, even though in the past the majority of nuns could not read or write. Among the monks the candidate should have a strong recommendation if he is not college educated. In fact, he "should have possessed previous gainful employment" as well in order to be eligible as a successful candidate.[5] The future novice, male or female, should be healthy in body and mind, and, since the revival started, unmarried (and never have been married). In other words, the candidates should be virgins. They must not be afflicted with a mental disease nor be deemed to be possessed by an evil spirit. Men must have completed their military service and must not be fleeing from the authorities because of having committed a crime.[6]

There are some obstacles to entering the monastic life.[7] Candidates are expected to come to the convent or monastery without possessions, money, or other material goods or to give all their worldly goods to the convent or monastery. When candidates are allowed (for a probational period) to enter the convent or monastery, they take a one-year unpaid leave from their jobs in order to keep open the option to return to the world.

The Active Community

A woman who wants to join the active community is required to spend one week in the mother house where she will participate in the daily life, work, and devotions of the sisters. If after that week she is still interested in joining the community, she receives permission to visit the convent regularly over the period of *ziyāra* (one year). During this year the candidate continues her regular job and is not required to change her lifestyle in any way. Anytime she makes up her mind about entering the community she has to apply for a six months' leave from her job and can start her probationary period at the convent. Until recently, illiterate women were allowed to enter the convent. With the increase of candidates, the Banāt Maryam has stopped accepting illiterate women because the process to educate them proved too time-consuming. Because of this increase, women are being asked to produce medical statements attesting to their physical health. With regard to the candidate's age, there is only the minimum age of eighteen with no limit on the maximum age. Some women join the active community upon early retirement after a full career. The candidate should be unmarried and never have been married.

ON PROBATION

There are three levels of initiation into the monastic life in all forms of monasticism. There is a *taḥt al-ikhtibār* (precandidacy period which literally means "under examination"); the *ṭālibāt rahbana* (actual novitiate or female monastic students); and the initiation into monasticism. Actually, there are no separate terms for the period of precandidacy and the novitiate. The difference between a postulant and a novice is mainly noticeable in clothing.

During the precandidacy period the young woman or man (the postulant) has not yet been accepted for a potential initiation. They keep their own names, and the contemplative and active women retain their normal clothing but wear an obligatory headscarf, while male candidates dress in a *gallābīya,* the long caftanlike garment the Egyptian farmers wear.

In the active community the postulants are required to participate in all the activities and projects of the community. They are also required to perform daily chores in the active convent. A postulant in a contemplative nunnery lives among the other nuns. She is required to do certain chores that fully initiated nuns do not perform (such as prepare snacks for the convent's guests). A man who is on probation lives in a special wing of the monastic guest house. He eats in the same area as the laborers and does cleaning and cooking for the guests while performing menial tasks that are usually required of the laborers only.

The candidate serves the monastic community through works of menial labor. The rationale for this is to help him or her acquire the virtues of *iḥtimāl* (endurance) and perfect *ṭā'a* (obedience). A classic illustration of this training that is widely used among all monastic communities is the story of the spiritual father of the Monastery of Baramūs, ʿAbd al-Masīḥ al-Masʿūdī (d. 1905). This spiritual father made a new novice sweep the whole monastery (then around 5,000 square meters). At night, when the novice was required to recite his share of the daily psalms, he was found to know none of them by heart. The next day he was made to scrub all the floors. Again at night he did not know his psalms. The monks complained about his ignorance whereupon the spiritual father answered them: "During the first year I will teach him endurance, the second year obedience, the third year humility and in the fourth year the psalms will follow."[8]

While menial work is seen as a normal activity for women, the menial work a male postulant performs is deeply admired among Coptic visitors to a monastery. These visitors are quite aware that in a nonmonastic setting, they would never see a man cook, serve the meals, and wash the dishes as these young male candidates. These are activities that, due to the rigidity of gender roles in Egypt, seldom are carried out by men.[9]

Another point of difference between the monastic life and the secular world is that the majority of the novices are not uneducated or illiterate; rather they are highly qualified professionals. Not only are gender roles rigidly divided in Egypt, but the division in class structures is also strict. A well-educated monastic candidate from an upper-or upper-middle-class background would never consider servants to be on the same level as himself—he would never clean the dining table for people who were not his superiors.[10] And, as the story from the Monastery of Baramūs suggests, in addition to lessons in humility, postulants must learn a number of psalms by heart.

Ideally speaking, the period of precandidacy should be approximately six months. In reality, however, the length of this period varies. Especially among the monks, precandidacy might last less than a week or more than a year.[11] After this period, when the candidate is approved (either by the spiritual guide or by the abbess), he or she is promoted to the novitiate during a brief, unofficial ceremony in the church. The male novice changes the color of his *gallābīya,* while the female novice dresses in a grey floor-length garment with a high collar and long sleeves. Around her head she tightly wraps a black scarf. A novice retains his or her former name, but the name is preceded by the word *ākh* (brother) or *tāsūnī* (my sister). A novice is not considered a member of the community yet. During the periods of precandidacy and the novitiate the aspirant is still allowed to leave the convent or monastery, though it is preferred that she or he leave before becoming a novice.

While the responsibility of accepting or rejecting a candidate in the contemplative convent or the monastery lies solely with the abbess or abbot, in the active community a committee is formed to decide on the promotion of postulants. The committee consists of the bishop, the mother superior, and the supervisors of the annexes and projects. This committee discusses the eligibility of the candidates, and in the process of accepting a candidate the community stresses the point that the choice comes from both the postulant and the community. The postulant has to feel comfortable with the other sisters and to feel encouraged to develop her talents, knowledge, and skills in an organized community life. Once it has been agreed upon that the candidate is ready for promotion, a special ceremony (the details of which will be discussed below) takes place during which she takes preliminary vows and dresses in a beige ankle-length dress and a short veil of the same color for her head. The candidate is called *tāsūnī.* As is the case in the contemplative convents, the novice can leave the active community as long as she has not been fully initiated.

A look at the differences between male and female monastic candidates, especially in the precandidacy, shows that the male candidates are put in a more liminal position—outside of any defined social group.

This position of outsider is less prevalent among the female contemplatives and hardly exists in the active community at all, while male candidates are forced to stay outside the actual community and are expected to do tasks they would never perform in secular life. This situation suggests that for the men one feels that there is more at stake than there is for the women. The men not only are nearly all college graduates, but, considering the age of entry, they must be successful professionals as well.[12] A man who has an impressive career in the secular world is believed to be giving up more when he becomes a monk. In other words, he is believed to be making a bigger sacrifice than a woman who has to make up her mind to become a nun before she is twenty-seven years of age. Concurrently, the monk will be in a better position to gain more respect and admiration than a nun. It is likely that a fully initiated monk will proceed to be ordained into priesthood; he might one day even become a bishop. The ordination into priesthood gives him the power to administer the sacraments that are vital for the spiritual, religious, and social life of the Copts. Furthermore, priesthood automatically grants him a power of *baraka* (blessing) that is not easy for a woman to acquire. The liminality of a male candidate truly "humbles and generalizes the aspirant to higher structural status."[13] A woman can only reach a position of power (of sorts) by becoming a mother superior or an extremely saintly nun; only in this way is she able to reach a state where believers perceive her personality or position as giving *baraka*. Contemplative nuns are in a better position to reach this state than are active sisters, whose life is considered to be an impediment to a high degree of asceticism. This situation is shown by the active sisters' position as postulants and by the process of promoting the sisters into the novitiate.

MOTIVATION AND RECRUITMENT

Motives for Entering the Contemplative or Active Nunnery

The personal motives for entering a convent, as given by contemplative and active nuns, are diverse. Spiritually, all of the nuns see entering a convent as a matter of *mauhiba* (which means literally "gift" or "talent"). As Umminā Irīnī explained it: "The desire to become a monastic can be seen as a natural desire that was implanted in the human being from the day of his or her birth." She shares the opinion of Anbā Matā'us in his book *Sumūw al-Rahbana* (The Excellency of Monasticism). Anbā Matā'us writes that one discovers a calling to the monastic life because from the earliest age onward one detects in oneself "a great love for celibacy, . . . the inclination to turn away from worldly goods . . . and family relations," and "a preference for meditation, prayer and seclusion."[14] In some cases, the natural inclination in a person for the monastic life is evident to the outside world from very early on. For example, a friend of Umminā Maryam recalls: "When we were in our teens, in the 1950s, we once went together to summer camps organized by our church. Maryam did not like it at all. She considered all this swimming and playing in the sand a useless waste of time. I was not surprised at all when one day she decided to become a nun."

Umminā Rifka called her wish to take the habit a *niʿma Rabbinā* (special grace from Our Lord). According to her, the calling to monastic life is an experience, almost an inspiration, from God who invites a person to dedicate her whole life to Him. According to Rifka, the person thus called is not obliged to follow this calling by entering the convent. Some people, she said, "choose to stay in the world and lead an exemplary life or a life of service there."

The monastic call can also be induced by a supernatural event. In the case of one of the current abbesses, the call, turned out to be already evident at the time of her birth. She related the following story concerning the events that occurred during her birth:

> My mother was having a very hard time; the delivery was extremely painful and difficult, and she had been in labor for many hours. At a certain moment, when everybody had lost hope that I would ever come out alive, Māri Girgis [St. George] and St. Mary appeared to her. Māri Girgis tapped three times on my mother's back and I fell out. Then the Holy Virgin made the sign of the cross on my forehead and said: "This child will not be yours, for she is mine." My parents used to think this meant that I would die as a child, but I entered the convent at the age of thirteen and later on we understood that St. Mary had destined me to become a nun.

Although I cannot generalize about each nun's reasoning for entering a convent (especially since there was no opportunity to interview all the nuns on this subject), from the nuns interviewed for this study I can distill three motivations: a wish that had been dormant from a young age; a special calling; or a miraculous event. Most of the time a woman enters the convent for a combination of reasons. Some of the contemplative nuns claimed to have entered the convent because they had had a vision or witnessed an apparition of a saint. Most of them, with personal variations, said they only wanted to work for God. And, according to their stories, they had shown ascetic dispositions from their early childhood. These women had learned about the monastic way of life from books, were fond of the stories with lives of the saints, or had role models in the Catholic nuns who were their teachers in school. Many of them had never visited a convent before they decided to become nuns.[15]

The story of Umminā Alexandra illustrates the experience and background of the majority of nuns:

> My father and mother always took me to church and read the stories of the saints for my brother and me. They fascinated us and as soon as I was able to read, I read them myself. My brother loved to go to church. He became a deacon and even after he married, he participated in every mass. Marriage never attracted me; actually, from the time I left elementary school it was clear to me that I did not want to get married and raise a family. Neither did I like to go out of the house and meet friends. I preferred to stay at home and read books about religious topics and the lives of the saints. I was lucky. My mother allowed me to live this way and fenced me off from too many people.

According to Suzanne Campbell-Jones in a study about Catholic nuns in Great Britain, on the decision to become a nun, the "emphasis on the positive value of the religious life in the upbringing of young . . . girls cannot be stressed too much."[16] Several of the Coptic nuns had been educated in Catholic schools where the example of the foreign teaching nuns inspired them to join the monastic life. For Coptic women fifty years ago, this decision meant that they had to opt for a contemplative life. When contemplation did not attract them, they tried to remain unmarried and stay with their parents.

So far I have provided examples about the contemplative nuns that are just as applicable to the active sisters. Several active sisters had wished to join a contemplative convent when they first believed they wanted to become a nun. The reasons that made these nuns change their minds were manifold: there was no place to join a contemplative convent; they never managed to see the abbess; they did not feel comfortable in the traditional convent; their confessional fathers suggested they become active nuns. Especially in its formative years the active community was too much of a novelty to be first choice for a young woman who had only heard about the traditional convents. Nowadays this situation has changed. The majority of sisters who have joined the community have deliberately chosen the active form of monasticism because they want to be of service to the community and to those people in need.

The Socialization Process of Nuns

While young men who wanted to pursue a monastic career traditionally could find models in the married priests that served their parish and in public figures such as celibate bishops, there were few visible role models for young women. Contemplative nuns were stowed away in the convents, and, until two decades ago, not even the lay Copts were conscious of the nuns' existence. The question arose, then, as to what influenced these women's decisions to become nuns. Nowadays, there are several channels that bring women to the monastic life within and outside of the Coptic Church. Important gatherings where young women can find information and inspiration about the monastic life are the Sunday schools, youth clubs, and church programs for university students. All of these social activities have developed as a result of a conscious effort to give children an opportunity to find their Coptic identity and culture and for them to feel comfortable and secure in their church.[17] When the children become adolescents they can participate in one of the manifold charity programs run by the church, or they can become Sunday school teachers or teachers of Coptic themselves.[18]

In Sunday school sessions students sit in groups divided by age. These groups start when the child is four and continue to the university level. The university students themselves study to become teachers in the Sunday school. The young children spend their time singing Christian songs, praying, listening to Bible stories and the stories about saints. The lessons and readings are interwoven with studies of Christian ethics and values: how to be a good young man or woman by becoming educated, respected, and properly dressed. The saints, including child saints, are set as examples for the young Coptic community; these child saints were steadfast in their faith, often converted their pagan families to Christianity, and had no fear of dying for what they believed.[19]

From the youngest age possible, children become familiar with the prototypes of the saints' faithful lives. Moreover, the children are encouraged to identify themselves with "the Saint of the Day" and to try to imitate the saint's asceticism and courage. When one Sunday school teacher asked her clan of four-year-olds, "*Ḥaddu khāyef*" (if any of them was afraid to die as a martyr), the whole class roared back in one voice, "Lᶜa!" (no one).[20]

In hagiographies of the early saints, women who were interested in ascetic or monastic life could always find male and female role models. More recent female role models, however, have been lacking among the nuns, so that some of the present leading nuns took the guidance of a charismatic monk. For example, in the beginning of her own monastic career, Umminā Irīnī used to spend her retreats in the Monastery of St. Antony where she observed the example of Abūnā Yusṭus and received regular advice from the prior and spiritual guide, Abūnā Ebskhayrūn, whom the monks of St. Antony's consider a holy monk. According to the monks, it was the advice and guidance of the two monks that taught and inspired Irīnī to become the independent and innovative superior of the Convent of Abū Saifein.

In the active community one finds several members who, before they became nuns, were involved in the programs that were run by their churches. Often the local priest encouraged these women to become active sisters. Coptic priests are in a position to convince young women to become nuns because the priests are believed to mediate between the world and God. There are many different types of confessors, some more authoritarian than others. In the system where the confessional father holds the power to mediate between the young woman and heaven on the one hand and the young woman and the visible church on the other, the confessor's word is accepted by many as directly inspired by God.

Before the renewal in the Coptic Church started to bear fruit, the Catholic schools were places where young women could find female monastic models. The schools teach in Arabic and French and are frequented by many Coptic children from the upper and upper-middle class. The majority of teachers in the young women's schools are Egyptian Catholic nuns who themselves were educated in the same French-speaking system. Several of the nuns who are now in their fifties and entered the convents before the revival were inspired by the Catholics. The Coptic Church's recruitment of nuns through Coptic sources became effective about twenty years ago.

THE SELECTION OF CANDIDATES

The Educational Level of Nuns

With the decreasing amount of space and the increasing numbers of aspiring monastics, the contemplative convents' directors are very careful in their selection of candidates. The directors' decisiveness is not solely based on personal preference. In the process of selection, the mother superiors have to take into account educational and social factors of each candidate as well as spiritual factors.

From an educational point of view, on the whole women who are university graduates are preferred over women with a lower education. However, the process of selecting educated female novices did not start in the 1940s, as it did with the monks, when highly educated young candidates presented themselves to the monasteries. The ideal of the uneducated, nearly illiterate holy one, represented by Abūnā Yusṭus, persisted in the convents for much longer than it persisted in the monasteries and thus took longer to change the convents. Many of the present elder nuns had to learn how to read and write in the convent, as this became a prerequisite to accomplish daily devotions. Of course, this situation was related to the general level of literacy among Egyptian women. With the monks, it was the abbot of Deir al-Suryān, Bishop Tī'ufīlus (d. 1989), who during the 1950s, allowed candidates with a higher education to enter his monastery. The change in educational levels for nuns was brought about almost single-handedly by Mother Irīnī. The following story tells how this change came about.

> One day our abbess needed an operation. She had suffered from an ulcer in her stomach for over seven years. The abbess was brought to the hospital accompanied by a nun. This nun was a university graduate. She had wished to enter the convent for many years but the abbess refused her at first because of her high education. In the hospital she took care of the abbess with a kindness and skill that impressed the abbess. When the abbess came out of the hospital, she went to the Patriarch Kyrillos VI and told him that from now on she would only accept novices who had higher education.

This incident occurred about 1965, which means that the influx of university-educated nuns has taken place for thirty years. In 1970 a visitor to a convent recorded that there were several highly educated women among the nuns: "There is a doctor, a dentist, a pharmacist, an artist, a secretary, and two agricultural engineers among their number."[21] The other convents were quick to follow this example and rapidly began to accept women with university educations. As a result, the educational level of the nuns today sharply contrasts with that of the early nuns: where the majority of nuns in previous ages were widows and old or handicapped maidens, now most nuns hold university degrees. A similar situation took place in the men's monasteries. After the plague in the fifteenth century decimated the monasteries' population, the number of monks declined and the educational level of novices dropped; it did not recover until this century.[22] Nowadays education has become a decisive factor in assessing whether the motivation to enter the convent is related to the candidate's failure in secular life or not. The fact that she is willing to give up her career is considered a proof of the sincerity of her call.

The candidates for the active community, as discussed earlier, do not necessarily have to be college or university graduates. The bishop holds the opinion that the religious community should be a reflection of the society: since there are more university graduates than ever before in Egypt, they are highly represented in this community, but anybody with true motivations is welcome. The educational level naturally has an impact on the kind of work both contemplative and active nuns undertake nowadays.[23]

Social Factors in the Selection of Candidates

In the selection of monastic candidates, superiors of convents (whether contemplative or active) naturally are conditioned by the cultural expectations concerning the behavior of women. In Egypt, girls and women have to be extremely honorable and constantly attentive to guard their virginity and honor. One of the basic strategies used to regulate and control the behavior of women is the set of normative restrictions embodied in the "nice girl" standards of Egyptian society.[24] The two other strategies are confinement ("which restricts a woman to the vicinity of her household and proscribes much independent movement outside") and protection ("by designated protectors who accompany a woman out into areas where her virtue may be comprised").[25] These strategies of confinement and protection are often related to the "nice girl" standards. A woman ideally should not walk alone in the streets; however, if she must, it should be with a clear destination or purpose such as going shopping or to her job. Preferably, a woman is accompanied by a man or another women. Engaged couples are allowed to go out walking together as long as they are clearly not involved in shameful activities, such as kissing or holding hands. The responsibility of self-control falls upon the young woman who is eager to keep her reputation as a "nice girl," because her "nice" behavior enhances her possibilities for finding a good husband.

Coptic women live under the same normative restrictions as Egyptian Muslim women. Coptic women are not only concerned with their honor in the secular world—due to their Coptic identity and to the fact that the Coptic Church comments upon every aspect of life—but they are also concerned with the religious ideal of what kind of behavior is honorable. A "nice Coptic girl" spends most of her free time in church, attending the liturgy, Bible studies, social gatherings, and charitable activities. In the summer, she joins a Coptic youth group and has a spiritual retreat somewhere near the seaside. She always tries to look clean and well kept. Her highest goal is to be saintly in thought and behavior. To fulfill this ideal she might want to become a nun.

The Coptic Church encourages young women both to be perfectly honorable and to cherish the ideal of as saintly a life as possible, whether in marriage or in a single life. When a young woman does something that is considered wrong and loses her honor (for example, becoming pregnant before marriage), her shameful behavior is seen to reflect on the whole church.

For monastic candidates, the standards required of behavior are even higher than they are for women in secular life. A mother superior's first impression of a young woman is derived from the candidate's clothes, her behavior, and her way of moving and talking. But a candidate's outward appearance may be deceiving. If a young woman has been accepted as a novice and is found unsuitable for monastic life, she is seen as a failure. Because of this failure, it is shameful for her to go back to her parents, especially if she has been a novice for several years. One elderly woman in the church explained the situation as follows: "A nun has to be very sure of her call. It is just like in a marriage. When a girl does not feel happy in her marriage and wants a divorce [although this is forbidden in the Coptic Church], everybody will say, 'What did she do wrong? Why did she not behave well?' It is always the woman who is to blame." One can conclude that the choice of candidates is strongly connected to the respectability of the convent. If the dishonorable behavior of a woman reflects on the church as a whole, imagine the convent's dishonor. A convent will lose its reputation if many of its women have to be sent away. But in the final analysis, the shame falls on the woman who now must find a way to make up for her loss of honor. In her process of searching, however, she will find support from the Coptic society as a whole, since every Copt has an interest in the honor and respectability of a single member.

Motives for the Candidate's Preference

In spite of the fact that, because of crowdedness and other factors, monastic candidates have limited choice in deciding which contemplative convent to enter, they do express preferences. These preferences are connected with the image of each convent and how that ranks among the Coptic people.

For the topic of recruitment it is important to note that in Cairo Umminā Irīnī's Convent of Abū Saifein ranks highest, followed by those convents with new superiors who were recruited recently from Deir Abū Saifein. These convents are as follows: Deir Māri Girgis in Old Cairo, with Umminā Yo'annā as the superior; Deir al-ʿAdhrā' in Ḥārat Zuweilah, headed by Umminā Maryam; and, most recently, Deir Amīr Tādrus in Ḥārat al-Rūm where Umminā Odrosīs became the superior in September 1990. Deir Māri Girgis in Ḥārat Zuweilah is headed by Umminā Aghāpī, an "old-style" abbess (which means that she became the superior before the revival became visible). At the moment, Umminā Aghāpī's convent seems to be the least popular among candidates, although it attracts sufficient numbers because candidates have been rejected in other places. Many of the novices in Umminā Aghāpī's convent come from lower- and middle-class families, several come from Upper Egypt, and not all novices hold advanced degrees.

For many reasons, the Convent of Abū Saifein receives a lot of attention from the outside world. As a result, the convent is well known and thus the most sought after by monastic candidates. Most of the candidates are women from upper- and upper-middle-class families who hold university degrees. Recruiting young women from these classes automatically implies more income for the convent in the form of endowments and financial donations. Relationships with high Coptic families result in favors for the convent and, most important, in personal intervention on the convent's behalf to government authorities, thus facilitating a smooth flow of bureaucratic paperwork. The other three convents offer alternatives for candidates who cannot not be placed in Deir Abū Saifein. The superiors follow the Convent of Deir Abū Saifein's example and try to buy plots of land to build annexes; they celebrate feast days in similar ways and receive guests according to the same pattern.

In spite of the fact that her convent is less popular and less frequented than the other ones in Cairo, Umminā Aghāpī has access to a steady circle of people who support the convent. She managed to raise enough money to purchase a small farm in the vicinity of Alexandria, to initiate several building projects in her convent, and to renovate the abbey.

The convents outside Cairo, Deir Sitt Dimyānah and the convents in Upper Egypt, are less subject to a rating system from the Coptic lay population. In both places one finds novices and nuns who have moved from Cairo and specifically sought out these convents because they wanted to be removed from the Cairene crowd to lead a more austere life. These convents also receive many local candidates who do not wish to move to Cairo.

Among the active community in Beni Suef and the consecrated women, one regularly finds women who started their quest for a monastic career with an orientation visit to Deir Abū Saifein. These women were either rejected or advised to use their talents in an active vocation. The majority of the sisters I interviewed, however, wanted to pursue an active vocation. The sisters from the active community often justified their choice for the convent of the Banāt Maryam because it offered them a regulated community life. The community also fulfills a local need by receiving several members from the area of Beni Suef.

BARRIERS TO THE MONASTIC LIFE

Monasteries and nunneries in Egypt are regarded as not being of this world. The concept of leaving the world symbolically represents for many Copts leaving behind the secular and Islamic realms of the nation. The high, thick, windowless walls around the monasteries in the desert are an especially powerful symbol of this separation from the world.[26] In Egypt, leaving the world also means separating from one's family—a separation from the social system that gives a person his or her identity and security.

The prospective monastic assumes the position of an outsider and forgoes the highly esteemed marital state, giving up the chance to fulfill the role of wife, mother, husband, father. Sons often represent the hopes of their parents for economic security, especially when the son has completed higher studies at the expense of his family. The reaction of family can be vehement when they first hear of their daughter's or son's decision to become a monastic, especially when she or he is the guardian of the parents' future. The Coptic Church understands that, in the case of the son or daughter who provides a substantial means of income, it can be disastrous for a family whose child enters a monastery. In order to provide for such cases, there are rules concerning the personal situation of the monastic candidate. When a person is the only child or has elderly parents, he or she is not allowed to enter the monastic life because Egyptian society does not provide for its old or disabled people. After consultation with the superior, the candidate is then advised to return to the family and come back when the family does not need the younger person's support.[27]

Sometimes a woman must substitute for a deceased or absent sister, or, if this woman is the eldest, she might have to substitute for a deceased mother. Whatever the situation, because a woman in Egypt needs a valid excuse to remain single, it is important that she has connections with a convent even if circumstances prevent her from entering in the immediate future. A woman who chooses to remain celibate for religious reasons without having a relationship with a convent, or even a church, creates a serious problem for her family. The obligation to safeguard her virginity rests on her male relatives. This means that in the case of the death of her father, this obligation will fall on her brothers.[28]

In some cases the family's reactions to a child's vocation can be especially fierce. One Coptic author makes the comparison between a future monk or nun and their family with the exodus of Israel out of Egypt: the family represents the raging pharaoh who will do anything to prevent the leaving. Furthermore, since it is believed that the devil will try to lure the candidate back into his or her familiar environment and activities, monastic candidates need a "special spiritual energy" that enables them to leave behind everything that represents "the world" including their family.[29] Inside both the monastery and the convent, there are strict rules concerning receiving visitors. The candidate's family might come and try to make the candidate change his or her mind.[30] In the case of a future nun, the family might try to convince her that she cannot leave the prospective husband whom the family had arranged for her. The restrictions concerning visits become more lenient once the family has accepted and appreciates their child's vocational choice.

In the case of a monk, the family tends to be proud of him when he eventually is ordained a priest or bishop and regards his monastic status as a kind of blessing for the whole household. These kinds of promotion, of course, never happen to a nun. Nevertheless, apart from an initial objection, one would suspect that a family might tend to be relieved and to rejoice when a daughter has become a nun. Her decision alleviates the burden to take care of her, procure a husband for her, and guard her virginity. However, the reverse of what we might expect turns out to be true. One mother of a nun expressed the general attitude as follows:

> From the outside, the Copts consider the convent a holy place. They love to visit it and benefit from its blessing and admire the nuns. They consider them [the nuns] to be perfect creatures. But when their daughter wants to become a nun, they get furious.
>
> My family was very angry with me that I allowed my daughter to enter the convent and did not even try to stop her. Some members of the family never visit us anymore. They say that I should have persuaded her to use her university degree in a better way. Now it is a loss for society.
>
> But my daughter is a wise and intelligent woman who knows what she wants. And what if she would have emigrated or died? Or if she would have married a

man who would not allow her to see me frequently. After all, she would have to obey her husband! I would have made her miserable by going against her wish.

Thirty-five years ago, this mother wanted to become a nun herself. She went to the convent as an eighteen-year-old, and the abbess told her to come back when she had reached the age of twenty-one. "Then my parents were quick to find me a husband, and they forced me to marry before my twenty-first. In those days, you blindly obeyed your parents."

A few decades ago, the main reason for the parents' anxiety seemed to be the notorious backwardness of the inhabitants of the convents. Especially when a young woman came from a middle-or upper-class family, her family would not allow her to become a nun. Because it had not been usual for people to make visits to the convents, the lifestyle of monasteries was virtually unknown. For a child to consider going to such an unknown place caused parents to say of these strange worlds "Eddeir ghalaṭ"—monasteries are no good.

As a result of this situation, the majority of women who entered the convent more than twenty years ago belonged either to society's misfits (unable to find a suitable husband or widowed without means of income) or they were strong and powerful and thus considered unsuitable brides. These women often possessed a familiarity with the convents, had encouraging family members, or had experienced a supernatural invitation to the monastic life.[31] The first two factors are the result of a strong presocialization, while the supernatural invitation reaffirms the monastic call. One story told about a nun whose sister and several brothers already had entered the monastic life combines all three factors. When the future nun in this story broke the news to her parents that she too wished to become a nun, they refused to acknowledge her wish, arguing that they would lose all their children if she were to follow her wishes. The parents quickly arranged for the daughter to become engaged, and the wedding was planned. But the moment that the engagement ring was put on her finger, the finger started to swell so much that the skin nearly burst. This incident was repeated three times. After the third time, the parents understood that they should allow their daughter to become a nun.

Today, for different reasons, the atmosphere of reluctant parents still prevails, so that a young woman may find it worrisome when her parents actually do encourage her plans to become a nun. One nun told about her mother's reaction when she announced her wish to become a nun: "My mother reacted with, '*mabrūk, yā Monā*' [congratulations, Mona], when I told her about my plans to enter the convent. I became very worried because either your parents are against your choice or you become a bad nun." The special energy that a monastic candidate gets in turning away from the world indeed seems to be indispensable and remains with the monastic candidate throughout the rest of his or her life.

The situation in which the family objects against the monastic choice of a daughter or a son seems to be more current among the contemplative monastics than among the active monastics. It should be mentioned, however, that almost all the sisters had to face some resistance from their families. Egyptian families simply do not like to lose a member, and often the parents were suspicious at first about this new kind of active monasticism. However, families tended to be more lenient when they discovered that the members of the active community are allowed to spend time with their families regularly and that they all seem to pursue a career. When a medical doctor, for example, becomes a contemplative nun, she might be forced to give up her profession. The other nuns might become her patients, but she can never be sure. A medical doctor who joins the active community has a good chance to be sent abroad for further education after which she will work in one of the clinics run by the convent.

I have tried to describe and explain the strong reactions, based on social or economic reasons, that families sometimes have against the monastic vocations of their children. The tendency for future nuns to expect, even hope for, a negative response from their families that eventually changes into support for the daughters' choice indicates that this negative reaction is almost ritualized. The stronger the family's reaction, the bigger sacrifice a nun makes when she trades the secular world for the convent. In most cases the family's attitude changes, and they become proud of their monastic child. The family especially comes to terms with their child's choice upon discovering that she is actually happy in the convent.

When the Vocation Fails

A novice can always leave the convent and be rehabilitated back into secular society, but an initiated nun can never return to her family home.[32] This circumstance, however, does not prevent nuns from being sent away for certain reasons or from leaving by their own choice. In such cases, different strategies have had to be developed by the church authorities for providing for the uncloistered nun.

An estranged nun is suddenly deprived of the protection and sustenance of the convent. In most circumstances, the family would receive their daughter or sister back and take care of her. But since the nun, who has been initiated into monasticism, is considered dead to the world, she can never return to the secular world, and therefore her family cannot take her back. This is a basic rule in Orthodox monasticism, practiced since its early days. Coptic canon law precludes monastics from leaving the monastic life after their initiation rite. The only solution for a nun who is sent away from her original convent is to transfer to another convent or to a monastic site.[33]

The problem with the canon law is that it does not provide clear guidelines for situations in which another convent or monastic site is not available. As René-Georges Coquin explains the law: "The Coptic church has no *codex juris canonici,* as the Roman church does, but it has remained closer to its sources, which it has grouped in chronological or systematic collections. . . . Thus there are the Apostolic Canons and the Ecclesiastical Canons of the Apostles, or the Didascalia and the Testament of the Lord."[34]

In the event that a nun wants to leave the convent after being initiated, she must present her case to the patriarch who, in his capacity as head of the Coptic nation, has to design a solution for her. The nun must also inform the patriarch if she herself finds a solution to this dilemma. This solution, however, can never be a return to her secular life.

A monk who feels compelled to leave the monastery for any reason has the option to work as a priest or conduct other tasks within the church system. Even though he is not permitted to stay with his family, he can more or less live a normal life as a clergyman in the world. For a nun, however, it is preferred that she continue to live as a secluded monastic no matter how her situation is solved. In reality this means that the women monastics' problems are solved on an ad hoc basis and differ according to each case.

The fact that there are no clear-cut precedents for these situations can provide a certain freedom in finding creative solutions; however, the lack of guidelines can just as well have a negative impact. The following story helps to illustrate this point:

> One of the nuns had to leave her convent and presented her case to Patriarch Shenouda III, who had no idea how to solve her problem. She was lucky to be offered living quarters by a relative, but for the most part [she] was in limbo concerning several aspects of her life as a nun. Without a convent or monastic connection, she could not attend church services regularly, and thus had to forgo the Sacrament of Communion. Not having a car, it was impossible for her to reach the church closest to her house. As a nun she could not walk or ride the public buses, and taxis were beyond her budget. By leaving she had also lost her

> confessor, and, as long as the patriarch had not taken a decision concerning her case, no priest or monk was willing to become her confessor. Apart from this, she had lost her means of sustenance and for the time being had to rely on her family's charity.
>
> When queried about her legal rights and options, she said she had no idea and simply was waiting for an answer from the patriarch. She explained that because fixed rules and regulations never played an important role in the convent, nuns were unaware of possible rights.[35]

The fact that monastics have no access to possible legal solutions indicates that they are totally dependent on the church hierarchy if things go wrong in their monastic careers. The majority of monks I interviewed about this topic were not aware either of their legal rights or of regulations concerning the monastic life. But since monks have more options in changing their ecclesiastical careers, their position is less distressing than the nuns' position. In fact, a contemplative nun who has left, or wants to leave, her convent runs the risk of becoming a sort of outlaw and is totally dependent on the church hierarchy to obtain a satisfactory solution.

The exiled nun then must find suitable housing. This is a problem with only a few solutions. She may purchase a small apartment with some other nuns who are in the same situation as she, or she may occupy a closed-off room in a retreat center on the edge of a village in Upper Egypt. In either case she lives an ascetic, anchoritic life. For day-to-day business, like shopping, the nun has to rely on a layperson to provide her regularly with goods and services. For her spiritual life and general supervision, she is either placed under the jurisdiction of the patriarch (in the event that she lives in Cairo) or she is assigned to a bishop who will be her spiritual guide and see to it that her needs are met. Sometimes arrangements are made that enable the nun to pursue a more active vocation.

The whole process of resocializing an exiled nun into an honorable way of life outside the convent is carried out in utmost secrecy and silence. Trying to discuss the matter with the nun herself or with one of the other people involved in the matter is taboo. The nuns I met who had been forced to find other modes of living a monastic life would discuss the matter only after I had known them for a year. Most of them did not feel that their life as a monastic had failed. They felt they had valid reasons for leaving their convents.[36] Some had literally escaped in the car of visiting relatives because they felt overwhelmed by the mother superior's demands. For example, one nun had been denied Communion for a whole week as punishment for missing a daily devotion. Some of the exiled nuns suffered from zealous colleagues who interpreted the Coptic revival fanatically. These overzealous nuns would accuse others of eating too much or of looking up during the prayers, and the accusations were so often made that some nuns felt badgered into leaving.

All exiled nuns I met became accustomed to their new conditions and accepted their situations. Their silence concerning the events that precipitated their leaving the convents was influenced by a fear of social backlash. They worried that their stories might cast negative impressions on their former convents and their mother superiors. Further, they felt anxious and embarrassed toward their families. The father of one of the nuns had not been able to cope with the stress of his daughter's being sent away from her convent and died during the process of finding a solution. Of course, the exiled nuns were also concerned about their own image and the public image of nuns in general.

This attitude of the nuns coincides with Andrea Rugh's observation about the "nice girl" constructs that "are characterized in Egypt by their stress on public image. The self-controls people internalize are ones that usually stress how to present oneself to the world rather than how to satisfy purely personal moral standards."[37] By attempting to keep the estrangement of a nun from her original convent away from the public, the possible sanctions of the public eye are averted. This is a process that saves the honor of the Coptic Church, the nun concerned, the mother superior, and the convent itself. The mother superior, for her part, tries to prevent the recurrence of this kind of embarrassing situation by being more careful in her selection of monastic candidates.

The active community does not have to cope with such situations. This is probably due to the fact that the sisters have more freedom to move around and to fulfill a task that is satisfying to them. In the case of discord between a sister and her superiors or colleagues, there is always the possibility of transfer to another one of the convent's branches. Nevertheless, the same observations that were made about the contemplative nuns are applicable to the members of the active community: active nuns cannot return to the family, are prohibited from leaving the monastic state after initiation, and are held above all to the importance of remaining honorable.

NUNS AS ROLE MODELS

The Coptic convents, both contemplative and active, have an enduring appeal to young women. The question arises then: To what extent do the nuns serve as role models to young Coptic women?

In a 1989 anthropological study of adolescent Coptic girls, Berit Thorbjørnsrud argues that new social conditions, such as increased educational opportunities and newly created options in church work for young Coptic women, have created a serious identity crisis for young women in their teens and twenties. As a result of these young women's higher education and the growing influence of the West, traditional cultural structures, such as marriages arranged by the parents, are no longer acceptable. The age at which young women marry has been pushed forward by five to ten years, and better educated women have more work opportunities outside the home, even after marriage.[38]

The Coptic mothers, on the contrary, still belong to a generation of housewives who are bound to their homes and are not accustomed to being active in the church. As a result of this generation gap, today's girls and young women have to look for other role models to follow. The Coptic Church is gradually trying to fill this gap with special programs for both girls and women. Young women who are not satisfied with staying at home and watching television or standing on the balcony and chatting with the neighbors on the other balconies often turn to the church to fill their free time. They participate in meetings and perform services not only to fill their days but also to experience for themselves what it means to be useful outside the home. At the same time the young women gain the prestige of being good Christians who work for the betterment of the church. Another reason young people find their home situation frustrating is that the parents often show a laxity in performing the religious practices and are more concerned with customs and *taqālīd* (conventions) than with the life of the church.[39]

Since young women cannot go out alone or socialize with strangers (even Coptic strangers), the worship and meetings at the church allow some form of socialization for the restricted young women. Consequently, the church and its meetings serve the function of safekeeping the young woman's decency. Above all, whatever the young woman's motivation for participating in the life of the church, it helps constantly to reaffirm her Coptic identity.

As students, the young Copts must reassess their identity and behavior in view of the Muslim environment, especially in times of strained interreligious relations. The result of this reassessment is a greater sense of Coptic identity. Young women stress their Coptic identity in the process of overcoming their earlier confusion by belonging to a well-defined group. As a result, the Muslim culture becomes increasingly seen as "the other" to them. This process has been described and analyzed in Thorbjørnsrud's dissertation. She points to the fact that the parents often cannot guide their daughters. The parent's role model becomes replaced by the role models the young women find in their church. The traditional mothers cannot influence their daughters' activities and behavior as the church's models for women can. As one mother commented: "Now they are like men; they have full freedom."[40]

In the chapters to come, I will discuss more extensively the role of nuns like the Mother Martha, Mother Irīnī, and Sister Hannah who, in the eyes of the Copts as well as of their nuns and sisters, enjoy special authority in the church and embody both the church's mission and its ideas. As one Coptic young woman expressed it: "They have chosen the best, the most right. They spend all their time and energy in serving God."[41] Nevertheless, the attitude of women like Martha, Irīnī, and Hannah is diametrically opposed to the expectations of Egyptian society for women. A so-called independent woman is anathema, in light of the rigid sex roles: "Men don't like strong women."[42] This is the attitude that the nuns contradict. They have bypassed the general expectations for women of marriage and motherhood and have gained almost full independence from their male protectors. Their fathers or brothers have no say over them any longer. Within their convents the nuns have an all-female society where no man can gain entrance. The only men they have to deal with are the confessor and the patriarch who seldom intrude in the nuns' lives. The most important factor of their independence, however, is that they prove successful in creating a full and satisfactory life which gains them respect and authority from outsiders. As such, in spite of their relatively small number, the nuns exercise a considerable influence on young women's ideas about women's roles. Nuns behave respectfully and modestly (by covering their bodies and abiding by the church rules) and yet they take up challenging tasks. Their choice of celibacy and their quest for holiness has moved them into the realm where "there is neither male nor female" (Gal. 3:28). They are more or less re-creating heaven on earth and showing that women can rise above the cultural, religious, and social restrictions of their environment. The fulfillment of their lives is no longer measured in terms of marriage and children. In the mind of a young Coptic woman, to join an all-female community is to become part of a group which is independent yet respected and completely Coptic.

SUMMARY

Contemplative and active nuns pass through a probation time that is similar for both groups. Although she is not a member of the community yet, the novice already lives among the nuns and participates fully in the daily activities—in contrast to the male novice who lives in separate quarters until the time of initiation. The difference between the process of selecting candidates in an active and contemplative convent is that a more democratic system is used by the active nuns.

Monastic life is a calling, a gift, and often a predisposition. It has to be very clear that the calling is true because much is at stake. First, there is the reaction of the family, followed by cultural prejudices, and, finally, one has to give up a social life that is difficult to return to because of cultural factors. To succeed in the monastic life, the socialization process of a future nun, which primarily takes place at home, seems to be important. Church activities that have been developed as a result of the Coptic revival also form an important element of this socialization process. Young women are able to participate in these activities because of their higher educational level.

Since women are still subject to the general restrictions of the Egyptian society, a convent's mother superior is careful in the selection of candidates, using precautions in order to filter out any woman who she feels might leave the convent. A nun who fails in her vocation can find herself in a desperate situation; not only are her own credibility and honor at stake but also the honor of her family and of her convent. In addition, she has no definite system to fall back on. Once these nuns succeed in the convent, they become role models for Coptic laywomen, showing them that life's fulfillment can involve more than the traditional requirements of marriage and motherhood.

CHAPTER 5

Dead to the World

The Initiation Rites

When the minimum years of precandidacy and novitiate have passed, the prayers of the rite of initiation into monasticism (or prayers for the dead, as they are called) can be said over the novice. After this rite of initiation the nun becomes dead to the world. This chapter will discuss different rites, the implications of certain texts, the symbolism of the monastic habit, and the significance of receiving a new monastic name. The chapter closes with the end of the monastic struggle and the true fulfillment of a nun's life—physical death.

RITES FOR THE CONTEMPLATIVE AND ACTIVE NUNS

Because the initiation rite used for both the contemplative and the active nuns is the same, I will discuss this rite first. After that I will explain the vows of the active sisters and the liturgy that is used to promote a precandidate to the novitiate.

After a novice has been on probation for a minimum of one year and has proved to be worthy of the monastic habit, she is told that the rite of initiation may now be performed. In the convents the ceremony can be presided over by the monk who hears the nuns' confessions, by a bishop, or by the patriarch.[1] The active sisters are always initiated by their abbot, Bishop Athanasius. In a monastery it is the abbot who usually performs the ceremony.[2] Sometimes the contemplative novice is given only a day's notice informing her that she will be initiated. Since the active sisters have to take a retreat for three days prior to the ceremony, they are notified earlier. While at some monasteries relatives of the novice are welcome to attend the ceremony (if the message can be sent to them in time), no family member is allowed to be present during the initiation at the convents.

The day before the initiation the novice has a special session with the spiritual father and confessor in order to confess her sins. This is an extremely important step in the preparation since the candidates cannot enter the monastic state without having received *taḥlīl* (absolution). The higher state of life the novices are going to enter requires them to be cleansed from even the smallest transgression.[3] By that time—in case of the contemplative nuns—the new habit has been secretly placed inside the altar for three days. The day before the ceremony, the mother superior or the abbot will counsel the novice concerning monastic life in general and will give the appropriate personal admonitions. While the candidate prepares for the event, ideally, she will also be informed of the new name that will be given. This name will not be made public until after the next day's celebration. The night before the actual initiation ceremony, the contemplative novice keeps vigil in the church and meditates on the lives of the saints, especially the saint whose name she will bear. This reflection is particularly important since this monastic name signifies the heavenly patron whose ascetic lifestyle the novice will try to imitate. The sleepless night combined with many hours of prayer are meant to prepare the candidates properly for the ceremony. Sleep is believed to be the time when a person is most vulnerable to the devil, who can whisper inappropriate thoughts into the mind and thus, for example, cause a man to produce nocturnal pollution. So the novice remains awake in order to ward off mental and bodily impurities and thus imitates the passion of Christ, who remained sleepless in prayer as his disciples slept in the Garden of Gethsemane. "Passion and death are indeed the themes of the consecration ceremony."[4] After the office of the morning prayers and the raising of the incense have taken place, the initiation begins. During the ceremony the novices lie on their backs, with their heads toward the east facing the shrine that contains the relics of the monastery's patron saint. Father Mark Gruber describes the ceremony for the monks:

> The wool covering of the coffin-like reliquary is removed and placed over the reclining man. He remains in that state of intense heat, excitement, weariness, motionless, and near airlessness for over one and a half hours. Above him and his funerary pall, the monastic community chants the funeral prayers for the dead. That is to say, these are the same prayers and chants of the Coptic funeral, invoking the saints to assist their brother who has died. Therein is the essential part of the consecration, which is accomplished not so much by vows uttered, as the willingness to lay down in ritual death.[5]

The ceremony for the women is similar to the one described above, except for the Gospel readings and the chanting. A liturgical chanting is also performed by the members of a female monastic community, but they are not allowed to raise their voices.

In the active community the novice does not have to spend the night in vigil in the church. Excitement about this important event might induce the whole community to retire somewhat later than the usual 9:00 P.M. The novice has been told her new monastic name because she has already gone through a ceremony of promotion from postulant to novice. The new name does not necessarily have to be that of a Coptic saint. The initiation ceremony's liturgy is exactly the same as the one for the contemplative nuns, although the active nuns' chanting is faster (which means that the novice has to spend less time under the suffocating wool cover). Because their patron saint is St. Mary, the novices simply recline in front of the altar where a picture of the Holy Virgin is standing.

After the initiation, the monastics, contemplative and active, are not allowed to move to another monastery or convent. In principle they dedicate themselves to the place where they are initiated.

Some Nuns' Reflections on the Initiation Ceremony

For most of the nuns, contemplative and active, the initiation ceremony is an emotional event full of tensions and doubts. The novices are nervous and do not feel pure enough to enter this high spiritual state—especially since being initiated into monasticism does not mean that one will not make mistakes or fall into sin. A monastic's life is always threatened by the possibility of falling. And the higher the state one has reached, the steeper one can fall. Some nuns said that they had felt the urge to run and hide when they heard that the ceremony was coming up for them. "I almost wanted to leave the church," claimed one nun. Another had cried when she was covered by the funerary pall because she felt unworthy of the ceremony through which Christ would become her bridegroom and she would be set apart for a life of worship: "I felt like a poor girl who got married to a king." The majority of the nuns had experienced the funerary prayers as "a special grace and power" from the Holy Spirit. This feeling had taken away their fears and doubts and had given them the reassurance that they would not have to bear their special responsibility alone.

Many members of the active community said that the initiation of new sisters provided them with an occasion to contemplate their own monastic life and vows. It more or less meant a renewal of their vows.

The Initiation Rite

Because the monastic rank does not belong to the seven Coptic ecclesiastical orders of reader, subdeacon, deacon, archdeacon, priest, hegoumenos, and bishop, the rite of initiation is not a sacrament. A male monk can only be ordained into one of the holy orders after his initiation into monasticism. The Arabic term for the ceremony is *Ṭaqs al-Risāma* or *Ṭaqs al-Siyāma* (the consecration rite), the same term that is used for the ordination of a priest or for the consecration into any of the seven orders. The text that is used, both for monks and nuns, is based on a manuscript from 1761, edited by Raphael Tūkhī.[6] Slightly different versions are used in different nunneries and monasteries.[7] The main difference between the rites for nuns and those for monks are the different Bible passages and exhortations that are read.

Because through the initiation rite the nun or monk becomes "dead to the world," the first part of the service (until the bestowing of the habit) is chanted in mournful tones. In total, the rite consists of forty-four sections of prayers, doxologies (including the doxology of St. Antony), Bible readings, and the singing of the Kyrie Eleison. The central readings are: Psalm 51 on the basis of God's judgment; Psalm 119 on meditations on the Law; and several Bible readings. For a monk, the readings include the passage from Paul's letter to the Ephesians (6:10–17) concerning the spiritual armor which God provides to His people and verses from the Gospel of John (3:1–21). The readings for a nun come from 1 Corinthians (7:25–34) and from Matthew (25:1–13); however, it should also be noted that in the Convent of St. Dimyānah the reading from Ephesians (6:10–17) is used. After the attendants of the service have said the creed, the leader of the service prays that God may grant the nuns or monks goodness and mercy so that they may be perfect and able to flee from passions and to overcome all evil spirits. Then the novices stand up with their faces toward the east and the sign of the cross is scissored out of their hair. While a monk lets the hair of his beard and head grow freely after initiation, a nun cuts her hair off and keeps it short for the rest of her life. Her long hair that once was the sign of her femininity and beauty has to be trimmed to delete her feminine attractiveness. Furthermore, as many of the nuns have stressed, cutting the hair is a sacrifice to God. After cutting the sign of the cross in the hair, the clothing ceremony begins and from hereafter the chanting is joyful. After the whole congregation has chanted the Kyrie Eleison forty-one times, the abbess or abbot takes the novices to the altar and reads a set of monastic instructions to them. The novice is now considered dead to the world and only in case of extreme circumstances will leave the monastery. According to the instructions at the end of the ceremony, the new nun or monk is "cleansed from the filth of the world . . . [and] clothed in the attire of the angels."[8] A nun is furthermore reminded of the parable of the ten maidens and of the fact that she is called to be a wise maiden. The monk hears at the end of the ceremony that he is "appointed a soldier of Christ" and should "fight the good fight, . . . combat the devil." Both the nun's and monk's foreheads are anointed with oil and the nuns receive a burning candle that they carry in the church during a *zaffa*, or festive procession. After the initiation ceremony, the mass is celebrated and the new nuns and monks enjoy their first communion after being initiated.

MONASTIC CLOTHES FOR CONTEMPLATIVE NUNS AND MONKS

After the sign of the cross is made three times over the monastic garments, the new nun or monk is first clothed with the *qalansūwa* (cowl) for the head and then with the *gallābīya* (habit), under which a leather girdle with three plaited crosses is worn (*minṭaqa* or *ḥizām*). Contemplative nuns and monks are dressed in black and their basic garments are virtually the same. Nuns however add three other pieces to their habits: the *taltīma* (a square scarf that is folded into the shape of a wimple) that covers their breast and thus their femininity; a *mandīl* (a triangular scarf that is fastened at the back of the head) to keep the *qalansūwa* and the *taltīma* in place; and, finally, a long black *ṭarḥa* (veil) that reaches down to the waist and is draped over the head. This is to remind the nuns of the veil of the Virgin Mary.

The monastic garb for women strongly resembles the traditional outfit of the women in Upper Egypt that is still worn today. Actually, until about two decades ago, nuns did not wear distinctive clothing. With the Coptic revival, monastics looked for appropriate clothes to symbolize their vocation. The cowl that is called *qalansūwa* was reintroduced in its present shape by Patriarch Shenouda during the time he was still a monk. According to Shenouda, the *qalansūwa* resembles the skullcap St. Antony used to wear.[9] All the nuns wear it, but it is not accepted at every monastery, because some monks believe it to be Syrian rather than Coptic.

During the initiation rite itself the nun wears a special garment called the *zaʿabūṭ*; this is a *gallābīya* made of coarse wool that eventually will serve as a nun's shroud. The garment is a vivid symbol of the dead-to-the-world notion.

The black habit advertises the monastic life while at the same time insulating the monastic from the world. The basic garments of a monk and nun are the same, and for both their clothes represent St. Paul's "garment of righteousness, the breastplate of salvation," while the cowl is "the cowl of humility and the helmet of salvation."[10] The symbolic explanation of these images is a vivid reminder to the monk that he is a "warrior of Christ." Like the former desert fathers, the monk has moved into the desert to combat the devil and the demonic powers. For the nun the symbolic clothing is an indication that she is also engaged in a spiritual battle that can be won only by being a wise virgin.

The *qalansūwa* (cowl) covers the head and the back of the neck. It is black, divided into halves by a sewn line in the middle, and has twelve crosses (reminiscent of the twelve apostles), six on each side, embroidered on it in a contrasting color. The cowl is kept on the head by means of strings that can be tied under the chin. According to the nuns and monks, the shape of the cowl resembles a bib for young children by which they are reminded of Jesus' words that "one should become like a child in order to enter the kingdom of God" (Mark 10:15). In the surrounding Muslim world the embroidered crosses on the cowl stress the nun's or monk's removal from the world.[11] The two halves of the cowl are explained from St. Antony's hagiography. It is said that St. Antony's cowl was torn in two during a fight between him and demons. For the monk it suffices only to wear the cowl, while a nun covers her head with four layers of cloth. By covering her head and breasts, she makes sure never to be a source of temptation. In other words, she is forced to be more modest than a monk simply because she is a woman.

The *minṭaqa* or *ḥizām* (leather belt) that is worn around the waist under the outer garment is to remind the nun or monk of the symbolic death—because the leather is made from the flesh of an animal. Furthermore, the belt beneath the habit is a symbol of purity and chastity. Its closeness to the body warns the monastic against bodily satisfactions (such as eating too much) and protects the bearer against attacks of the evil one who may "arouse sexual desires and physical unrest."[12]

The clothes are not just a symbolic reminder to the monastics of their special state. The monastics need their habits as weapons against the attacks of evil. Popular legend holds that the three basic elements of the outfit as described above were revealed to St. Antony by an angel. Monastics wear the habit of St. Antony (and lie in front of the relics of a saint during the initiation ceremony) in order to be strengthened by the saint's spiritual power. This is analogous to the Old Testament story of Elisha, who asked the prophet Elijah before Elijah departed: "Let me inherit a double share of your spirit."[13] Apart from being a repository of the saint's spiritual power, the symbolic clothing of the monastic habit is believed to be imbued with the power of the Holy Spirit. According to a story that is widely spread among monastics, St. Antony once dressed a dummy in the clothes of a monk. Immediately devils appeared and attacked the dummy with arrows. Antony asked them why they attacked it while they could see that it was not a real monk. They answered that it was not the person but the clothes that bothered them and the monastic costume was the armor that made the demons suffer.[14]

MONASTIC CLOTHES OF THE ACTIVE SISTERS

Although active nuns are initiated by a similar ceremony and wear the same type of leather belt as the contemplative nuns, the active nun's outer monastic clothing is utterly different from the black floor-length dress the contemplative nuns wear. The necessity to design a new dress was due to Patriarch Kyrillos VI's stipulation that he was willing to bless the community only if the nuns would wear habits that differed from the traditional monastic one. Since the active community's work was not so much involved in continuous prayer or combatting spiritual evil as it was in serving humankind and combatting the evils of poverty, sickness, and social injustice, the nuns' habits were made to symbolize their specific tasks. The outfit is an ankle-length dress with a broad pleat on each side and a small white collar. It is comfortable so that it does not hinder the nuns' in their work; the broad pleat on each side of the front gives the impression that an apron is tied over the dress. In Egypt an apron is generally worn by servants who work in the kitchen. So by wearing this "apron" a sister indicates that she is a servant who is always ready to obey and to do God's work. The small white detachable collar, similar to the ones found on the dresses of children, is a sign of purity. The active sister does not wear a cowl but a short veil that reaches to her shoulders. The sisters explain the symbolism of the veil: first, it covers their hair as a sign of modesty; second, it reminds them of a soldier's protective helmet worn in battle; and finally, the veil covers the back of the head and the neck, indicating that the active nun has turned her back to the secular world. The color of the outfit is beige for novices and grey for initiated sisters. Both wear the same model of dress. Although an active nun is considered dead to the world, the grey rather than black color of the habit is an indicator that to a certain degree she still participates in the world.

THE MONASTIC NAME

The monastic name becomes a crucial factor in the nun's identity, as it is supposed to serve as a kind of alter ego for the nun so that she will try to emulate the lifestyle and virtues of the saint whose name she receives. During his stay in the Wādī Rayān, Father Mattā al-Meskīn related the following concerning the names of the other hermits living with him: "The names are not given haphazardly, but according to the marks of the person's spirit and the marks of his heart, which are not easily seen by every man. Moreover, the name which is chosen will leave a powerful and lasting impression on the monk. When we determine which name shall be given to a monk, we assemble and pray, and then we decide."[15] That a monastic name is the bearer of a new identity is also reflected in the way monks and nuns speak about "the name I had in my former life" when mentioning their birth names.

One of the consequences of the increase of monastic vocations is the need for new names. Especially since the nuns in a convent are regarded as one family, no two nuns in the same convent can have the same name. Broadly speaking, names for Coptic clergy and monastics used to come from three main sources: (1) the Bible; (2) the Coptic saints and church fathers; and (3) the names derived from Biblical Greek and their Arabic equivalents. To expand the pool of appropriate names, the present Coptic leaders turn to these three sources and try to discover existing though lesser-known saints and personalities. Since the Coptic Church has always had more male than female saints, models, and, of course, church leaders, a degree of inventiveness is required to find or create names for the new nuns.

The active community is more open to the choice of "foreign" names. However, this non-Coptic naming can lead to a situation in which a nun may not be familiar with the name she has been given. For example, some of the novices in the active community received biblical names that had not been traditionally used for monastics (Eve), or not widely known (Asenath, the wife of Joseph). One sister got the name of the midwife (Salome) who, according to the legend, accompanied the Holy Family on their flight to Egypt. Some other nuns received the names of saints or personalities that are mostly known only in the West—Therese, for example, or Basilia. This choice of unfamiliar names led to deep disappointment among some of the sisters who either felt no relation with the person whose name they now bore or had problems with an un-Coptic name. The choice of un-Coptic names also lead to remarks from the Coptic laypeople. The people had problems remembering certain names and somehow felt that the use of these foreign names formed a threat to true Coptic identity.

Name giving is also an indicator of the extent to which a certain new monastic group has been accepted and incorporated into the monastic system. The names of the *mukarrasāt* (the consecrated women) serve to illustrate this point. A woman who joins the monastic project at Luxor often receives a new name within a few weeks upon arrival. But the *mukarrasāt* in Deir St. Dimyānah, as in several other bishoprics, keep their birth names until they are dedicated. This means that until 1992, when a new rite for the initiation of *mukarrasāt* was introduced, none of the dedicated women of St. Dimyānah had received a monastic name. Although their installation is perceived as binding, these women are neither active nuns, nor are they regular laypeople. The fact that in some places *mukarrasāt* keep their birth names indicates that the attitudes toward their positions in the church are still ambivalent.

THE CEREMONY FOR THE PROMOTION FROM CANDIDATE TO NOVICE IN THE ACTIVE COMMUNITY

The liturgy used for the promotion of a candidate to the novitiate is similar to the one used to dedicate *mukarrasāt*. A novelty in the active community is the taking of vows, or, better, the making of promises. During the ceremony, the novice promises to keep the community's seven vows and reaffirms these vows when she is initiated. There are three vows that are considered basic for monasticism: *al-ʿiffa* (chastity), *al-ṭāʿa* (obedience), and *al-tajarrud* (poverty). These vows are dealt with extensively in the handbook for monastics, *Bustān al-Ruhbān* (The Garden of the Monks).[16] These vows are, of course, valid for every monk or nun, whether contemplative or active. The active sisters compare their vows to the three nails used in Christ's crucifixion. By being reminded constantly of Jesus' suffering, they feel drawn closer to Him.

The four other vows the nuns take are connected with specific philosophy the community has in regards to work: *al-hudūʾ* (quietness or peacefulness), combined with *al-ʿamal* (work), *al-khedma* (service), and *al-sharika* (community life). An active nun should try to maintain her inner peace in whatever work she does. She can reach this peace by constantly concentrating on God's commandments, the psalms, and prayer.[17] Work and service are interconnected and indicate that the nun is active and not contemplative. The promise that she accepts community life means that she has to participate in the communal meals and activities—in other words, she is not allowed to live a semianchoritic life.

The ceremony during which a postulant is promoted to the novitiate is called the *ʿahd al-irtibāṭ* (vow of affiliation or promise of commitment). The ceremony consists mainly of Bible readings with an opening prayer and the presentation of the postulant to the community by means of a *al-tazkiya* (recommendation) read by the mother superior. The novice then agrees to the vows, with the understanding that they are not yet binding, and promises to keep the community's rule. The ceremony ends with the blessing and then the novice puts on her new monastic clothing (the beige dress and a veil).

The ceremony is considered to be similar to the consecration of a deacon, although the diaconate is not open to women. As a symbol of this similarity the novice gets a plaited leather cross on a leather band that she wears under her dress, crossed over her body, like a deacon would wear his sash over his liturgical garment. The leather cross precedes the leather belt that the novice will get at her initiation.

OTHER INITIATIONS: ESKĪM AND THE MOTHER SUPERIOR

In the chapter on hierarchy and administration of the convents, I discussed a higher degree of initiation that hermits, or people holding certain position in the church, would take: the *eskīm,* or great skema. Bishops, abbots, and abbesses used to receive the great skema before they were installed in their positions. Because of the tasks such a position entails nowadays, bishops, abbots, and abbesses no longer are great-skema-bearers. The present-day abbesses are promoted to their office during a ceremony of blessing for which a new type of liturgy has been designed. The first abbess to be blessed this way was Umminā Yoʾannā, the Abbess of Deir Māri Girgis in Old Cairo (11 September 1980).

The main readings for the service of the eskīm, the great skema, for nuns are passages from 2 Corinthians (10:1–18) and Luke (14:25–35) (about renouncing everything to follow Christ.) The Bible readings for a monk are Hebrews 13:7–25 (Remember your leaders, obey your leaders, and submit to them, and continually offer up a sacrifice of praise to God).[18]

In the texts used for nuns and monks there is no particular point of reference to the candidate's gender. The main themes of the texts are renouncing worldly goods and following Christ in continuous prayer and sacrifice.[19] This study is not the place for an extensive discussion of the service for the great skema, especially since the ceremony is hardly ever conducted today. Nevertheless, there are some relevant points that should be mentioned. The most crucial difference between the texts for a nun and those for a monk is the admonishment to the male skema-bearer to obey his leaders and to submit to them. The use of this text from Hebrews 13 acknowledges the potential anticlerical state of a skema-bearer, keeping in mind that originally this degree of monasticism was conferred on hermits. The true nature of a hermit is stressed by the use of this Bible text; a hermit has chosen to be radically removed not only from society but also from the institutional church. The letter to the Hebrews warns: "Do not be lead away by diverse and strange teachings" (13:9). A hermit who wears the great skema, the sign of a great asceticism from which he derives charismatic authority, has the potential to draw a crowd of followers, even to form his own group. This means that he has the potential to break away from the church. Thus one can observe that in this ceremony, which recognizes the highest degree of spirituality, there is indirect reference to the intricacies of church politics and hierarchy. The text indirectly refers to the two types of authority that were recognized in the early church: the authority of clergy belonging to the institutional church and the charismatic authority of monks. This means that when the degree of great skema is no longer bestowed, the only valid authority left is the official church clergy. At present, this situation suits Patriarch Shenouda's autocratic style of ruling the Coptic Church.

The fact that no admonition is made to the female skema bearer to obey and submit to her leaders indicates that women are not expected or considered to be capable of disobedience to their church leaders, nor are they thought to have the charismatic authority to set up their own order. Since women do not belong to the institutional hierarchy, bestowing the great skema on them was the only way to recognize and formalize their spiritual authority by means of an institutionalized initiation. This was also the only institution that could place the nuns on a level where gender differences no longer counted. A female hermit in a cave lives in the same way as a male hermit. An abbess holds the same authority and power in her convent as does an abbot in his monastery. Moreover, the great skema was a powerful link with tradition. Redefining tradition means in this case that women are deprived of the only initiation that invested them with some sort of official spiritual power and authority.

THE INSTALLATION CEREMONY FOR AN ABBESS

In the past for the installation of an abbess a short blessing would follow the ceremony for the great skema during which the laying-on-of-hands would take place. The newly designed text for this installation service can be divided in two parts. During the first part female personalities from the Bible are mentioned for the specific tasks God had given them. Some examples are St. Mary, Elizabeth, Deborah, Tabitha, Sarah, Mary, Lidya, and Priscilla. The second part is mainly a prayer during which God is beseeched to grant the new abbess "the spirit of wisdom and consultation to administer the convent."[20] The text acknowledges the role of mother superior as an organizer and administrator who must deal with a range of responsibilities (which do not leave room for the ascetic exercises required of an eskīm bearer). Finally, it has to be noted that the position of mother superior in the active community potentially rotates; every two years a new superior can be chosen. The ceremony as described above will not be used for her installation.

RETURNING TO THE WORLD: ORDINATION TO PRIESTHOOD

The contemplative nuns I interviewed did not regret that they had no access to any degree of ordination within the church. They said that they "were lucky" because being barred from ordination to them meant that they could never be called away to serve outside the convent. Concurrent with the process of clericalization, the majority of monks now go on to ordination to priesthood.[21] This means that the monks nowadays play a greater social role in the Coptic community than they used to. At the same time a monk is supposed to have come to the monastery to seek God in solitude and pursue the ideal of eremitism.[22] The attitude goes back to the earliest monastic history that recognizes the very original state of monasticism as a lay movement with anti-ecclesiastical tendencies. Among the early monks some were ordained to the priesthood only as they were needed to celebrate the Eucharist. The preference of the Coptic Church in this matter dates back to Pachomius who is said to have "disappeared into the midst of a crowd so as not to be discovered" when St. Athanasius came to ordain him into the priesthood.[23] A monk has the freedom to flee from ordination as Pachomius did.[24] The same argument of the pure eremitic state is used to keep monasticism outside the holy orders of the church.

This unwillingness to be ordained and to be forced to leave the "true monastic state" has become a genre in the history of monasticism. For example, in Coptic history, patriarchal candidates had to be brought from the desert in fetters due to their presumed unwillingness to trade the desert for the patriarchal throne.[25] The present Patriarch Shenouda III claims that while he was living as a hermit, the then Patriarch Kyrillos VI called him to Cairo and ordained him a bishop by surprise. Patriarch Shenouda likes to express his grief about this promotion with the words that "the most beautiful years of my life, when I lived alone in a cave, ended there." Father Gruber has found in his research among the monks that stories abound of how a monk was called by the patriarch or a bishop "to serve as a deacon assistant during the liturgy, and that in place of a simple blessing . . . , the bishop imposed his hands on the head of the unsuspecting monk, and made him a priest."[26]

The Coptic nuns consider their (socially imposed) gender limitation—which prevents them from ordination and thus from reaching a place for themselves in the ecclesiastical hierarchy—a benefit. When one looks at the Coptic practice of avoiding ordination, it seems that the nuns' opinion on their exemption from priesthood is based on more than just the idea that they are free to live out the true monastic ideal. Their gender also spares the nuns from a subtle and intricate play of "power eschewed"[27] in which monks willingly, or unwillingly, participate. Nuns can link their present life directly to the early monastic history and consider themselves symbolically as the "bearers of the true monastic ideal." The nuns uphold the ideology that they have nothing to do with the world and that nothing can force them away from their true contemplative life.

Among the active sisters asked, none wished for ordination to the priesthood. One of them had researched the position of women in the early church in order to provide the community with more information about this topic, however.[28] Her conclusion was that the church should grant women more opportunities to participate on committees and in decision making. She stressed the point that for the early Christians "all were alike."[29] But she did not feel attracted to "extremists" who wanted equal rights for men and women in the church.[30] Most of the active nuns felt that certain responsibilities were incompatible with their heavy work loads. Furthermore, many sisters gave the standard biblical answer most Coptic women give to the question or whether or not women can work as priests: "If God wanted women to have certain positions in the church, He would have given an active role to St. Mary and Jesus would have chosen women to be among the apostles." One also often hears the remark: "We have never had female priests; we are not used to it. What should we call her? Abūnā?!"

THE MONASTIC STRUGGLE AND PHYSICAL DEATH

In discussing the different rites of initiation I observed that the monastic "dies to the world." He or she moves to the level of "an angel on earth." The monastic has to protect him or herself from potential incursions into this pure state. In this lifelong struggle the monastic uses certain symbolic and real mechanisms to shield him or herself from disturbances. Defensive mechanisms are clothing, the inaccessible locations of monasteries and convents, continuous reflection upon prayers and scriptures, and recitations from the tradition.

One can distinguish two main sources of disturbance for monastics. First, the outside world regularly disturbs the convent or monastery. Visitors and tasks that have to be done in and outside the monastery force the monastic to encounter the secular world. This situation is nothing new. Even the most remote hermits in the earliest days of Christianity had regular contact with people who came to them for advice, prayers, and healing. The nuns and monks today see spiritual and material assistance and hospitality to visitors as part of their vocation; however, it is not their main task.

The second source of disturbance for monastics belongs more to the monastic vocation than anything else. It is combatting against the attacks of the devil and demonic powers. This struggle was an important theme in the conversations and daily lives of the desert fathers. A considerable part of the life of St. Antony consists of descriptions of his fights with the demons who appeared to him in different shapes—from seductive women, to other monks, to wild beasts and reptiles.[31] In this context the readings that are performed during a monk's initiation become clear: monks are warriors but, as Antony said, "*not against blood and flesh,* but against destructive demons."[32] Antony exhorted his disciples with the words from Ephesians to "take the whole armor of God, that you may be able to withstand in the evil day" (6:13).[33] In early monastic life fighting the demonic played an important role. One of the reasons monks preferred to live in the desert was the belief that there was the preeminent dwelling place of the demons.[34] While ordinary Coptic believers are urged to ignore the devil and his demons, present-day monks still consider this struggle as one of the crucial points of their vocation. One monk in the Monastery of Baramūs expressed this as follows:

> Some of us leave the monastery to live in a small group as hermits out in the desert. Originally that is the habitat of the demons. Then they start to fill the

place with worship and prayers. At the same time, monks from the monastery supply them with water with which they cultivate the soil and make it fertile. After a while the demons will leave because that spot is no longer theirs; it now belongs to the monks.

The question now concerns the nuns. They are not allowed to live in the desert because it is considered a dangerous place for a woman and also because they are women, and women embody temptation. Although some of the nuns have moved into desertlike areas, the majority of nuns still live in the city. Nevertheless, they hold the same views as the monks concerning their monastic vocation: a fundamental issue is fighting against evil. According to the sisters, evil attacks them with disturbing *afkār* (thoughts) such as: "should I go back to my family and normal life?" Contemplative nuns might think: "should I not be out there doing charitable work?," while active nuns might be obsessed with the thought that they do not devote enough time to prayers. According to the nuns, these kinds of thoughts require as much spiritual struggle as do the demons who appear to the monks in the desert. Contemplative nuns especially describe their monastic life with words like *ṣaʿb*, (hard, difficult) and *taʿab* (troublesome, tiring). By this they mean that they lead a difficult life that requires immense efforts. Their behavior can be explained as a redefinition of the old model of "the athlete for Christ," a concept first used to describe the ascetic efforts of St. Antony.

It is obvious that the life of a monastic is full of pitfalls from both inside and outside of monastery or convent, and it is accepted that the devil is always after the monk or nun to make him or her fall. In this context the nuns like to quote the following story from the early fathers about a meeting of the devils:

> Satan said [to one of the lesser devils], "Where have you come from?" The devil answered, "I was in a certain place and made much blood flow, and I have come to tell you about it." Satan asked, "How long did it take you to do this?" The devil replied, "Thirty days." Then Satan commanded him to be flogged, saying, "In so long a time have you done only that?" After several devils had related the achievements of disturbances they created and people they killed, the last devil gave his report: "I was in the desert forty years fighting against a monk, and this night I made him fall into fornication." When he heard this, Satan arose, embraced him, and put a crown he was wearing on the devil's head and made him sit on his throne, saying, "You have been able to do a very great deed!"[35]

The battle nuns and monks face does not end until they die. Death is seen by the monastics as a joyful occasion. When al-umm Safīna was informed about her death three days in advance she:

> Got up over joyful . . . and cleaned her cell and washed her clothes. The [other] nuns heard her repeat to herself: "a day of farewell, a day of struggle and a day of raising up and carrying away." . . . Then she went to each of the nuns . . . to tell them: "oh my sister, I will go on a trip; forgive me and remember me in your prayers." Then a mass was celebrated after which she announced that it was the last one she would attend (a day of farewell). The following day she fell ill (a day of struggle) and the third day she died (a day of raising up and carrying away). And all the nuns were filled with awe and joy.[36]

A monk who was told in the early morning that he would die before dawn reacted with tears of joy and words of praise. It is said that his brothers in the monastery were shedding tears at the same time because they were not able to join him.[37]

SUMMARY

From the traditional initiation texts that are still in use today, one can distill information about the expected role of a female monastic—a wise virgin. One observes also that the spectrum of monastic possibilities within the Coptic Church has widened. Although the ascetic hermit still serves as the prototype, the virtual abolition of the great skema indicates that in reality other priorities have come into place. With the abolition of the great skema, spiritual authority now solely belongs to the members of the institutionalized church. The original anticlerical monastic attitude and the ideal of the hermit still exist but mostly in Coptic heritage and in wistful desert tales. The reality of life is that the Coptic community needs more priests, more people to administer sacraments to a growing population, and more spiritual guides and social workers to meet the needs of the people at this time. Hence one can observe that the clericalization of the monastic profession has lead to a wider social role, especially for monks and active nuns. All these activities have resulted in a stronger position for the official church in the Coptic community. In this shifting monastic landscape the contemplative nuns have managed to stay closest to the original monastic ideal.

For women this trend of clericalization and concentration on the institutional church has resulted in an active community whose members are initiated into monasticism by the old, traditional service. The use of this service signifies their intention to maintain a link with their monastic heritage. Only in the readings given during the promotion ceremony of a postulant to the novitiate does one see textual indication of the specific vocation of the active nuns: "to go out and serve." The clericalization of Coptic social work is symbolized by the leather cross the active novice wears under her dress which is analogous to the deacon's sash.

Contemplative and active nuns are reminded daily of their role as wise virgins. The veil they wear is one of the indicators of this state. St. Mary, from whom they derive the veil, is considered the "new Eve." It is a nun's vocation to overcome the "old Eve."

According to the texts read at initiation, combatting the devil is the monk's job. But the use of the alternative text from Ephesians by the Convent of St. Dimyānah shows that contemplative nuns have started to join the ranks of the "warriors for Christ" as well.

Contemplative nuns design their own activities and meet the spiritual and social needs of believers; they are headed by abbesses who are now acknowledged as organizers and administrators. At the same time the contemplative nuns are the keepers of the old monastic ideals. The "lucky" contemplative nun at heart is a Coptic believer who strives to reinforce her church and its identity. Apart from their spiritual work, contemplative and active nuns create their own spheres of activity. What exactly their activities comprise will be dealt with in the next chapter.

CHAPTER 6

Work and Income

Traditionally monastics have worked for several reasons: for daily sustenance, in order to provide for guests or people in need, or because social work was their vocation. While the contemplative nuns try to develop "traditional" monastic tasks (producing arts and crafts), the work of the active nuns has more to do with the development of social work and projects that were initiated during the Coptic revival. Both contemplative and active nuns consider their work as *khedma* (pious service) to the Coptic community at large. I will begin this chapter with a discussion of *khedma* and what this notion implies in the work of active sisters. I will then discuss the types of work contemplative nuns have developed and end the chapter with some observations on how today's nuns obtain their funding.

KHEDMA

Khedma, or *khidma,* means to serve, be at service, do or render a service, work or have a job.[1] In ordinary language the word means "service," as, for example, in the frequently heard question: "*Ayye khedma?,*" which is translated "Can I be of any service or do anything for you?" In Coptic circles *khedma* has acquired the connotation of "service as an act for God"; hence I have translated it as "pious service" or "Godly service." *Khedma* in its various forms can be performed by any Copt: laypeople who teach Sunday school, collect clothes for the poor, or regularly provide goods or services to a monastery or convent are all performing *khedma.* Consecrated individuals (married deacons, for example) who assist in the liturgy and priests who serve the community through their words, deeds, and the sacraments perform *khedma.* Contemplative nuns and monks can perform *khedma* by exercising charity and receiving guests. When Mother Martha built a church next to her convent, this accomplishment was considered an act of *khedma* to the Coptic community at large. Finally, the active nuns and the *mukarrasāt* and *mukarrasīn* (consecrated women and men) have devoted their lives to the performance of different types of *khedma* in their social work.

In order to get a better understanding of the nature and the spirit of the present work of the active community, I will investigate how the concept of *khedma* has developed. Looking at Coptic Church history, one can detect two main lines that lead to *khedma* as it is known today: (1) the Coptic charitable organizations and (2) the so-called deaconry movement.

The *gamʿīyāt al-sayyidāt al-qibṭīya* (Coptic charitable organizations), mostly run by women from the upper and middle classes, were founded at the end of the nineteenth century. These organizations established schools, hospitals, and orphanages and set up social welfare programs. The development of these charities was not restricted to Coptic women only; many Muslim women were active in the field of Muslim charities as well.[2] An extra goal for the Coptic organizations was to help "keep a dispersed community in touch" and to provide "services that the state either was unable to provide due to limited resources, or was unwilling to provide for non-Muslims."[3]

The members of the active community in Beni Suef see these charitable organizations as their actual forerunners, although the community's work principles were considerably influenced by the deaconry movement. About half a century later, in 1945, the first conference about *khedma* was held under the guidance of the late Bishop Bāsiliūs, then bishop of Luxor, Esna, and Aswan.[4] Young people who were active volunteers in Sunday school and other projects of the church gathered together to discuss the impact of these activities on their daily lives. For example, they decided that they should live in communal groups and share whatever they possessed. An example of such a communal house was the *Beit-al-Takrīs* (House of Consecration) in *Ḥelwān*, opened in 1958. The seven young men who lived this communal life were dedicated to celibacy and were active in missionary work among Coptic youth. The initiative for this new project came from Father Mattā al-Meskīn.[5]

The main issue in the 1950s was the plight of the Coptic villagers who lived in poverty and ignorance and were often unaware of what it meant to be a Copt.[6] Under the guidance of people like the monk Makārī al-Suryānī and others the so-called rural *al-dīākūnīya al-rīfīya* (diaconal projects) were launched. Makārī al-Suryānī later became a well-known representative of the Coptic Church as Bishop Ṣamūʾīl, the bishop for social and ecumenical affairs. The young men who called themselves *khādim* (deacon or server) moved from village to village five days a week providing spiritual, social, and educational services. They were followed by priests who toured the villages with their mobile altars in order to celebrate the Eucharist in places that had no access to regular church services.[7] All kinds of people were involved in these projects. Some men were already monks, others entered a monastery later, a few experimented with a communal lifestyle, and others simply called themselves *khādim*. Apart from Anbā Ṣamūʾīl and Mattā al-Meskīn who lead the Ḥelwān project, the main exponents of this movement were Anbā Athanasius, the abbot of the active community, and the priest Ṣalīb Sūryāl, the leader of a communal house in Gizeh for men and women who wanted to lead lives of service.

Women participated in these projects as well. They were often involved in pioneer projects that were set up locally. For example, Sister Hannah, the first mother superior of the active community and one of its first two members, participated in a project that aimed at teaching young women to read, write, and master a skill such as embroidery. As Sister Hannah remembered: "Since most girls came from poor families that did not have a proper source of light in their houses, we used to go to the village square at night and teach the girls to embroider handkerchiefs under the light of the public gas lanterns."[8] Later on the young women were given a dowry (making them attractive candidates for marriage) and a sewing machine that could provide them with an income after their marriage.[9]

Part of the program for the servers or deacons of these projects were regular meetings and spiritual retreats during which topics such as the goals and means of *khedma* were discussed together with questions concerning the concepts of orthodoxy and the importance of *khedma* in the life of the church. At this point one must remember that, traditionally, the Coptic Church (like most Orthodox churches) stressed the administration of the sacraments and the preaching of "the word." Social and developmental projects were a novelty, imported from the West by the Protestant and Catholic missionaries.

From the records of these meetings one can form an idea of what *khedma* stands for. The first question that preoccupied the attendants of these meetings was "whom should we serve?" The prevailing answer was the person "nobody else wants to receive . . . and who is not loved by anybody."[10] Furthermore, the servers also became directly responsible for their neighbors and for anybody who stood next to them.[11] Their approach to life, and thus their way of serving, was to be *naẓra kullīya* (holistic). In other words, there was no difference between:

(1) "The church and the (human) body; one human being is as a whole"; (2) "The present life and the eternal life; . . . we stepped into eternity by our union with Christ"; (3) between the "Church and society"; (4) between "proclaiming the faith and living it"; and (5) finally, between the "Past, present, and future . . . because history is an important part of the present church life and influences it."[12] With these holistic principles as a starting point, *khedma* found a place among the recognized church ministries of liturgy, pastoral care, and preaching the biblical word.[13] By referring to the importance of Coptic history, the new type of church service was placed within the Coptic tradition.

The tasks of the *khuddām* (the ones who serve) were inventoried; they had to live an exemplary life, to be joyful in fully giving themselves to the people they served, and to pray night and day for these people.[14] The *khuddām* should teach the people how to read and write and how to sing hymns, and they should provide the people with books, like the Bible, in order to lead them to Christ. Furthermore the *khuddām* should organize religious meetings and work on a cohesive relationship between the clergy and their Coptic followers. The servers should train local leaders in the Coptic faith and conduct spiritual retreats and trips to churches and monasteries and set up small libraries. Finally, all Coptic believers should be made aware of the fact that they hold the position of *ishbīn* (godfather or godmother) to the people around them, giving them the responsibility to reach out to family and neighbors.[15] The goal of *khedma* was to bring isolated people back to the church by improving social and spiritual conditions; hence the stress on administering the sacraments, which was called "the Godly service of the Sacraments" and was the backbone of their services. Visiting the people who did not attend church activities and convincing them that they should come to church were important aspects of the *khedma*. However, the real goal was to bring the people "the message of the Resurrection."[16] As Father Mattā al-Meskīn expressed it: "The essence of *khedma* is the communication of the eternal life to the ones we serve whom God has put in our responsibility."[17]

This introduction into the history of *khedma* shows that originally their activities were directed at groups of poor, illiterate, and often passive Copts. The projects were more pastoral than social and eventually played an important role in the renewal of the church. Laypeople became more involved in a structure that no longer originated from discontent with the church's poor performance, but was rather set up by the church itself. In the process, a definite clericalization of the different positions that had been originally held by laypeople took place. Dedicated volunteers became consecrated deacons, priests, and monks. The monks often left their monastery later to serve as priests or bishops.

For women who chose to be nuns in the 1960s, to be involved in this renewal meant joining the active community. Several of the first members of the active community were older women who had been involved in church projects for decades already. Later on, in the 1980s, projects with the *mukarrasāt,* or consecrated women, were launched.

Another effect of the clericalization was that the church hierarchy gradually took charge of the social activities. First, a special bishop for social and ecumenical affairs was consecrated (the first one was Bishop Ṣamūʾīl in 1962). Then not only were the servers divided into subgroups (each within their own specific field) but also the people they served were split up into specific categories. For example, the laypeople served were: children (divided according to age), university students (divided by gender), newlyweds, young mothers, apostates, and the poor. For each group appropriate educational, pastoral, and social programs were designed, all under the guidance of the central bishop in Cairo. The activities are conducted from a hierarchal pyramid with the bishop of social and ecumenical affairs at the top. The bishop's responsibility is represented locally by the diocesan bishops or priests who run the social projects with the bishop's approval.[18]

Khedma in the Active Community

When the active sisterhood officially started in 1965, it was not an isolated project of active ministry within the Coptic Church. Nowadays the services of these nuns are part of an overall diocesan program with pastoral, social, and developmental projects. Nevertheless, at the start the active community had to overcome severe criticism. Some critics noted that the sisters called themselves nuns and used the same initiation rite as the traditional nuns. Others were suspicious of nuns who went around in active service, instead of leading the enclosed, contemplative life the laypeople had equated with true monasticism for centuries. This last point might indicate what the real objection against the active monastic communities were: they were not perceived as "really Coptic."

In the footsteps of the *khuddām,* the nuns, under the guidance of Bishop Athanasius, started to convene spiritual meetings and organize retreats for outsiders, during which the principles of the active community were explained and discussed. In 1971 the records of these meetings were published in a book called *Al-Batūlīya wa al-Khidma* (Celibacy and Service). Apart from the monastic ideals of chastity, obedience, and poverty, the issues discussed in this book have to do with legitimizing a place for active monastic women in the Coptic Church. Examples were drawn from the Old and New Testaments to show how both women and men had combined their active vocations with their celibate lives.[19] Mary, the sister of Lazarus, is among the women mentioned as a model for both contemplative and active nuns. Contemplative nuns often claim to model their lifestyles after Mary because she "has chosen the good portion, which shall not be taken away from her."[20] But according to the active sisters Mary divided her life between work and prayer. And, quoting from the *Bustān al-Ruhbān*, the active sisters said: "No doubt Mary needed Martha. Because Mary said praises together with Martha."[21] Furthermore, the examples from the New Testament serve to prove the point that women were active in the early church.

After the biblical examples are discussed, a discourse on the early fathers St. Antony, St. Pachomius, and St. Shenute follows. This material shows how they lived an anchoritic or enclosed life and nevertheless cared for others.[22] Another reason these heroes of monasticism are discussed is to create a connection between the active community and the original ideals of monastic life. This connection is maintained in the sisters' daily lives when they study and contemplate the sayings of the early fathers.

On the basis of the Old and New Testaments, Coptic tradition, and the theories concerning *khedma*, the active community has developed its own work ethic.[23] The sisters hold that "we don't detest any kind of work, even though [it might] be lowly. Since we are the children of a carpenter."[24] They then divide their time between work and prayer.

The projects that are run by the nuns are clinics and mobile clinics, nurseries, elementary schools, schools for vocational training, a crafts center, and projects for mentally retarded, for elderly people who are mentally or physically disabled, and for young women and men from broken families. The nuns' run centers for retreats, conferences, and social clubs and provide pastoral care for various groups of people, including unmarried mothers and Copts who want to convert to Islam. Furthermore, they are involved in the "Mobile Evangelism Teams" and provide pastoral and social care for the families that are involved in the different projects. The nuns also provide young people who want to get married with a dowry and items for their new house. Their service can go as far as furnishing a whole apartment.

The sisters want to serve the groups that are most needy and for whom there are few service institutions available; this is their motto when the sisters are invited to start up a project or serve as consultants—they never refuse on the basis of lack of money or space.

Their clinics, for example, are open to the poorest (the price of treatment is lower than the cheap governmental facilities), and the patients get the best treatment available. Their mobile clinics go to the most remote villages, their home for the elderly accepts people who are not able to take care of themselves, and their nurseries are capable of caring for babies from three months old. The sheer fact that the sisters run a home for the elderly is a novelty in Egyptian society because the idea of old people living apart from their families is alien to the culture. However, Egyptian society is changing, and, as trends such as increased emigration and higher divorce rates are splitting up families, these homes may become more familiar.

Also a relatively new and developing project in Egypt is the professional program for the mentally retarded. Sister Rauth who is in charge of this project received her training in Canada, the United States, and England; there was no adequate education on this subject available in Egypt. Sister Rauth expressed the theology of this kind of service as follows:

> We don't choose the retarded kids, they choose us. When they come it means that they need us. These kids suffer. Nobody wants or accepts them, they are hurting. Like the nails were hurting the body of Christ on the cross. His wounds were part of the body too, holy places. And we are all members of the body of Christ. These kids are like the hurting wounds. So we have to treat them as if we were touching the body of Christ. And, in the same way that we never leave Christ, we have to stay with them their whole life.

The project for the mentally retarded started with a handful of children and has grown steadily, in part because none of the students ever leaves. Often these children came from homes where parents, because of lack of information on mental retardation, did not know how to raise them. Mentally retarded children are seen as social outcasts in Egypt, and until a few years ago it was difficult to find appropriate facilities to care for and educate them. The most efficient projects for the mentally retarded are found in big cities like Cairo and Assiyut and are run by the Catholic organization Caritas. In smaller towns like Beni Suef there was a dire need for assistance with retarded children. Because of frequent intermarriage within families and problems at birth, the percentage of mentally retarded children is relatively high in certain areas of Egypt.

The original concept of *khedma* was to serve Christians who had drifted away from the Coptic Church. In the sisters' projects, however, both Christian and Muslim people benefit. Beni Suef is situated in the southern region of Egypt, fairly close to Minya and Assiyut, an area where interreligious conflicts can be rampant. Having members of both religions involved in certain projects asks for certain adaptations to be made and for some flexibility and tolerance from the community. Expanding the original ideas of *khedma* even further is the fact that these social projects are implemented from an ecumenical approach. The philosophy of the sisters serving the most needy people first overrides the idea that only Coptic ideology should prevail. To date the best examples of ecumenical cooperation are the community development projects that serve the garbage collectors in Cairo. These were started in the 1970s by a Catholic nun, Sister Emmanuelle, who sought assistance from several local church groups before she found the community in Beni Suef.[25]

The active nuns do not lead all the projects themselves; it is their goal to train locally recruited staff members who at first participate in the projects and then eventually take over. On most projects the sisters hold positions of trainer, superviser, administrator. The nuns themselves do not receive salaries, but their co-workers are paid from money raised through program fees. A difference between the active and the contemplative communities of nuns is that the active community does not depend on regular donations from the Coptic Church. For big projects they raise their own money through fund drives in Egypt and abroad. This principle has ruled from the start and is directly connected with the vow of poverty and the earliest ideal that monastics should earn their own livings.

After having discussed several aspects of *khedma* and the work of the active community, a description of how one of the convent's clinics is operated might serve to draw a final picture of how *khedma* comes together in daily work. The medical clinic that is situated on the premises of the mother house was opened about 1979. It offers general treatment, mother and child care, dentistry, and several specialties. Recently it moved from four rooms on the ground level to a spacious three-storied apartment where each specialist has a room. An operating room is being set up, and the old building has been turned into a health information center. Sister Virginia runs the clinic. She joined the community twenty years ago, and after medical training under the guidance of a French nurse, she started her own work in health care. She broadened her knowledge by taking different courses on preventive health care. Her staff consists of local assistant nurses who were all trained in the clinic and a group of medical doctors with different specialties. Most of the doctors are volunteers who have jobs in another hospital or who own private clinics. Sister Virginia starts her day in the clinic at 9:00 A.M. By that time the assistant nurses have already sterilized the instruments and prepared the rooms for patients. From 9:00–9:30 the assistants have a Bible study and read the story of a saint, after which the doctors usually arrive and everyone starts work.

Work in the clinic is to differ from the way things operate in the public facilities. This means that instruments are sterilized, that the whole facility is clean, and that the patients are treated cordially and respectfully.

On Fridays, Saturdays, and Sundays Sister Virginia spends her afternoon in the so-called mobile clinic that goes around to the villages. The mobile clinic consists of a few cars loaded with nurses, a doctor, medical equipment, and tools to give practical, primary health-care lessons. The villages visited do not have paved roads, and the housing is crowded with extended families living in the same room with the livestock. Upon arrival Sister Virginia first walks around the whole village, greeting people and announcing the times the doctor will be giving consultation and when the information session and Bible study will start. These activities take place in the local church or in the community center, which are often the most spacious and presentable places. While the doctor sees the patients who quickly have lined up, Sister Virginia prepares for the information and Bible study session. Slowly, people file in and when the room or church is full, Sister Virginia opens the meeting with a prayer. A religious song is then sung after which she discusses health-care topics such as the importance of proper nutrition for infants and why babies' bottles should not be washed in the local canal. When the doctor is ready, he or she joins the discussion, giving more information and answering questions. After symptoms of current children's diseases are dealt with, the meeting proceeds to the Bible study. Before she conducts the Bible study herself, Sister Virginia makes sure that the local priest is not available in case he might prefer to do it. She reads a story from the Bible and explains its contents and implications for daily life. More songs are sung, and the meeting ends with a prayer and the announcement of the next mobile clinic visit. Before departure Sister Virginia leaves a small pile of books behind with stories from the Bible and tales about the saints. She has brought books to encourage the local priest and the people who can read to set up a small library. On the way back to the convent Sister Virginia says that she is satisfied with the result of the afternoon. Almost all the Christian villagers attended the meeting in church, and, according to her, "most important is that we gain souls; it is not necessary to gain money."

The process of how the clinic and its extended activities work is a blueprint for how *khedma* was visualized by its designers from the beginning. Most of the elements that have been discussed are present in the clinic's ideal: care for the neighbor in the form of concrete medical assistance, which is the link with the true goal of *khedma*—to provide the people with a means to salvation. Faith and Coptic tradition are proclaimed by means of the Bible, religious songs, and the living of an exemplary life. Those who serve try to improve the relationship between the priest and his congregation by involving him in their activities, and, finally, they attempt to solidify their work by providing regular access to religious literature in the form of books that eventually might lead to the creation of a small library. There are no conditions for Muslims who only benefit from the medical assistance. They are not expected to attend Bible studies. Still, the practice of serving both Christians and Muslims can be tricky at times because of the looming danger of being accused of proselytizing.

Work of the Contemplative Nuns

Monastics consider their main work to be daily prayers, praises, and devotions. Nevertheless, daily chores and handicraft activities are seen to be important also. The early desert fathers and mothers made it clear that monastics are supposed to work for their food.

Both monks and nuns work to provide a living for themselves, to give alms to the poor, and to be generous to guests.[26] Work is also seen as an excellent weapon against one of the most feared states of mind in monasticism; in Arabic it is called *biṭāla* or *malal,* idleness or inactivity. Helen Waddell describes this state as: "tedium or perturbation of heart. . . . When this besieges the unhappy mind, it begets aversion from the place, boredom with one's cell, and scorn and contempt for one's brethren. . . . Also, towards any work that may be done within the enclosure of our own lair, we become listless and inert."[27]

The modern monastics, contemplative and active, see *biṭāla* as the breeding ground for evil thoughts and eventually evil actions.[28] This state should be avoided by all means; hence the importance of work in monasticism.

The original work of a monk was the plaiting of palm leaves in order to weave baskets. According to the legend, St. Antony was tired of sitting idle in his cell and of being attacked by disturbing thoughts. Thereupon, God showed him a vision of a man, dressed like a monk who was plaiting palm leaves.[29]

Nuns seem to have pursued other activities. The records of female anchorites such as de Ammās Sarah, Syncletica, and Alexandra do not mention that they plaited palm leaves.[30] And the nuns of the community that was founded by Mary, Pachomius' sister, sewed garments for the monks.

Following the traditions of the early fathers and mothers, the contemplative nuns today exercise several activities that serve the mandates of keeping the monastic busy while at the same time raising money. Preferably, the activities are such that they allow the nun continually to recite an unspoken prayer (called the "Jesus prayer"). Generally speaking, the nuns' ordinary activities can be divided into seven categories: daily chores, traditional handiwork, gardening and farming, commercial activities, study, research, and, finally, caring for guests (an activity that can include the running of a retreat house for young women).

Other types of activities that are directly connected with the convent's patron saint(s) are organizing and managing *ʿeids* (feasts) commemorating the saint's martyrdom or the opening of a church. Furthermore, the nuns maintain and refurbish the relics of the saints. They are in charge of preparing the holy oil, the wine for the Eucharist, and the ingredients for fragrant *ḥanūṭ* (spices) to be placed on the containers of the relics. People come to the convents for healing and the intercession of the saints. Apart from these activities, nuns undertake building activities. They design and enlarge their own abbeys, build churches, and start new farms.

The daily chores consist of tasks that have become very familiar to women. The cleaning of the convent and the church as well as cooking are all tasks done by nuns on a rotating basis. Each nun performs these tasks for a certain period of time, in addition to or instead of her regular work. Unlike the monks, the nuns perform these activities without assistance from the outside. And novices are not the only ones to do menial tasks. This means that each nun is personally responsible for a part of the convent's cleanliness. As a result, most convents, unlike monasteries, are impeccably clean.

The nuns' traditional handiwork is the embroidery of altar curtains, liturgical vestments, and other articles connected with church life such as baptismal dresses and covers for the sacramental bread. In some convents, embroidery results in truly ingenious pieces of art. Another much practiced art is the weaving of leather crosses.

A traditional task of one of the monastics is to serve as the *bawwāb* or *bawwāba* (doorkeeper). For a monastic this is a precarious job because it entails direct contact with the world outside the convent. The doorkeeper sees to it that no nun leaves the convent without permission from the abbess. However, the doorkeeper is forbidden to speak with guests about news from the outside world. Hence she opens the door, locks it again, and disappears in silence after instructing the novice who helps her to serve the guests drinks or snacks.[31]

A newly developed activity among the nuns is icon painting. Nuns have been trained in the techniques of painting icons as well as fashioning them by mosaic and woodcarving. Often the nuns are trained by the Coptic artist Izaaq Fannūs, who is associated with the Coptic Institute. This training is partly designed to enable the nuns to make images in honor of their patron saints. For example, the nuns of the Convent of Abū Saifein have made an enormous mosaic of their saint which hangs in the entrance hall of the convent.[32]

In 1990, the Convents of St. Dimyānah and Abū Saifein intended to open a small clinic where nuns who were medical doctors could treat their colleagues and patients living in the convent.

Since the locations of the convents (in the middle of crowded Cairo) do not allow much room for gardens, the activities of gardening and farming mainly take place on the convents' farms outside of Cairo. Again, a rotating system of tasks moves some nuns to the farm for a period of two months. The phenomenon of an agricultural dependency is not new to monasticism; however, it is new to the convents.

The design of the gardens in Cairo and the layout of the dependencies are done by the nuns themselves. To till the ground properly, the nuns need assistance from local workers. In case the farm is too far away from a city or an inhabited area, these workers stay in special quarters in the convent. However, they normally leave the convent at night. This situation is in contrast to that in the monasteries. There, there is a constant crowd of paid workers who actually do the work, while the monks supervise their activities.[33] Nuns also need the assistance of local workers to make the desert flourish. Nuns do supervise the workers and work in the fields as well. Due to the lack of sufficient fresh water, the nuns have to experiment with different crops to find out what flourishes on brackish soil. So far the farm of Deir Abū Saifein is the oldest and the largest. Trees that proved feasible in this area are olive, fig, date, almond, and lemon trees. The nuns grow vegetables for their own use and keep some dairy cows and chickens. In the midst of well-tended flowerbeds stand beehives as well. When the nuns show visitors the gardens, they insist on mentioning that the secret behind the abundance of their fields lies in the constant prayers said during work. "The plants feel the continuous prayerful attention they get," one nun explained. From the produce and milk that is not destined for the convent's use, the nuns make marmalades, pickles, and cheese. Eggs, milk, and meat from the animals is for sale, both at the farm and in Cairo. During the summer, a stroll around the premises leads to spacious boxes where flowers dry in the sun. The dried leaves will be used to mix fragrant oils and other substances into the herbal mix called *ḥanūṭ*, which is first used to rub the containers that hold the relics of saints. This act remotely reminds one of the pharaonic habit of embalming. Every year, during the feast day of the saint, the old *ḥanūṭ* is removed and divided into tiny pieces that are given to the believers. Since the substance has been in touch with the saint's relics, it is thought to contain an extraordinary power of *baraka* (blessing). The produce and the different products from handicraft are for sale in a small kiosk inside the convent.

INCOME AND GIFTS

Whenever the contemplative monastics of Egypt are asked how they finance the management of their convent or their building activities, which seem inexhaustible, they answer that it is God who provides everything. Actually, until recently the nuns did not have to worry about their income. In 1955 Father Giamberardini wrote that: "For no reason at all should work stop nuns from their spiritual exercise. Whatever they need must be provided to them."[34] According to Father Giamberardini, "In the past it was up to the monks to provide supplies for the nuns; in exchange they used to sew clothes for the monks; if there is a convent of monks close to the nuns, they will provide them with provisions, and the nuns will repair the clothes of the monks."[35]

Indeed, since the days of St. Pachomius, it was the custom that the men's monasteries sent the nuns fixed quantities of products such as grain from their farms, and twice a year, a cow. Nowadays this arrangement is still in place for some convents. For example, the Convent of Abū Saifein receives this yearly gift from the monks of St. Antony's Monastery as part of a *waqf* (a religious endowment). This custom, however, seems less organized than it used to be, and the nuns in fact insist that they generate most of their income themselves. Gifts today seem to be more the result of collegial respect and gratitude than of obligation.

Today, apart from a monthly allowance from the patriarch, contemplative nuns mostly provide their own living by selling the products they make, with money novices bring in (although there is no official amount of money required), and through gifts from believers. These gifts can vary from a few Egyptian piaster to a plot of ground, a car, or a building. According to many Copts I asked about this topic, Copts in Egypt still favor monastic places as recipients for their gifts, because the prayers of monks and nuns are perceived as powerful for the well-being of the believers. Of course, to the monastics all the gifts come straight from God. For big undertakings such as building a church or a new abbey or furnishing a farm, special money is raised. While mostly by word of mouth, sometimes fundraising is done through an organized effort; the Convent of St. Dimyānah, for example, has raised funds for a new abbey by means of special drive to secure pledges.

The most important point to be observed in this context is that contemplative nuns have emancipated themselves from the traditional dependent relationship that they had with their ecclesiastical male protectors. The nuns for the most part earn their own income and raise their own funds, which means that they can undertake activities like building new abbeys or churches. For the actual building they still have to depend on the services of male Copts, clerical, and laypeople to facilitate and arrange their affairs, but today these relationships are of their own dictating.

The active sisters rely for their income on the fees people pay at the various social projects they oversee. This income is extremely low, which means that for large-scale projects, such as the construction of a new mother house, the sisters have to raise funds as well. Like the contemplatives, they receive gifts from benefactors, and in some cases they apply for funds from organizations abroad. From the start the active community has refused gifts from the Coptic Church itself.

STUDY, RESEARCH, AND MODERN LIFE

Scholarly activities are undertaken by all monastics, but more so by the monks than among the nuns. For nuns the way in which the inhabitants of a convent have managed to organize their day-to-day life (the chores, handicrafts, and so on) determines whether or not there is time for studies. Some of the monasteries regularly publish books on different religious topics and some also produces a monthly youth magazine.

For contemplative nuns the primary aim of study is to gain access to their Coptic heritage. This includes getting to know more about the desert and church fathers and mothers, about the history of the Coptic Church and the lives of the saints (their patron saint in particular), and about the extraordinary lives of monks and nuns. In order to pursue these studies, nuns learn languages such as Coptic, English, French, and biblical Greek. Gradually, all the contemplative convents have become keen on recording the stories of their patron saint, the miracles that happened at their convent, and the life stories of extraordinary nuns. Several booklets about these topics have been produced by the convents themselves. Furthermore, the convents are in the process of designing brochures about their convents similar to the ones for sale in the monasteries. These are colorful picture books that contain some facts about the history of the convent, about monasticism, and about the convent's patron saint.

The high level of education among the nuns certainly implies that there is an ample supply of talent, especially technical talent, available to the convents. I have already mentioned the engineering nuns who design their own abbeys and those who are medical doctors and work in small-scale clinics. For nuns who are teachers or who know certain languages, there are not yet sufficient opportunities to exercise their skills and talents. So it is possible that a contemplative nun who is educated in these areas may not be able to use her knowledge after entering the convent. She will have to limit herself to menial duties or handicrafts.

In the active community the situation is not the same because every member of the community is challenged to discover her own talents and encouraged to develop them. This results in sisters pursuing further studies in Egypt or abroad.[36] In Egypt several active nuns take courses to become certified nurses or teachers or they follow special programs in community development. Some nuns have studied abroad, in community development, primary health care, and similar areas.

As we have noted, the sisters are active in producing books that give theological and spiritual reflections about their work. One nun that I spoke with was preparing a short meditation on St. Mary, her convent's patron saint.

All monastics in Egypt nowadays have access to the conveniences of modern technology. In spite of the monastics' firm adherence to the teaching of the church, saints, and martyrs of early Christianity, there is no inhibition in using all the technological means available for religious purposes. Monastics transport themselves in cars or mini buses, use telephones, electricity, cassette recorders (to listen to the taped sermons of the patriarch or a bishop), and videotapes. On a saint's feastday video cameras tape the celebrations and monitors are placed at different locations in the convent to show the public what is going on in the church.

The use of modern technology has opened many possibilities for female monastics. The active community could hardly have existed without it. And now even the contemplative nuns can move around and arrange their own business. With a telephone they can shop around for advice, explain problems, and advocate their causes. Videos and cassettes are wonderful means to promote their convent and their patron saint among the laypeople. For the Coptic community at large it is reassuring that when the bishops take a retreat in a remote cave in the desert, they carry a walkie talkie that can be used to call them back to their pastoral duty at any time.

Modern technology also has unexpected consequences for certain female monastics. Mother Alexandra, a female hermit who lives in a mausoleum, can store her food in a refrigerator. The water for the cup of tea her incidental guests are offered is heated with a little electric device. She has a fan that can keep her abode cool in the summer and in winter she can turn on an electric heater. Modern means of living have smoothed out the harsh edges of anchoritic life. This means that women can opt for anchorite living even though the church had declared it difficult for them.

SUMMARY

The emancipation of Coptic nuns that is reflected in their work runs parallel with the revival within the Coptic Church, the wider educational possibilities offered by Egyptian society for women, and the development of modern technology. Within certain limits, the nuns are able to pursue areas of work they could never have considered before, and thus they are able to play an active part in bringing about the revival of their own convents. An important side effect of successful activities is that the nuns gain respect from the Coptic population, which can be transformed into considerable donations for a convent. Many of the contemplatives' products, their icons, their buildings, and their reinhabitation of the old monastic sites in Upper Egypt enhance the Coptic heritage.

The active sisters never launch a project without their bishop's instigation, although he encourages them to propose new ideas. While still maintaining traditional monastic handicrafts, these active nuns also perform duties based on the development of the concept of *khedma,* or service in the sense of social work, which is still considered something new to the Copts. This concept of service is believed to have been imported by the Catholic and Protestant missionaries. This belief is reflected in a remark one of the Coptic bishops made when he tried to define the active community: "They operate like Catholic nuns; we never had this phenomenon in our church." These active sisters are, however, credited with sufficient spiritual authority to be allowed to give religious speeches at church meetings.

An active form of monasticism first serves the Coptic Church by incorporating the former charity programs of Coptic laity; second, it provides a chance for monastics to participate in social and developmental projects in Egypt; and, finally, it serves to keep social activities within the Coptic tradition.

Traditionally, the activities of both the contemplative and active nuns have been limited to what has been labeled women's work: domestic skills, teaching children, nursing, and social work. By pursuing their own activities, the nuns have reinstated the old ideal of the desert fathers that monastics, including women, should earn their own bread. The active sisters even go back further in time to legitimize their activities, pointing out that in the Bible several women are mentioned who had active ministries.

Sister Aghape, present mother superior of the Banāt Maryam, and Bishop Athanasius, abbot of the Banāt Maryam.

The Garden in Deir Abū Saifein.

The alley leading to Deir Amīr Tādrus in Ḥārat al-Rūm.

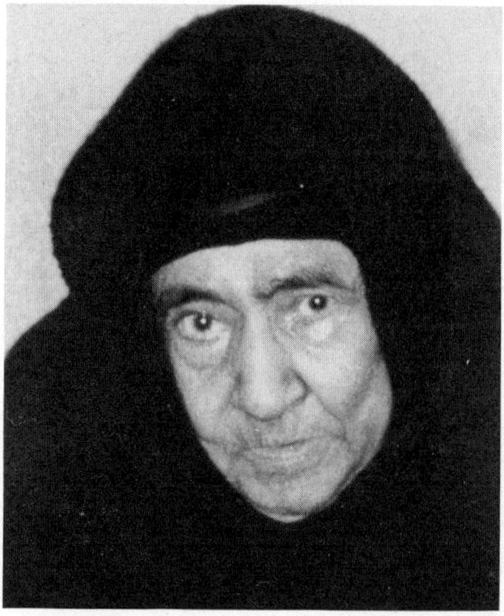

Mother Martha, former mother superior of Deir Amīr Tādrus.

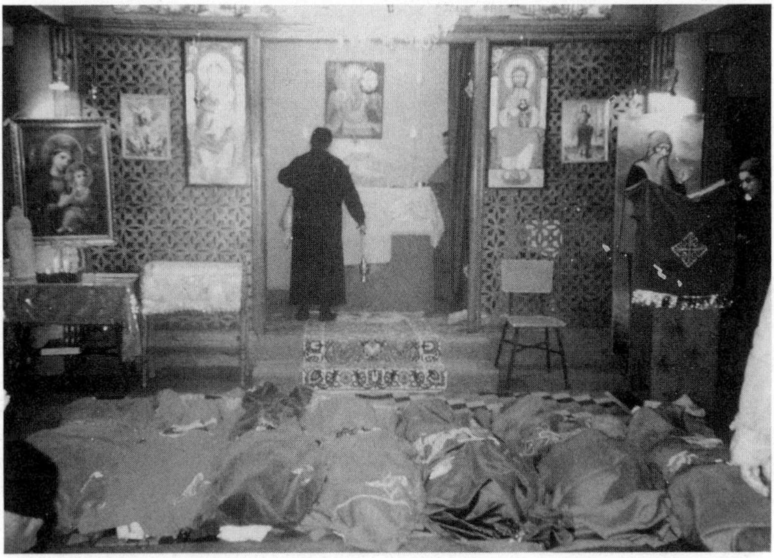

Celebrating the initiation rite.

Sister Hannah (far right), former mother superior of Banāt Maryam, with Bishop Athanasius.

Newly initiated novices and nuns at Banāt Maryam. The monastic belt is put symbolically over the grey dress.

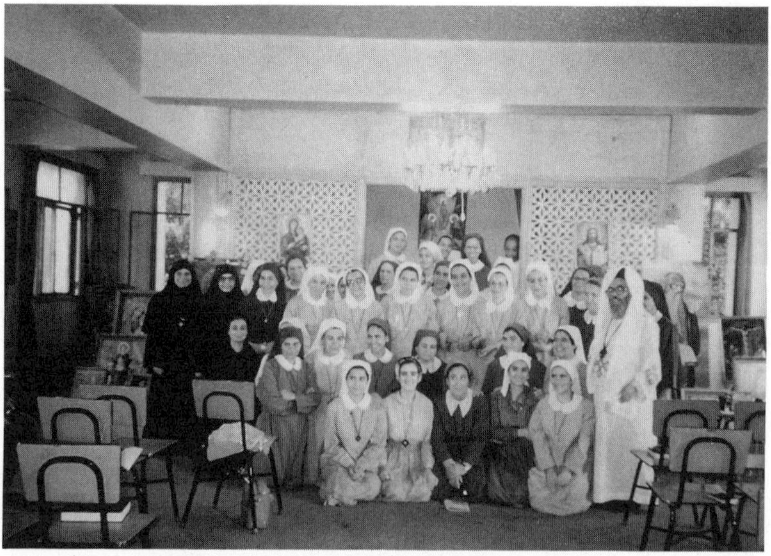

Group photo including the new novices at Banāt Maryam.

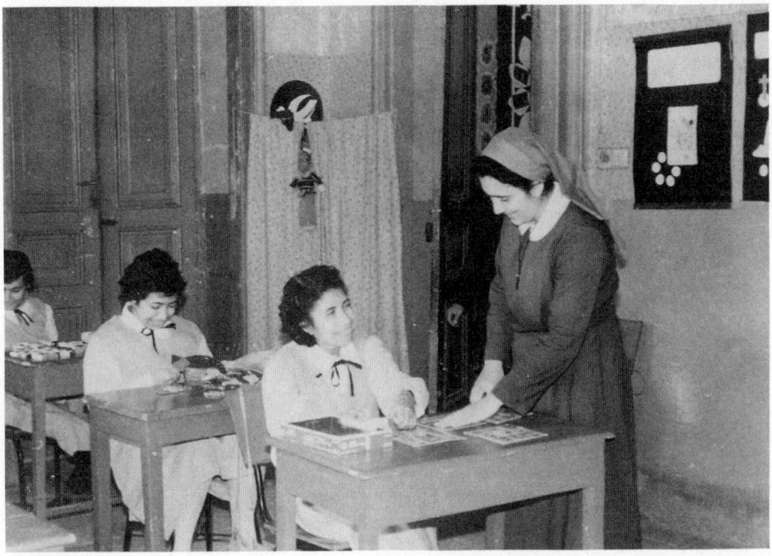

Sister Rauth of Banāt Maryam working with mentally handicapped children.

A sister of Banāt Maryam displays handicrafts the sisters have made.

The door leading into Deir Māri Girgis at Ḥārat Zuweilah.

A chapel in Deir Māri Girgis.

The entrance to the al-ʿAdhrāʾ Church in Ḥārat Zuweilah. The church is connected to the convent.

Deir Drunka in Assiyut.

Bishop Yusṭus, abbot of the Monastery of St. Antony (holding a handcross and bishop's staff), and monks wearing the *qalansūwa* (cowl).

CHAPTER 7

The Spiritual Life

This chapter consists of two parts: the first part is about spiritual guidance and the second about the monastics' devotional life. The concept of spiritual guidance has been mentioned several times in earlier parts of this study. In connection with the rule, we saw the importance of the spiritual guide who more or less replaces the rule. And in the context of the novice's initiation rite, a session with the spiritual guide forms an indispensable part of the ceremony. In this chapter I will review the history, roles, and models of spiritual guidance. In particular I will try to focus on female guides and their influence on the monastic goals. After an excursus on St. Mary's role as a model, I will describe the place of prayers, Psalmodia, the Eucharist, and fasting in the nuns' devotional life.

THE SPIRITUAL FATHER OR MOTHER

Spiritual guidance is an important concept in the economy of faith in the Coptic Church. For the average believer, guidance is closely allied with *sirr al-iʿtirāf* (confession) and communion since the *sirr al-taḥlīl* (absolution after confession) necessarily precedes the Sacrament of Communion. During confession, the Coptic believer habitually asks for guidance in spiritual and day-to-day matters. The priest is expected to guide in matters ranging from daily devotions to the choice of school or a prospective spouse.[1] In fact, many Copts turn to their priests before making important decisions. The aim of *irshād rūḥī* (spiritual guidance) is to promote the spiritual growth of the believer. The Coptic layperson does not devote him or herself purely to spiritual growth but has to cope with many day-to-day affairs. Consequently, most of the priest's advice concerns practical matters. In this process, the priest is seen as a representative from God, and his words are considered to be divinely inspired. In reality the priest has little time for extensive spiritual guidance. Laypeople ask a priest for spiritual guidance voluntarily, while monastics are obliged to follow the instructions of their spiritual guide.

Strictly speaking, then, only monastics have a *murshid rūḥī* (spiritual guide) in the full sense of the word. For the monks, this is primarily the monastery's abbot; for the contemplative nuns, the spiritual guide is their abbess. In the life of a monk or a nun, the role of the spiritual guide is pivotal. The spiritual growth of a monastic depends on the guidance received from the spiritual guide, and the guidance consists of instructions concerning devotion, work, and study. The spiritual father or mother embodies the rule and teaches the novice the whole way of the monastic life. The spiritual father or mother guides the pupil in discovering the will of God in his or her personal life, and the guide is personally responsible for the pupil's salvation.[2] The guide decides on the daily devotions; the number and length of prayers, vigil, and prostrations; the rules for fasting; what kind of books the monastic should read; and what kind of work he or she should do. Reading spiritual literature is considered beneficial for the monastic. As one of the nuns expressed it: "Reading the words of the heroes of the monastic life is like daily bread. It sustains your mind and spirit and helps you to grow spiritually." Studying the Bible is an especially crucial activity, because one can only determine the will of God by reading these scriptures. Next to the Bible, the *Bustān al-Ruhbān* (The Garden of the Monks) is indispensable. From it, the monastic can learn the desert fathers' and mothers' opinion on each stage of spiritual growth. This book lists the order in which spiritual exercises should be done and goes as far as detailing points as to how one should pray and why one makes the sign of the cross prior to praying.[3]

The concept of spiritual guidance as practiced today stems from the fourth-century desert fathers. The fact that their sayings still form an important part of the process of guidance exemplifies the present-day monastic ideal of following these early examples. St. Antony taught his disciples that "the Kingdom of God is within you."[4] And, as Benedicta Ward explains, "this conviction that the kingdom of God is to be discovered within the human heart lies at the center of the spiritual teaching of the desert."[5] Nowadays one finds this conviction expressed in the constant advice to the monastics that they should "keep the heart." The desert fathers also stressed the importance of constant reading and memorization of the Bible.[6] Furthermore, the words of a father (an abbā) had to be taken seriously: "The 'word' was not to be discussed or analyzed or disputed in any way; at times, it was not even understood; but it was to be memorized and absorbed into life, as a sure way towards God."[7] Today's monastics still ask for a *kilma manfiʿa* (useful word), but they also seek out their spiritual guide to discuss problems, decisions, and the like. But the real spiritual guide is God Himself. His guidance can be understood by reading His words and by continuous prayer, and it is important that the monastic seek God's presence alone—hence the importance of the cell.

At the same time, the spiritual father is the one who hears confession and absolves—the most crucial difference between the spritual direction of monks and that of nuns. The spiritual mother can never administer the sacrament of absolution. Thus there is a need for a priest to hear the sacramental confession and administer absolution.

In order to be guided in a fruitful way, the pupils have to strip themselves of their own wills and completely submit themselves to the orders of their spiritual guide. Not one thought or deed can be hidden from the spiritual guide and the pupils should confide the most minor details to him or her. Since the spiritual father or mother is believed to speak in the name of God, his or her word has to be obeyed without further thought or discussion. Even if the judgment or advice seems unwise (as was sometimes the case with the desert fathers), a monk or a nun can never trust his or her own thoughts since it is believed that it is through trusting their own judgment that monastics fall.

This blind obedience has been a topic of discussion among the monks since the earliest days of Christian monasticism. The most feared pitfalls for a monastic are false claims to virtue and vainglory. Manifold and fearsome are the stories of monks who became conceited because of their rigid asceticism. One of the publications of the Baramūs Monastery gives a vivid account of a monk at the end of the nineteenth century, Abūnā Mūsā, who loved prayer so much that he outdid all the other monks in hours and numbers of prayers. His spiritual father came to understand that he did not pray out of sincere love for God but because he liked it as a way to pass his time in the monastery. Abūnā Mūsā gained immense respect from the other monks who felt shamed by his zeal. One day the spiritual father ordered Abūnā Mūsā to limit his prayers to the morning and midnight prayers only. Abūnā Mūsā chose to disobey the order, assuming that his spiritual father was envious of his ardor. This disobedient monk began to receive visions from demons who had assumed the form of angels. One night these demons told him that he would receive the reward for his virtuous life by being taken up into heaven in chariots of fire like the prophet Elijah.[8] In order to embark upon the chariots, Abūnā Mūsā had to climb on the wall of the monastery at midnight. Deluded by the demons' visions of chariots, he jumped from the wall. A few days later he died from his wounds, after repenting of his vainglory and pride.[9]

THE EARLY FEMALE MODELS

Here and there one finds some remarks about the desert mothers—women who were able to reach the same spiritual level as men and thus were qualified to act as spiritual directors and be addressed as "ammā." One hears about the ammās indirectly. For example, Irenee Hausherr mentions the Egyptian father Bessarion who was struck by the aptitude of certain women for the ascetic life. According to Hausherr, stories of such female saints as St. Mārīnā, St. Theodora, and St. Hilaria, who spent their lives incognito in male monasteries, are intended "to make us admire the courage of their heroines."[10] And indeed these women are still known and venerated by Copts today who are eager to read and retell the life stories of St. Mārīnā al-Rāhib or Mārīnā the Monk. The endurance, patience, and humility of these saints are greatly appreciated by the Copts. St. Mārīnā al-Rāhib, who was living in a male monastery in the disguise of a monk, was accused of impregnating a young woman in the nearby village. She was forced to take care of the baby and was expelled from the monastery. Only upon her death was her true identity revealed. The words of some of the ammās are mentioned in the *Sayings of the Desert Fathers*. The sayings of Ammā Sarah can be found in the *Bustān al-Ruhbān*.[11]

Women who had reached a high level of spirituality, pursued, more so than men, the ideal of hiding their intense spirituality. One of the best examples of such a holy woman in Egypt was from the fifth century: St. Syncletica, a daughter of wealthy parents who defied her parents' attempts to marry her off and lived an ascetic life at home. After her parents died, she moved outside the city and lived with her sister near a tomb. Her "Life" by Pseudo-Athanasius is a rare document of the spiritual teachings of a woman. The story of St. Syncletica is known among the Copts, but unfortunately her story has only been available in Greek and French until recently.[12] The story provides an illustration of how, after her fame as an ascetic had spread, people came to St. Syncletica and pressed her for "a word." At first she refused to answer their question: " 'In what way is it necessary [to be] saved.' But she, having sighed heavily and let flow a multitude of tears, withdrew into herself, and as if she had made an answer by means of tears, she practiced . . . a second silence."[13] But the ones who had come to her did not give up and pressed her to speak, with the result that the "blessed one, . . . after sufficient time, and after a great silence, spoke in a humble voice this scriptural word: 'Do not do violence to the poor, for he is poor.' And those who were present, receiving the word gladly as if tasting honey and honeycomb, had a great many further questions."[14]

AL-UMM EFRŪSĪNĀ, AL-UMM SAFĪNA, AND THE PRESENT-DAY SPIRITUAL MOTHERS

There are three accounts of contemplative nuns who conducted the spiritual life of their communities: al-Umm Efrūsīnā (1228–1308), who was the abbess of Deir Māri Girgis in Ḥārat Zuweilah; al-Umm Safīna (1850–1900), who was the spiritual guide of the nuns in Deir Abū Saifein in Old Cairo (where her sister al-Umm Dimyānah was the abbess); and al-Umm Marthā, who was the abbess of Deir Amīr Tādrus in Ḥārat al-Rūm (1900–1988). Their lives give a picture of the tasks of a spiritual director and of the way in which that direction was carried out.

Discussing this topic while the main actors are still alive is considered taboo. Speaking about one's spiritual gifts is not considered appropriate, and people wish to hide these gifts in the same way that St. Syncletica did. Most of the information one receives about the abbess comes from the pupils who tell about words from their spiritual director or about visions during which the director received information or advice for herself, her community, or for one of the nuns. Apart from the fact that spiritual guides do not wish to discuss their guidance, these guides are often not able to recall what specific advice was given to a certain nun. As we have noted, the director merely serves as a channel to pass on the words of God. Since she has not thought out the message herself, the director often simply forgets what she told her pupil.

The written accounts of the three female directors provide one with some clues about the directors themselves and the way they guided their pupils. First of all, their high calling seems to have been confirmed in some supernatural way. At the moment of her initiation as a nun, al-Umm Efrūsīnā had a vision in which she "saw a bishop who came towards her, holding a cross and a censer filled with incense. He made the sign of the cross over her and 'sprinkled' her with the incense; then he handed her the cross and the censer and left."[15] Al-Umm Marthā became a nun after a vision was experienced by the superior of the convent she entered, who happened to be her aunt.[16] The appointment to superior of Umminā Irīnī (whom we already mentioned) was affirmed by a dream of Patriarch Kryllos VI. An awareness of a special calling induced these nuns, even before they became abbesses, to live lives of great austerity. Al-

Umm Efrūsīnā "led a life of *al-nusk* (asceticism), and she tired her body out (*al-ta'ab*), in a way that surpassed all human potentials."[17] In order to intensify her suffering, the saint begged God to strike her with a disease, because the "enemy of good" (the devil) attacked her with gluttony. One day, while she was praying in the company of the mother superior, a radiant light came down from heaven, and she "begged the Lord passionately to remove from her the 'lethal thing' [the habit of overeating], and the Lord answered her and tested her . . . for thirty years with severe diseases, and she fervently thanked the Lord and never took any medicine. . . . so she broke down her body with this battle, and made it an altar for the Holy Spirit."[18] Al-Umm Marthā is said to "have increased her prayers and fasts more and more" during her time in the convent.[19] And after she had become the abbess she "never gave her body any rest, nor her eyes sleep."[20] Following the early fathers she strove to "protect the heart": "Her life began in her heart, her inner life was the most important."[21] Of the contemporary al-Umm Irīnī, who is renowned for her high degree of asceticism, people whisper that she hardly eats more than half a zucchini a day and seldom sleeps over four hours a night on a bed that is only half a meter wide meant to be as uncomfortable as possible.[22]

The main work of these spiritual guides is to pray for their pupils and for anyone who asks for their intercession. These guides also devote special prayers to certain groups. Al-Umm Efrūsīnā always interceded for people who wanted to leave their religion or had lost their jobs because they were Christians.[23] Al-Umm Marthā relentlessly prayed for people who had stopped going to church.[24] The mothers had spiritual gifts, or there were miracles that occurred upon their intercession. Al-Umm Efrūsīnā had "the gift of reading people's minds, the working of miracles and healings."[25] People say about al-Umm Marthā that "it looked as if heaven stood open for the requests she made for her children."[26] She had the gift of clairvoyance and often told visitors how they could solve certain problems, even before they had mentioned them.[27] Many prayers were answered and healings took place after the intercession of al-Umm Marthā—ranging from passing exams at school to the birth of a child after alleged barrenness for many years, the choice of a right marriage candidate, and the healing of lethal diseases. The same is true of al-Umm Irīnī of whom people say that she "looks straight through you. It is as if you cannot hide anything from her." So many healings, rescues, and other kinds of miracles have happened through her intercession that her convent has special days during which she sits with the guests and tells them about the latest miracles that have happened.

Often the superior's prayers are reinforced by symbolic actions or devises that their pupils or laypeople can use or hold. Al-Umm Efrūsīnā "would pray over a vessel filled with water and give it to the sick person who would bathe in it and be healed."[28] Al-Umm Marthā lit candles in the shrine of the convent's patron saint, Amīr Tādrus; gave the people pieces of blessed *qurbān* (bread) and water from the well of Abū Nūfer or holy oil.[29] Today al-Umm Irīnī still gives the same things to strengthen her pupils as well as those who seek her advice and intercessions.

Apart from the ascetic practices and advancement of their spiritual capacities, which can lead to healings and clairvoyance, an important part of the spiritual mothers' duties is to be impeccable models for their nuns and for outsiders. Irīnī serves as a model among her nuns and the Coptic community because of her patience in suffering from many diseases. According to the Copts, by praising the Lord in sickness and bearing pain without complaining, people can acquire a higher level in heaven. Actually, these people are believed to reach the same level as anchorites—which spiritually is held to be the highest level, because anchorites have devoted their whole lives to giving praise to God only.[30]

One of the recurring themes in the lessons of al-Umm Marthā was the influence of a good spiritual example. She used to say: "Service for Our Lord Christ, to Him be the glory, does not go by words (*kalām*); words are easy. No, service of the Lord consists of a sanctified way of life and a holy model. . . . Early Christianity was not spread by moving sermons, . . . but because of the moral excellence of the Christians and their steadfastness in faith. . . . They were the practical and visible Gospel, read by everybody."[31] The example she set for her nuns was to practice continuous prayer, silence, and hard work. She insisted on participation in the construction of a new church next to the convent and would spend the day carrying baskets filled with heavy stones while reciting psalms.[32]

One century earlier, al-Umm Safīna had stressed a similar message. She set the example by constant hard work carried out in silence so that she could pray continuously. In her cell, she copied psalm books in calligraphic script. She took care of the sick nuns and arose in the morning before anyone else in order to prepare the dough for bread.[33]

Concurrent with their own spiritual devotions, spiritual mothers meticulously supervise the spiritual life of their nuns. Al-Umm Safīna started her day with the tolling of the convent's bell to call the nuns to the midnight office of prayer. On Sunday, after the celebration of the Eucharist, she would spend the entire day teaching and explaining to the nuns about the scriptures and the *Bustān al-Ruhbān*, and reciting the lives of the saints and martyrs. In addition, as a good spiritual director should be, she was in constant prayers on behalf of the mothers and fasted for their troubles and temptations by "the evil one."[34] The spiritual guide al-Umm Marthā spent Sundays in the same fashion.[35] She also set the example for attending church services and taking communion. According to her biographers, al-Umm Marthā never missed the celebration of one Eucharist in her life.[36] The present-day mother superiors have regular meetings with the whole community during which they discuss spiritual topics. In some convents the community has become so large that the superior needs a microphone to be heard.

In their guidance, the mother superiors used recurring expressions that conveyed their basic beliefs. Some of these expressions have been recorded and can be considered as apophthegmata or sayings. Since sayings of women are seldom preserved, I will give all those that have been recorded in writing. Two sayings ascribed to al-Umm Efrūsīnā are: "Someone who seeks the salvation of his soul should give silver [money] to the one who scolds, despises or grieves him, so that he can gain the virtue of humility" and "the Kingdom of God cannot be purchased with gold or silver, but with humility, a pure heart and genuine love for every one."[37]

In her spiritual instructions, al-Umm Marthā stressed the use of suffering. Thus, her sayings:

> "We ourselves are responsible for our own pain. When we bear it with courage, . . . it will become a constant source of many blessings."
> "Do not wish for a life without troubles (*ḍīqa*); that will hold nothing good for you."
> "The ones who play tricks [against you] are our brothers and not [our] enemies, because we only have one enemy, which is the sin that destroys our peace. God allows these tricks against us, not to make us suffer, but that we might gain a crown, through our pains we will reap the eternal glory."
> "Let us regard the troubles of this low world and [then] consider the heavenly rewards."
> "Let us accept pains as accepting medicines from a doctor for the benefit of our salvation, as a chastisement of the Father so that we will be glorified."
> "Remember that you left your mother's womb naked, and that you will leave the world naked."
> "Remember the words: 'Woe to you, when all men speak well of you' (Luke 6:26), 'Rejoice and be glad' (Matthew 5:12) 'when men . . . utter all kinds of evil against you' " (Matthew 5:11).

"Were you sent into exile? Remember that there is no place for you here [in the world] that befits you; if you were wise you would regard the whole world as a place of exile."[38]

Both Safīna and Marthā were considered "true mothers" whose hearts were pure as the "hearts of children."[39] As one of the contemporary mothers Ummināa Maryam expressed it: "it is necessary to become simple, to leave worldly cares and to abandon complex concerns; . . . God speaks through our hearts and not through our heads."[40]

From the historical sources, regarding the spiritual mothers one can deduce that they possessed an unquestioned spiritual authority built on a life of asceticism and prayers. Often their specific mission was reinforced by extraordinary phenomena such as visions and foresight. Apart from being barred from administering the Eucharist and confession, these women were fully equal to their male counterparts. In some cases the mothers must have been quite famous since their lives were recorded, while the actions of male spiritual directors who lived in the same period went into oblivion.

Another reason why the deeds of Efrūsīnā, Safīna, and Marthā were not lost for posterity might be the period of time in which they lived. Al-Umm Efrūsīnā lived during the beginning of the reign of the Mamluks (1250–1517). The documents that mention the Christian population during that period point out that the Mamluks rescinded the liberties that the Christians and Jews enjoyed during the preceding years.[41] From a document by Ibn Naqqash (d. 1362) one learns that in 1301 the Christians and the Jews were informed that "they would no longer be employed either in the public administration or in the service of the emirs. They were to change their turbans: blue ones for the Christians, who were moreover to wear a special *zunnar* (belt) about their waists; and yellow turbans for the Jews. Thus the Christians and Jews suffered in Cairo and Egypt a grievous return to the past. . . . Consequently, many of them were converted to Islam."[42] Al-Umm Efrūsīnā lived during these years; hence her special vocation for people who had lost their jobs on account of their religion. The reason why she was sought out for advice and guidance probably had to do with the fact that the see of the patriarch was next to her convent. From 1300 to 1660 the patriarch's residence was in Ḥārat Zuweilah. Many Copts in distress must have sought refuge with the patriarch who might have drawn their attention to the special gifts of al-Umm Efrūsīnā.

Al-Umm Marthā became an abbess in 1938 and held this position until her death in 1988. She lived in the period during which several representatives of the Coptic Church began their efforts to revitalize the church. In the end of the 1950s she decided that a piece of unused land adjoining her convent should be used to build a new church. The church was consecrated 11 November 1961. This activity fits the general revival movement and must have drawn sufficient attention from the church members. From her activities to regain a part of the Coptic heritage, in combination with her special prayers for apathetic Copts and her spiritual gifts, al-Umm Marthā derived her considerable fame.

The recorded sayings of both Efrūsīnā and Marthā conform to the Coptic theology that stresses the value of suffering and the duty of the community of believers to strive for salvation while on earth. Hence these mothers are considered true spiritual representatives of the Coptic Church. Moreover, their sayings are appropriate for the demands of their time and the general position of the Coptic population. Still remarkable today is that whenever there are riots between Muslims and Copts, the Coptic authorities somehow manage to keep their flock from aggressive reprisals. When Copts were scolded for their faith, lost their jobs, and were deprived of substantial parts of their income, al-Umm Efrūsīnā exhorted them not to care about silver and gold because these cannot buy the kingdom of heaven. Material wealth is sufficiently unnecessary that it should be passed out freely to anybody who scolds or grieves you. The teachings of al-Umm Marthā also stress the virtues that lie in losing one's property and being slandered by others. Her apophthegm that one creates his or her own sufferings is an exhortation to Copts to ignore the world around them, improve their inner lives, and look ahead for the blessings that await them.

Nowadays the mothers' spiritual authority is recognized by the fact that in most of the convents no bishop is in charge. According to the patriarch, this construction is set up in order not to interfere with the spiritual direction of the mother superior and to avoid conflicts over who holds the (spiritual) authority. If there are problems of any sort, the superior can confide in the confessional father.[43]

THE NEW GENERATION

An important topic for spiritual direction is the problem presented by modernity. The spiritual mothers appreciate the dilemmas young women face when they compare their education, lifestyle, and social circumstances with their original role models—the early fathers and mothers of the church. Although outsiders are not allowed to attend the convents' spiritual sessions, in conversation the monks and nuns often mention what is called "the problem of the *al-gīl al-gedīd*" (the new generation). While laypeople are convinced that monastics live on a higher spiritual level than ordinary beings and consider monastics holy, the monastics themselves feel the burden of being members of this new generation. Those of the new generation of monks and nuns never seem to have the same vigor and strength as the original desert fathers and mothers; contemporary monastics are not capable of living alone in the desert, fasting as rigorously as the fathers did, having marathon vigils, and the like.

In fact this theme of *al-gīl al-gedīd* serves to explain the discrepancy between the ideal life and contemporary reality. Modern monastics do not have the stamina that the early models of piety had. Nowadays, minds wander and diversions are sought. A modern monk or nun does not manage to be content with simply plaiting ropes; he or she needs compelling work. As a result, one finds a wide range of different activities in the monasteries and convents—a diversification of activity foreign to the early monastic situation.

The idea of the problem of the new generation should not distress young monastics, however. The lapse of monastic vigor had already set in by the time of St. Antony. According to one of the apophthegms ascribed to him, he remarked about his contemporaries: "God does not allow the same warfare and temptations to this generation as he did formerly, for men are weaker now and cannot bear so much."[44] During an interview, Mother Irīnī explained this saying in an apocalyptic way. According to her, the fathers used to say that toward the end of time there will be no longer any true monastic life because the people will have become too weak to pursue its high ideals. When pressed on this point, she said: "No, monasticism will not disappear until the end, because God will not expect the same from the people then as he did from the Desert Fathers. As long as the monastics have true love for each other, there will be monasticism." In spite of this encouragement present-day monastics feel frustrated that they obviously can never reach the ascetic ideal of the early models.

SPIRITUAL DIRECTION IN THE ACTIVE COMMUNITY

The spiritual director of the active community at this time is the abbot, Bishop Athanasius. In contrast to the contemplative nuns who cannot choose their director, the active sisters are allowed to have a director other than the bishop. For practical reasons this spiritual guide should live in the environment of Beni Suef. As is the case in traditional direction, prayer, the Bible, and spiritual works like the *Bustān al-Ruhbān* are indispensable in the process of the monastic's spiritual growth. As is the case with the contemplatives, the bishop instructs the sisters concerning their devotional activities: how many prayers to say, how long and how strict their fasting should be, what they should read or not read. In addition, the bishop prays for his spiritual children.

Bishop Athanasius acknowledges the fact that sisters are not always close to their spiritual guide. When a sister works in a project away from Beni Suef or lives abroad for study, she may not be able to reach him at all. In order to assist the members of the community in their specific circumstances, the bishop encourages them to find God's will in their lives independent from a director. When the active nuns ask him how to solve a certain problem, the bishop often wants to know their own opinion or recommends that they should pray for guidance in order to hear God's voice in their lives. To quote Bishop Athanasius: "Go to your cell and pray, the Eternal Listener is in your cell." Often, before joining the community, the sisters had become used to having a confessional father who never asked anything but simply told them what to do. One of the sisters admitted that at first she had to get used to Bishop Athanasius' brand of spiritual guidance. She experienced the benefits of spiritual self-reliance when she worked in Ethiopia in 1973. Because of the revolution the airport was closed and the postal system did not work. There was no way to contact her spiritual director, and so it became a reality for her that she could indeed find guidance herself. This did not mean that she stopped seeking the bishop's guidance after she returned to Egypt; she simply became a pupil who was self-reliant when necessary.

This "self-reliant" way of spiritual direction is considered revolutionary in the Coptic Church, but in fact it has its roots in the earliest ways of directing. According to the desert fathers, the ultimate guide is the Holy Spirit; hence the stress on prayers, reading of scriptures, and staying alone in the cell.

Bishop Athanasius is regarded by the active sisters as a real father. As Father Mark Gruber has pointed out, the metaphor of fatherhood is not incidental for the spiritual director. "The Middle Eastern and Mediterranean role of father deeply though not exhaustively defines the spiritual fatherhood of monks."[45] In this context, Bishop Athanasius remarked that:

> Fathers of confession differ; it is like mothers and their families. There may be a mother who wants her orders to be obeyed and who thinks that she knows what is best for the child. Some spiritual or confessional fathers are from this type and some spiritual children are of this kind. There may be a nun who goes to the spiritual father and asks: "what shall I do in this fast?" And then she

wants him to tell her: "Fast until four o'clock in the afternoon." But many of the confessional and spiritual fathers work as a catalyst with the Holy Spirit and the pupil, so that the pupil can grow spiritually.[46]

The bishop further stressed the point that the early fathers never imposed their views on the pupils.[47]

The Sayings of Tāsūnī Ḥannah

In spite of the fact that Tāsūnī Ḥannah was not a spiritual guide, she was considered a spiritual and moral model—both for the sisters and for laypeople. As one of her biographers says: "She was a model of the seven principles of the convent: poverty, obedience, chastity, community life, work, service and silence."[48] To all who were in distress she used to teach the power of the "Our Father," "this prayer by which she had overcome many problems."[49] Always ready to serve anyone in need, she encouraged people until her last day. When she was ill with a terminal disease, "she served even more . . . than when she was healthy."[50] The sisters love to tell the story about how the doctors in the hospital had difficulties locating Sister Hannah because she was never in her bed but always going about encouraging other patients. She prayed incessantly and praised God—more so when she was afflicted by cancer, which she saw as "a forced holiday in order to read more [in the Bible] and pray."[51]

Like some of the spiritual mothers, Tāsūnī Ḥannah also had a repertoire of spiritual phrases that can be considered sayings. She used to admonish people to trust in God because "God can do everything"; "Our Lord is able to solve every business"; "We trust in the blessings of our Lord"; and "Our Lord will never forget us."[52] She tried to teach patience with her assertion that "Everything under the sky has its appointed time." And especially sisters who were exhausted from hard work were reminded of the fact that "God will not forget those who serve under hardship."[53] Finally, Hannah stressed the importance of giving freely and without grumbling to anybody in need, but one should give in such a way as to "help the people so they can help themselves."[54]

Hannah was especially important as a model and guide for the people around her and for young Coptic women who wanted to pursue an active vocation, because she was the head of a new project with a new ideology. Consequently, spiritual, moral, and material guidelines had to be developed and many problems had to be overcome. Her sayings are practical—to the point and directed to the needs of active nuns and the people they serve. Through her sickness, her status as a role model was extended to the Coptic community at large. Like Mother Irīnī, Hannah praised God in sickness and suffered great pain without complaining. Hence, according to Coptic theology, she could reach a high degree in heaven.

THE CONTEMPLATIVES' GOALS

Because the role of the spiritual director is crucial in showing the pupil the way in the monastic life, the director also influences the goals which monastics set for their ideological life as a community or for their personal lives. Monastic literature for both males and females gives some indication as to what the ideal goals should be. The monastic wants to reach a spiritual wisdom and Godly enlightenment, or *shafāfīya* (transparency); achieve union with God; or join the ranks of angels and tirelessly praise and glorify God.[55] By heroically fighting against their human passions, monastics become nonearthly creatures—perhaps heavenly ones who regain paradise lost while living on earth. For Copts, this transformation from ordinary human being to a creature that is closer to God is not only a theological concept, but has profound cultural and social implications. Mark Gruber expressed this as follows: "Monasticism, as the Copts practice it, is hardly then a private lifestyle or religious devotion. The institution has profound cultural ramifications inasmuch as it posits a compelling cosmological framework in which a beleaguered people can find survival."[56] By their asceticism and their continual sacrifice, monks and nuns give the Coptic community "a central religious value and operation upon which the discordant elements of their lives find order and meaning."[57] The monasteries and convents are places were the Coptic believer can fully identify him or herself—ignoring the Muslim world.

The monastics see their highest goal as upholding the greatest commandments—to love God and to love one another (Matthew 22:37–40). Because, as we have noted, this they believe is the only way the new generation will find acceptance in God's eyes. This same problem of the degeneration of ascetic capacities is an important theme in the discourse of laypeople as well. They uphold that the faith and performance of fasting, prayers, and vigils by laypeople was much more ardent during the first centuries of Christianity than it is today. Thus important tasks for monastics are to exercise the "commandment of love" and to be models of ascetic pursuits which guarantee the perpetuation of Coptic monasticism—an indispensable stronghold for the Copts.

The nuns mention one goal that differs from the goals they share with male monastics. These contemplatives like to explain their role by drawing the comparison between their own lives of prayer and the way Moses acted during the war with the Amalekites. In order to insure victory, Moses instructed Joshua to carry out the fighting, while he, accompanied by Aaron and Hur, climbed to the top of a hill. According to this story in Exodus 17:8–16, Moses held up his hand, and whenever he "held up his hand, Israel prevailed; and whenever he lowered his hand, Amalek prevailed." The nuns want their prayers to have the same effect as Moses' actions: the prayers help the people to fight the battle in the world. This comparison shows the nuns to be in a "defensive" role. By entering the convent, the mothers take a step that removes them even further from their traditional gender roles than the monks. Their sacrifice of virginity excludes them from the primary vocation for an Egyptian woman—to raise children. Instead of this role the nun now takes her place in the defensive line against evil and thus gains respect and admiration. Whereas a monk can show social commitment by becoming a priest, a contemplative nun has the option to excel as a model of virtue and spirituality and to be a medium to ward off evil.

ST. MARY AS A MODEL

The prime model for Coptic nuns, contemplative and active, is St. Mary, the Mother of Jesus. She enjoys a high degree of veneration among the Copts, and, especially after her apparition in Cairo (in the area called Zeitūn) in April 1968 and in Shubra in 1986, she is also deeply respected by the Egyptian Muslims.[58] For people from both religions she is seen as a powerful intercessor between God and humans. The Coptic Church praises St. Mary every day; she is commemorated and invoked during the liturgy and in every canonical hour.[59] Her veneration is based on the Bible verse of Luke 1:48: "For behold, henceforth all generations will call me blessed." The Copts consider St. Mary to be the first saint in Heaven. During the sacraments of matrimony, baptism, and healing of the sick, St. Mary is addressed and invoked in prayers.[60] During the year there are seven feasts dedicated to her. The most important, on 22 August, commemorates "the assumption of her body into heaven" and is preceded by a fortnight's fast that most Copts strictly keep—it is a special chance to give honor to St. Mary. The month of Kihāk (10 December–8 January) is dedicated to St. Mary, and special hymns of praise are sung for her daily in the churches. The monastics in particular spend long hours in the church singing her praise: "In the month of Kihāk you don't sleep, all you do is pray and praise."

St. Mary's symbolic value for female monastics is her virginity—the "law of the heavens"—and her personification of the "New Eve."[61] In addition to the virgin birth of Christ, the Copts hold that St. Mary's virginity was perpetual and that the brothers of Jesus were Joseph's children by a previous marriage.[62] St. Mary's is seen as the "New Eve" because she took Eve's place; "by her faith, obedience and humility she became, through the Holy Spirit, the mother of 'Life.' She offered Adam's children the 'Tree of Life' to eat, and thereby live forever."[63]

According to the nuns, St. Mary had taken an oath of *al-ʿiffa* (chastity), which made her appropriate to be chosen as the mother of Jesus. In her biography, Mother Martha is repeatedly compared to St. Mary; both are called *al-ʿafīfa* (the chaste one).[64] The virtues of St. Mary are *al-ṭāʿa* (obedience), *al-tawāḍuʿ* (humility), and *al-taslīm* (acceptance) of God's will, and these are the primary virtues every nun strives for.

The active nuns are also impressed by St. Mary's quickness to travel to Elizabeth upon hearing that the older woman was with child (Luke 1:36–40). This immediate response shows the sisters that they should never delay to help anybody who asks their assistance. The relationship of the active community with St. Mary is very close. According to the sisters, she is always watching them because they are her daughters. As Sister Basilia said: "I try to be like her daughter. When I feel down, I go to the chapel and talk with St. Mary. She understands our problems; she had many difficulties in her life and nevertheless lived a life of joy." In spite of their heavy workload, none of the sisters skips the special praises for Kihāk, because they consider this a special opportunity to show their gratitude to their patron saint, St. Mary.

DAILY DEVOTIONS

The monastic daily devotions—the prayers, the Psalmodia, and the liturgy—are kept or attended by Coptic laypeople as well. Robert Taft analyzed the liturgy and the offices of the Coptic Church as shaped by the concrete, popular, and ascetic monastic culture that the Coptic Church solidified as: "a native counterbalance to the cosmopolitan, theologically sophisticated, Hellenic Church of Alexandria, whose speculative, spiritualizing intellectualism stood in marked contrast to the popular, traditionalistic piety of the South, a largely oral culture transmitted through sayings, proverbs, ritual, rather than through theological treatises."[65]

The three main activities of the Coptic liturgy are: (1) the prayers from the *Agbīya* (the book with the prayers of the hours), (2) the *tesbiḥa* (Psalmodia), and (3) the celebration of the Eucharist. The differences between the laity and monastics is that the latter have one special prayer in the *Agbīya* and that they practice the so-called Jesus Prayer. Monastics pray these common prayers more regularly and with more intensity, but the "coincidence of monastic and lay prayer forms is one of the features which marks the Coptic church as thoroughly monastic in character."[66] Hence one can observe that there is little difference between the content of the prayers of contemplative and active nuns. In the end, only the quantity of the active nuns' prayers is less. All preferably recite the prayers by memory. The prayers and praises can take two to four hours (depending on the tone of singing which can be in a swift, punctuated staccato or in a slower tempo) and are performed standing. The *Bustān al-Ruhbān* states that the one who prays should be standing; "do not lean against the wall with wobbly legs, and do not stand on one leg only."[67] If the celebration of the Eucharist follows the daily devotions, the monastic actually spends about six hours standing.

Al-Agbīya: The Prayers of the Hours

After the bell tolls at 3 or 4 A.M., the contemplative nuns and monks pray the first four of the eight canonical hours in the *Agbīya*. The prayers are said in Arabic and start with the *ṣalāt niṣf-al-leil* (midnight prayer), followed by *ṣalāt bākir* (prime), *ṣalāt al-saʿa al-thālitha* (terce), and *ṣalāt al-saʿa al-sādisa* (sext). The morning prayers are followed by the *tasbiḥa* (Psalmodia), which is sung in Coptic (the Bohairic dialect). For nuns, the celebration of the Eucharist follows the office of morning devotions twice a week. Depending on the monastery, the monks celebrate it from every day to once a week. In some convents there is a *ṣalāt al-sāʿa al-tāsiʿa* (short prayer) at noon that is sometimes combined with special prayers for the sick and for people in distress. The day ends around 5:00 P.M. with *ṣalāt al-ghurūb* (vespers), *ṣalāt al-nawm* (compline), and a prayer called *ṣalāt al-sitār* (prayer of the veil) which is only prayed by monastics. The meaning of the word *veil* is not clear, but some writers have explained it in connection with the time of the prayer—when darkness veils the earth.[68] Each hour, starting from *ṣalāt bākir*, commemorates a moment of Jesus' passion. The first hour commemorates His being raised from the dead and the last hour ends with *ṣalāt al-nawm*, the hour that his dead body was placed in the tomb. Originally each hour only consisted of the recitation of twelve psalms.[69] Nowadays the structure of the hours, which is basically the same in all monastic places consists of: (1) fixed initial prayers, (2) twelve psalms, (3) gospel lesson, (4) troparia (poetic refrains), (5) the repetition of *Kyrie Eleison,* (6) Trisagion, (7) "Our Father," (8) dismissal prayer or absolution, and (9) final prayer.[70] The reading of the psalms is divided among the monastics who each silently recite the one assigned to them. After contemplative nuns say their prayers with the whole community, they repeat them all again alone in their cell. The communal way of praying is in contrast to the monks who are allowed to perform the prayers of the hours in their cells and come together only for the Eucharist. In the nunneries one would never conclude, as one visitor did at a monastery, that "the morning exercises are the most poorly attended common events."[71]

The prayers as described above are also said in the same order and length by the active sisters and by consecrated women. The only difference is that the active monastics start their day one or two hours later than contemplatives. Sometimes the way the prayers are divided during the day is slightly different. Depending on the communities they work with, the active sisters and consecrated women say part of the prayers with the people they work with. But, in contrast to the laity, at the end of the day a monastic must have prayed them all. Hence it is important to know the prayers by heart so that they can be recited during work. The sisters find the prayers from the *Agbīya* very important, because they help them in establishing "a relation between God and our hearts." Like other monastics, the actives find the recitation of the psalms a crucial part of their daily devotions. Praying the psalms binds the Coptic Church with other communities worldwide who also pray them: Jews, other Orthodox Christians, Catholics, and Protestants. in addition, the importance of reciting the psalms is reflected in a play on words that Coptic monastics like to make: "*Iḥfaẓ al-mazāmīr, taḥfaẓak al-mazāmīr*" (memorize the psalms; then you will be protected by the psalms).[72]

The Psalmodia: *Tasbiḥa*

Immediately following the morning prayers, the Psalmodia is sung. This office consists of several introductory prayers, different theotokies (songs of praise to St. Mary) for each day of the week, doxologies consisting of different hymns to be sung on certain days, and several other hymns.[73] The Psalmodia is divided into four parts based on readings from the Bible: (1) Exodus 15:1–21 (the song of Moses), (2) Psalm 135 (praise), (3) Daniel 3 (the story of the three youths in the fiery furnace), and (4) Psalms 148, 149, and 150 (all psalms of praise). Each part read is called a *hūs*. Around it the different prayers, theotokies, doxologies, and hymns are sung. For the month of Kihāk (10 December–8 January), the Copts use a special version of the Psalmodia. Singing the Psalmodia is seen as a means of being in touch with the communion of saints who have already gone to heaven. Bishop Athanasius explained this as follows: "We don't expect the saints to speak for us; it is more that they can not stop speaking for us, and we can not stop speaking about them. The singing of the Psalmodia expresses for us a life of communion of all the participants of the same faith, the ones who are alive and the ones who have already died."[74] The whole church sings the Psalmodia before the celebration of the Eucharist. Especially after a Psalmodia sung on a feast day, one can hear euphoric Copts say that it was as if the whole community from heaven had joined them in the singing, while they themselves had felt like "heavenly creatures."

Contemplatives sing the whole *Tasbiḥa* every day, whether the celebration of the Eucharist follows or not. The active sisters daily sing two of the four *hūs*, and in the event of a Eucharist they sing the whole Psalmodia on the night before the Eucharist.

People love to listen to tapes with recordings of the Psalmodias sung in the monasteries. Since the monks are already "angelic beings" on earth, their singing brings heaven closer than does the singing of ordinary laypersons. Taping the voices of the contemplative nuns is strictly forbidden. The reasons Copts give for this restriction is that listening to female voices can lead to distraction from the purpose of Psalmodia: to praise God. Somebody might fall in love with the nuns on the basis of their voices. Another reason the nuns themselves give is one of modesty: they do not want to make people think that they are singing the Psalmodia to show off their beautiful voices. Neither would they want to induce false praises or compliments for this. Although contemplative nuns also should have reached the state of "angelic being," their behavior is still influenced by the general rules of modesty from society—a woman should at all costs prevent becoming a source for temptation.

The Eucharist: *al-Quddās*

The partaking of the body and blood of Christ forms the core of the religious life of every Copt. A Copt cannot go without taking communion for more than forty days. The former Patriarch Kyrillos VI, for example, understood that in order to bind the Copts more closely to their church, one of the pillars of the church's revival had to be the frequent celebration of the Eucharist. Before he was appointed patriarch, he started a daily celebration in the church of St. Menas south of Cairo. One observes that in the Coptic religious view, heaven and earth meet during the singing of the Psalmodia. According to the Copts, what happens on the altar during the preparation of the Eucharist is heavenly. The angels are present, and just as God was encountered in the Holy of Holies in the Jewish temple, the priest perceives God's presence in the *haikal* (the sanctuary).[75] One can only approach this holy event in a state of ritual cleanliness after the proper preparation of fasting for at least nine hours (or from midnight)—which means that breakfast is eaten after communion. Confessing one's sins to receive absolution is a requirement before taking communion. Menstruating women and women who have recently delivered a child, because they are considered unclean, are not allowed to partake in the sacraments. Because such actions as eating and digesting belong to the realm of this world, even children fast before taking communion. But, so the Copts reason, because a child digests food much quicker than an adult, children are allowed to fast for fewer hours. In Sunday school the children are taught that "we fast because Jesus must come in a pure stomach, . . . and we confess our sins because He cannot be received in a body that is all dirty."[76] Fasting is furthermore a minor way of participating in Christ's suffering and His sacrifice.

The celebration itself often lasts more than three hours, which are mostly spent standing. The Copts see this as a proper way to honor the fact that Christ suffered many hours for their redemption and so His people should be willing to do the same for Him. Father Gruber analyzes the Coptic *quddās* as "the passion and cross of Christ [that] . . . carries the Copts through a divinely endorsed ritual medium into the mystery of Christ's sacrifice, into the zone of safety wherein the violence marked out for humanity was absorbed by the divine man."[77]

Partaking of communion, like singing the Psalmodia or the *taranīm* (hymns) during weekly meetings, provides reassuring moments for the Copts. In spite of their current precarious social status, Copts can feel part of a heavenly army and nurture solidarity within the community.

The performance of the ritual of the *quddās* requires the services of the ordained. For the mediation between God and the people, the Copts have to rely on a body of trained clergy to the extent that the *quddās* "is the public presentation of the institutional church's formal structure, order, and hierarchy."[78] One of the nuns explained how the ordinary believer perceives this situation: "Because of the Holy Spirit, the transubstantiation of the elements takes place: the bread and the wine become the body and blood of Christ. The priest, although he basically is a normal human being, is a vehicle in this process; when he puts his hands on the elements, his hands are blessed because of them. That is why we kiss the priest's hand: because they hold the elements."

For nuns the celebration of the Eucharist forms a crucial moment in their life of worship. The bread and wine are their spiritual food and connect them directly with the mystery of the Incarnation, which is what they live for. The nuns can only attend the *quddās* twice a week because it requires a priest or an ordained monk to come to the convent.[79] In the contemplative convents, the nuns are allowed to be involved in some parts of the liturgy; where in some cases a deacon would perform the responsory, the nuns can sing the response. In the active community a *muʿallim* (male liturgical singer) comes specially to do the singing. The contemplatives walk up to the altar to receive the communion in order of seniority—the eldest nun first and the postulants the very last. Like laypeople, nuns are extremely happy when they can partake of the body and blood of Christ. Unfortunately, their gender excludes them from entering into the inner sanctuary where "heaven is on earth." Monks are specifically invited to come into the inner sanctuary during the Eucharist, because "by their monastic life they are thought to be more intimately bound up in the liturgical sacrifice of Christ on the altar."[80]

The "Jesus Prayer" and the Daily Prostrations

Apart from the communal devotions as described above, every monastic—contemplative and active—has to pray the so-called *ṣalāt Yasūʿ* or *Al-ṣalāt al-Dāʾima* (Jesus Prayer, or "the continuous prayer"). The practice of this prayer is not unique for the Copts; it is known to monastics of all the Orthodox churches. Copts do not use the rosary but count the tips and joints of their fingers while performing the set praises or prayers. One hand stands for fifteen prayers; in each cycle, forty-one prayers are completed. The longer versions of the prayer that are used were reintroduced during the 1950s when monastics started to recapture orthodox traditions and history. Before that time monastics knew the practice of praying continuously, but they had the freedom to choose the text themselves. Often their prayers were limited to one or two short sentences such as: "Help me, oh Lord" or "I am a sinner."[81] For the practice of the continuous prayer, there is a precedent for this which goes back to the earliest desert fathers.[82]

An "old man" in the *Bustān al-Ruhbān* has the following to say to the beginning monk concerning the Jesus Prayer: "Now when the devil sees someone strive [to reach perfection], he stirs up the most terrible pains [in the monk's body], and God gives him free play to do so—lest he [the monk] will boast about his strife—until the continuous prayer clings to him, then he will know his weakness, and God will make the terrible pains stop, and his soul will pass to rest and peace."[83] The prayer does not belong to the official liturgy but is considered among the most important prayers for a monastic. Repeating the Jesus Prayer, like reciting the psalms and the "Our Father," gives the monastic rest in his or her soul, keeps the mind concentrated on God, and protects against the attacks of the devil. The text of the prayer is basically the same for all monastics:

"Yā Rabbī Yasūᶜ al-Mesīḥ irḥamnī."
"Yā Rabbī Yasūᶜ al-Mesīḥ a ᶜinnī."
"Yā Rabbī Yasūᶜ al-Mesīḥ khalliṣnī."

Which means:

"Oh my Lord Jesus Christ, have mercy on me."
"Oh my Lord Jesus Christ, help me."
"Oh my Lord Jesus Christ, deliver me."

Prostrations or *Meṭānīyāt*

Before the daily devotions start, the contemplative monastic gets out of bed to start the day with an hour of private prayer in the cell. Prayers sanctify the night, according to the nuns, since that is the time when the angels praise most. The private prayers are accompanied by *meṭānīyāt* (prostrations) that are made as an act of repentance; one moves from a standing position into deep kneeling with the forehead touching the floor and the arms stretched in front of the body. During the act of prostrating, the Jesus Prayer is often recited, while the monastic makes the sign of the cross before and after each prostration. The prostrations are also made to relieve the monastic of possible excessive energy.[84] The number of prostrations differs for each monastic and is decided in consultation with the spiritual director. This penitential act is so private that not even monastics know from one another how many prostrations another performs. If two nuns, for some reason, happen to share the same cell, one of them goes outside when the other performs her prostrations. As a general rule, a contemplative monastic has to perform 150 prostrations daily, except on Saturdays and Sundays. (Because Jesus was dead on Saturday and rose on Sunday, it is inappropriate to ask for forgiveness repeatedly on those days.) The active sisters perform the prostrations in the time between the morning devotions and breakfast. They do considerably fewer than the contemplatives because for most of them a day with physical work will follow.

Fasting

Fasting or controlling the body not to sleep too much are all acts of *nusk* (asceticism). These are seen as a sacrifice for Jesus which will be accepted according to the person's capacity. One can fast *al-ṣawm al-inqiṭāʾī* (severely), meaning that until a certain hour of the day one does not eat or drink anything. Or one can limit the fast to certain kinds of food; no animal products are allowed during a fast, which means that one must omit not only meat but also butter, milk, cheese, and eggs. Fish is allowed during the fasts (except during the fast for Lent). According to the Copts, their menu during the fasts is the same as Adam and Eve's when they lived in the Garden of Eden. The Coptic Church conducts about two hundred days of fasting a year—every Wednesday and Friday and on other occasions during certain periods of the year.[85] The specific rules concerning food effectively prohibit the Copts from having communal meals with Muslims. Certain types of snacks, such as the omnipresent *fūl* and *ṭaʿamīya* sandwiches (ground beans and ground chick peas), are eaten by every Egyptian. But the preparation for lunch and dinner requires special dishes and techniques so that it is difficult for those who fast to just join in with people who are not fasting. Also the fact that Copts follow their own calendar sets them apart from the other Egyptians.[86] Because the fasting periods are so long, many laypeople do not strictly keep them and start halfway through the period in order to complete the fasts for Advent, and Lent, and St. Mary.[87] Many religious authorities recognize the difficulty of long fasts; hence they often teach that God will accept the fast according to a person's capacity. One can, for example, help a neighbor in order to make up for a missed fast. The main goal is to control the body and to make a sacrifice for Jesus.

Copts also consider fasting a powerful means to invoke God's help in times of distress. For example, in the 1970s when Copts were often under attack from Muslim extremists and feeling that the government was ignoring their plight, Shenouda III mobilized the entire community to perform a fast.[88]

Contemplative monastics see it as part of their vocation to keep all the fasts strictly. Hence their motto: "*Kharāb al-nafs huwa ḥubb al-baṭn*" (the spirit is ruined by the love for the belly). Monastics especially become prone to attacks from the devil when they cannot control their desire for food. Eating too much food furthermore causes them to become sleepy and less alert to do their spiritual exercises. Monastics fast daily until noon, and many of them forego meat, even in periods when it is allowed. In times of fasting they do not eat until 3:00 p.m.—and then they have the only meal for the day. The average meal in a convent consists of *fūl, ṭaʿamīya,* lentil soup, vegetables (cooked or raw), fruit, olives, and bread. On nonfasting days, the nuns can eat eggs, butter, cheese, milk, fish, chicken, beef, and lamb. Guests are served fancier dishes, but the contemplative nuns never join guests for a meal. They have their own schedule, and they also do not want people to get the wrong impression concerning their eating habits. When a fasting period is drawing near, many monastics prepare themselves by abstaining from nonfasting food. To them, fasting does not mean that it is forbidden to eat certain things but that they can enjoy the absence of a desire for food.

Fasting for Lent is seen as a wonderful experience when abstaining from food is combined with a daily spiritual program and extra devotions. Most of the convents are closed for guests during periods of fasting so that the nuns will not be distracted in their spiritual exercises. All contact with the world outside is discouraged. The monastics are admonished, however, not to exaggerate and to try to imitate the early fathers in every aspect of fasting. The fathers and mothers, for example, considered fruits and vegetables a luxury, while nowadays people know that they contain elements that are necessary to keep the body healthy.[89] Fasting too rigidly is detrimental to one's health. Many diseases and ailments can be caused by rigid fasting. One result of extensive fasting can be a lack of calcium which, in combination with frequent prostrations, is the cause of weak bones and severe back problems among monastics.

In the active community the nuns are not allowed to fast too rigidly, because if they do they will not be able to complete their work. The actives always follow the rules concerning the types of food. Their menu is more or less identical with that of the contemplatives, but going without food until 3:00 p.m. is nearly impossible. The actives only forego breakfast during Lent, but for sisters who cannot cope without food until lunch (2:00 p.m.), there is food available that they can take when they wish. The time and amount of food one will have has been agreed upon in advance with the spiritual director. The active sisters also eat in the presence of guests, nonmonastic colleagues, and other outsiders. For Coptic outsiders, this rational way of handling the fasts by monastics is strange. For them the pinnacle of monasticism are monks and nuns who hardly eat and thus represent the old models of the desert fathers. Only in this way can one understand the criticism some have of the active community: "They are not nuns, they eat too much."

SUMMARY

The spiritual direction as practiced by the contemplative nuns is firmly rooted in a tradition that goes back to the desert fathers and mothers. The spiritual mother can acquire the same type of prominence in the spiritual hierarchy as her male counterparts—monks, priests, or bishops. Connected with this spirituality is an authority within her own convent. No male representative of the church hierarchy can interfere in cases of discord or trouble. For the ordinary nun the absolute authority of the spritual mother can turn out to be a situation full of pitfalls. What is the nun to do in case of incongruity with the spiritual director? Unlike monks, nuns have no alternatives for spiritual direction. Monastics express the nature of monastic life thus: "heaven when you can cope with it, but a prison when you can't."

The model of spiritual guidance in the active community is set up to avoid the problem of abuse of spiritual power. This system also claims to have direct links to the desert fathers. By granting a sister the freedom to find an alternative spiritual director, to develop her own relationship with the "Eternal Listener," and to freely express herself like Sister Hannah, the system has safeguards against the convent turning into a prison.

The contemplative nuns strive to become a body that strengthens the Coptic believers spiritually. In spite of a modern degeneration of the supposedly perfect spiritual gifts the desert fathers had, monastics uphold the standards of the Coptic community's spiritual heritage. Whereas the layperson attempts only to reach the standards for prayer and fasting, monastics excel in all of the disciplines. Contemplative nuns are capable of even more than monks, because they are less frequently disturbed. The Copts consider their nuns and monks to be set apart for spiritual goals. The contemplative nuns are considered the praying backbone of the community; without their incessant supplications the church might collapse. In combination with spiritual mothers who spread messages, such as the fruitfulness of suffering, convents have become strongholds for the Coptic faith.

Active nuns participate in this devotional system as well, but are absorbed by worries about their work and devotion to the needy. This makes their convent less of a wellspring of pure Coptic values. Consequently, Copts find it more difficult to grant the active sisters a firm place in the central value system. The publication of hagiographic booklets about Sister Hannah might be a first step toward changing this situation. Through these booklets, the Coptic community can become aware of Hannah's role as a model and as a potential candidate for sainthood.

CHAPTER 8

The Saints

In the Coptic tradition, saints are people who by virtue of their sacrifice and quest for God during their lifetimes have attained a prominent place in the divine hierarchy. The saints are thought to pray incessantly and to intercede for the community that struggles on earth. The saints have reached the ultimate goal, regardless of the positions they held during their life; they might have been patriarchs, monks, nuns, laywomen and laymen, or simply children when they died.

The saints figure prominently in this study. I mentioned the patron saints of convents and monasteries and saintly monks and nuns who could disrupt the established monastic hierarchy. I have also indicated that saints and saintly persons are members of a hierarchy that stands apart from the ecclesiastical or social hierarchy. In this chapter I will discuss the different types of saints venerated by the Copts, the concept of holiness, and the relationship of the nuns to the classic Coptic saints and holy persons. I will also look at nuns who themselves are perceived as holy and the implication of this holiness for their role in the Coptic Church and community.

POPULAR AND OFFICIAL VIEWS CONCERNING SAINTS

The belief in the presence and intervention of angels, prophets, and saints forms an important part of the popular cosmology of the Copts. The number of these venerated saints is relatively small. St. Mary, Jesus' mother, is considered to be at the head of the saintly hierarchy, followed by angels, prophets, martyrs, and holy people such as St. Antony the Great.

Using the term *popular* to describe the beliefs of the laypeople implies the existence of an "official" level which comprises the doctrinal view of the official church and the clergy. Both the popular and the official views recognize the existence of a saintly hierarchy. The differences between the two levels are concerned with the questions of who is considered a saint or saintly and when can a person be officially recognized as a saint.

In order to answer these questions, one first has to categorize the saints. The two main groups are: (1) saints from the first centuries of Christianity (until the sixth century) and (2) the modern and contemporary saints (from the second half of the nineteenth century until today). There are saints who lived in the period between the sixth and the nineteenth centuries, but their number is fewer and they are less known.

The main types of saints are the martyred saints and the modern saints. The *shuhadāʾ* (martyred saints) are those who died during the first centuries of Christianity, the desert fathers and mothers, and the church fathers. Since most of the Coptic martyrs died during the persecutions of the three Roman emperors Decius (249–251), Diocletian (285–305), and Julian the Apostate (361–363), this period of time accounts for a great number of martyrs.[1] Many martyrs were laypeople and included men, women, and children. In this group are the saints whose names have already been mentioned in this study: Māri Girgis, Abū Saifein, Amīr Tādrus al-Shuṭbī, and Dimyānah. Some of the saints who were desert fathers and mothers are St. Antony, St. Pachomius, St. Macarius, and St. Sarah. One of the famous church fathers is St. Athanasius.

The types of modern and contemporary saints can be divided into four groups: (1) saints who are dead and canonized (for example, ʾAnbā Abraam, the saintly bishop from Fayoum who was canonized in 1963); (2) saints who are dead but not yet canonized (ʾAnbā Kyrillos VI, the saintly patriarch who died in 1971); (3) people who are dead and considered very holy in popular opinion, but it is still to early to ascertain whether they will be canonized (Mother Martha and Sister Hannah and Abūnā Yusṭus belong to this group); and those people still alive (the present Patriarch Shenouda III belongs to this group, as do the bishops).

The official stand of the church concerning the first group of martyrs, desert saints, and church fathers is clear. These people have become part of the Coptic heritage and tradition, and their names are mentioned in the Synaxarion—the formal list of the names and lives of the martyrs and saints of the Coptic Church.[2] From the second group—the modern saints—only the canonized saints are officially recognized and have their names entered in the Synaxarion.

According to Coptic Church doctrine, a saint can be recognized officially by the Holy Synod fifty years after his or her death. That recognition means that the saint's name will be added to the Synaxarion. During every church service the lives of the saints commemorated that day are read publicly. Furthermore, the saint's relics can be placed in the church, and the priest is allowed to mention the saint's name in the daily prayers. One of the criteria of sainthood is the occurrence of miracles through the saint's intercession. When a miracle happens, the case has to be fully documented before it can be classified as a miracle. In case of a healing, doctor's reports and a detailed description of the course of the disease must be produced. For example, through the intercessions of the saintly patriarch like Kyrillos VI miracles proliferated, both during his life and after his death. All of these were recorded and published with documentation in a series of booklets that cover twelve volumes.[3] This means that Kyrillos virtually already belongs to the group of officially recognized saints.

The Popular Point of View and Contemporary Saints

The Coptic laity makes its own judgments concerning someone's holiness whether that person is dead or still alive. High church officials, the patriarch, and the bishops are considered holy by virtue of the offices they hold. Then there are monks, nuns, and some laypeople who are perceived as holy because of their saintly deeds. Patriarch Kyrillos VI combined of these two types of holiness. Another contemporary saint is Abūnā Yusṭus al-Anṭunī (d. 1979). Bishop Abraam (1829–1914) from Fayoum was considered saintly during his lifetime and was canonized fifty years later.[4] Another monk considered saintly was Abūnā Michael al-Buḥeiry (d. 1923) from the Muḥarraq Monastery. A monk from the Monastery of St. Paul, Abūnā Fānūs, although he is old, is still alive: "When he was about fifty, he began showing clairvoyance and working miracles, and his reputation became so great that his numerous visitors grew into a nuisance for his monastery."[5]

Among women, I point out the two contemporary saints who have been mentioned already: Mother Martha (d. 1988) and Sister Hannah (d. 1991). The basis for holiness varies for each of the contemporary saints, and not all might find official recognition after fifty years. Their actions, words, and environments differed considerably, but what they have in common is that laypeople regarded them as saintly. Their importance lies in the fact that they serve as contemporary models for certain groups and in some cases for the Coptic community at large. After these women passed away, admirers collected the stories that were known about them and published a booklet or hagiography.

The official church clashes with the laypeople when they start to venerate dead or living persons without the official prerequisites of sainthood being present. When a person is still alive, veneration is absolutely taboo since he or she has not joined the heavenly host yet. This means that too much attention goes to a human being instead of to God who should be the ultimate object of worship.

Holiness Beyond Persons

On the official level, holiness pervades the Coptic life through the distribution of the sacraments. This distribution is headed by the celebration of the Eucharist which takes place at the holiest place in the church—the altar. On the popular level, everything connected with the saints contains potential holiness or at least a *baraka* (blessing power). This power can be the saint's picture, a book about him or her, holy oil from the reliquary, *ḥanūṭ*, shreds of cloth from the relics' cover, an orange peel, or dust scraped from the bottom of a grave. Regardless of the objects or the circumstances, one can never rule out the possibility of a miraculous event. In fact, a miracle is to be expected. People regularly "see" saints, have talks with them, and are healed through a saint's intervention or intercession. From an early age children are taught to respect the saints, their relics, and icons. When the children are not yet able to touch an icon themselves, their mother or father guides the little hand to the icon in order for the child to receive the *baraka*. In the Coptic universe the extraordinary has nearly become the ordinary in day-to-day life.

THE MOST POPULAR EARLY CHRISTIAN SAINTS

Several of the most popular saints venerated today belong to the era of the martyrs which ended in the year 313. By that time, the country seems to have been littered with shrines—some containing the remnants of some unknown, possibly not Christian dead person. The cults and festivities that developed around these shrines seem to have adopted such outrageous characteristics to the extent that they were severely criticized by the great reforming abbot Shenute of Atrib (348–466).[6] Presently, the favorite male saints seem to be the martyrs Māri Girgis (St. George), Abū Saifein (St. Mercurius), Amīr Tādrus al-

Shuṭbī (St. Theodore Stratelates), and Māri Mīnā (St. Menas). All of these are so-called military saints, which means that they died while holding positions in the army. Apart from Māri Mīnā, these martyrs are portrayed on icons in the outfit of a soldier holding a lance or sword. Furthermore, there is Abā Nūb (St. Anub). The most popular female saints are St. Dimyānah and St. Mārīnā. Apart from these, there are many local saints. Sometimes a lesser-known local saint gains national popularity, as is the case with Abā Nūb, a child who died a gruesome death at the age of twelve. His fame seems to have spread during the last decade, probably because frequent appearances have been reported and miraculous healings of cancer have been connected with him and his reliquary in Samanūd (in the Delta). Another saint who achieved national popularity was St. Mārīnā, whose shrine is in Cairo.

St. George, St. Mercurius, and St. Theodore Stratelates were not originally Egyptian but Greek. Hence they are venerated in other Orthodox churches as well.[7] These saints became incorporated into the Coptic tradition and are now immensely popular in Egypt. They lived during the era of the martyrs, and the basic story of their passion is that they refused to obey the emperor's edict to reject Christ and worship pagan gods. Each was thrown into prison and, after suffering cruel torture, died, only to be consoled by Christ or an angel. Their martyrdom was surrounded by miraculous events that led to many spontaneous conversions to Christianity.[8] The same patterns can be found in the stories about the martyrdom of the female saints Mārīna and Dimyānah.[9]

The next group of venerated saints are the monks and desert fathers. The most well known are the ones to whom monasteries are dedicated: St. Antony the Great, St. Paul the First Hermit, St. Macarius, and St. Bishoy. Also well known are saints whose bodies can be found in the monasteries—St. Moses the Black, for example. The women who belong to this category are lesser known and rarely venerated. Most of them, like St. Sarah, lived as hermits, and often they were disguised as men, like St. Theodora, St. Hilaria, and St. Marina the Monk.

COPTIC AND MUSLIM COMMONALITIES CONCERNING VENERATION

Copts and Muslims have much in common in their acquaintances with saints, celebration of *maulids* and feasts, visiting graves, and in some cases witnessing apparitions. I have already mentioned that St. Mary is venerated by both traditions, and many Muslims witnessed her apparitions in Zeitoun (1968) and Shubra (1986). Several who have written about the Coptic Church have observed this phenomenon of joint veneration of the saints. Leeder writes about a Muslim woman "sitting in the Christian chapel nursing the relics and looking as intensely expectant of blessing as the Copt."[10] Meinardus observed in 1963, during the *maulid* of Māri Girgis at Mīt Damsīs, that a new altar curtain was donated by a Muslim merchant in gratitude to the saint for his cure during the *maulid* of the previous year.[11] Muslims attend Coptic *maulids* hoping for apparitions or healings through the saint's intercession. In times of sickness or distress or in cases when someone is believed to be possessed by an evil spirit, Muslims are not afraid to turn for help to one of the Coptic saints.[12] Occurrences of miraculous healings are not confined to the past. During the *ʿeid* (feast) of St. Mārīnā, 2 November 1990, the paralyzed legs of a Muslim man were apparently cured after he touched the saint's relics and spent time asking her intercession. As a proof of the miraculous event, the man's wheelchair was left hanging in the church.[13] In addition, Christian women visit the shrines of certain Muslim saints to encourage fertility.

A difference between the Muslims and the Christians concerns the frequent handling of relics. Relics are mostly preserved in wooden or metal cylinders. Christians lift the cylinders from the reliquaries and place them on their bodies so that the sick parts might be healed.[14] This fondness for saints' bodies stems from the fourth century, when certain Christians in Hellenistic Egypt used to keep the mummified remnants of the martyrs in their homes.[15] At the time of his death, St. Antony the Great was aware of the practice of venerating the martyr's body in the house. In order to prevent this from happening to his body, St. Antony asked two of his disciples to bury him in an unknown place.[16]

THE CONCEPT OF HOLINESS

In order to understand the position of the nuns in a Coptic cosmology filled with saints, angels, and spiritual beings, one first has to investigate what the essentials of holiness are for the Copts and to what extent there is a place for women. According to general studies concerning the concept of holiness or sainthood, the elements of sainthood can be broken into four categories: supernatural power, asceticism, charitable activity, and evangelical activity.[17] (The office of one who is part of the church hierarchy is itself considered saintly.) People who have exhibited these qualities during their lifetimes are perceived to be endowed with spiritual power, authority, and charisma.

For the Copts, supernatural power primarily means a deep faith in the power of God which is augmented by an active relationship with the saints. Asceticism involves a minimum of food, drink and sleep, as well as general distance from the world. For instance, Patriarch Kyrillos VI, during the fasting times, lived on one piece of bread daily with a little salt and cumin. Charitable activities are shown by great love and mercy for people which are motivated by the love of God. Evangelical activities include a model of obedience to God's commandments by which one is a constant model for fellow believers and outside observers.[18] These categories pose no objection to the participation of women in the system of sainthood.

Although ordained office in the official church body is not available to women, holiness can also be derived from this source. The origins of unquestioned spiritual power, authority, and charisma—habitually ascribed to the patriarch and bishops—are in the earliest days of monasticism in the time of the desert fathers. Many such situations are analyzed by Philip Rousseau in *Ascetics, Authority, and the Church* and are still applicable to the contemporary Coptic context. In the beginnings of monasticism, monks and nuns who strove to be holy came to a master (abbā) in order to "learn the way." Those masters held a spiritual authority, but Rousseau argues:

> No one took power for granted. A claim to the title of abba, spiritual father, depended on a wide range of qualifications, recognized throughout the desert. Ascetics of all types were convinced, first of all, that their leaders belonged to an historical tradition. . . . So Pachomius, and all those who followed this pattern of life, were seen by a later generation as descendants of patriarchs, of prophets, and of the apostles themselves. . . . The links between one generation and another were traced with care.[19]

The present members of the church hierarchy are perceived as saintly because their spiritual power, authority, and charisma are rooted in the monastic tradition. The holiness of church leaders is, according to the Copts, partly based on the fact that these leaders are directly guided by the Holy Spirit in their decision-making. Since these leaders are chosen from among the monks, one assumes that they have developed insight into and inspiration about the most high secrets of (Coptic) religion. By virtue of these qualities, the leaders are considered capable to serve as spiritual leaders and intermediates for the Coptic community.

HOLINESS OF PATRIARCHS AND BISHOPS: THE CASE OF ANBĀ KYRILLOS

Considering the components of sainthood, one can conclude that in fact all bishops and the patriarch can be considered holy, but that some who hold these offices are considered more holy than others. The saintly Patriarch Kyrillos VI is an excellent example of a patriarch whose life provides countless illustrations of his holiness. The Copts believe that it was not coincidental that during his reign St. Mary appeared for a long period of time on the dome of a church in Zeitūn, an apparition which resulted in many healings and miracles. According to the Copts, "God wanted to honor Pope Kyrillos VI with these apparitions."[20] As one of his numerous biographers writes, Kyrillos "despised all worldly goods and preferred to live as a poor, simple, fasting monk. He was in constant communion with God and the saints; his life was uninterrupted prayer and God gave him the gift to work miracles."[21] During and after his lifetime, innumerable healings took place through the intercession of this patriarch. Either he touched the afflicted while praying silently, or he gave people blessed water to drink, holy oil to rub on themselves, a piece of cotton drenched in holy oil, or half a loaf of *qurbān* (the blessed bread). The frequent use of his hand cross was also considered a powerful remedy for any affliction. He was famous for his clairvoyance. Personal contact was not necessary to acquire the patriarch's intercession. The story of Albert Y. Youssef shows that a picture might suffice:

> I always kept two pictures of Patriarch Kyrillos VI between my papers. One day I forgot a folder with important documents in the streetcar. I looked for them everywhere and asked the transportation authorities. There was no sign of the documents. In my thought I spoke with Patriarch Kyrillos: "Is it possible, Pope Kyrillos, that I put your pictures in my papers and you allow something like this to happen? When I don't find that folder, they'll take me to court." After saying this I boarded the first streetcar that arrived. There were my documents, in the same place where I had left them. I immediately drove to the patriarch to tell him what had happened. As soon as he saw me he said: "Have you found them? Why do you come to me? Get back to your work!"[22]

This story illustrates the deep trust Copts have in the power of their intercessors and the intimacy with which they discuss their day-to-day problems. The patriarch was obviously concerned with these practical matters as much as with brain tumors or paralyses that needed healing. The way Youssef spoke with Patriarch Kyrillos is similar to the way the patriarch himself addressed the saints from the early centuries of Christianity. For example, the patriarch had spent the period of Lent in the Monastery of St. Menas. The car that was going to take him back to Cairo would not start. Patriarch Kyrillos walked to the icon of St. Menas and said: "Why are you angry? Didn't we stay with you for 35 days? Don't be so sad."[23] After this the car started regularly. This ability to freely communicate with the saints is considered a proof of a high degree of holiness because the saints only grant this favor to those who rigorously fast and pray.

HOLINESS AND RELATIONSHIP WITH THE SAINTS AMONG THE CONTEMPLATIVE NUNS

With certain limitations, the one female saintly person who can be compared with Patriarch Kyrillos is Umminā Marthā. In the chapter about spiritual guidance, I mentioned her staunch ascetic life and the way she often reinforced her prayers by using water she had prayed over, holy oil, or a piece of *qurbān* (blessed bread). Several stories have been recorded of Mother Martha's intercessions: miraculous healings, women who gave birth to a long-hoped-for child, lost things that were found, students who passed their exams, and a thief who found himself seemingly nailed to the ground when trying to steal a car. Mother Martha's way of dealing with problems often was a mix of clairvoyance, common sense, and symbolic actions:

> A man whose brother was severely ill was concerned about his nephew's results at school. The family blamed the boy's poor performance on the father's sickness and decided to ask Umminā Marthā for advice. She called the boy to her and said: "Come here boy, . . . why don't you study? Shame on you for all these lost years, you have to find yourself a solution, for the sake of your sick father. Listen, drink water from the well of Abū Nūfer the wandering saint and come three times to take communion. After that, take some water from the well with you and wash yourself with it, then you will pass your exams." The boy, trembling with fear for this stern woman, quickly did as she had told him. Later on he passed his exams with results that were so excellent that he could enter the university.[24]

The Copts saw her advice to the young man and the fact that she foretold that he would pass his exams as a proof of her *shafāfīya* (clairvoyance or transparency). Mother Martha would also send St. Amīr Tādrus to someone in distress. For example, the saint would, in the shape of a small boy, deliver a medical instrument that was needed urgently for an operation but was not available in Egypt. When people went to the convent to thank Mother Martha for her intercession, she knew in advance what had happened.[25] When someone needed her, she could appear in dreams or phone that person unexpectedly.

Mother Martha was regularly visited by the saints. The archangel Raphael had announced to her that she was going to build a church. After she had purchased the plot of land where the church was projected, the Lord Jesus Christ himself visited her and said that the church was to have three altars.[26] Her nuns or visitors sometimes saw her in the company of St. Mary, St. Amīr Tādrus, or Pope Kyrillos. Like Kyrillos, Martha had a relationship with the saints based on mutual respect and the bonds of friendship. She counted on St. Amīr Tādrus to protect the convent and its inhabitants and to defend them in times of danger. For her part, Martha honored this saint by restoring "his" convent, building a church in his name, and spreading his fame among the Coptic community. As she used to express it, she wanted to create the Amīr as "a worthy place." One of the stories recorded by her biographers serves as an illustration of Martha's interaction with St. Amīr Tādrus:

> Martha had signed the agreement with the contractor for the construction of the church and the date to start the work was set. The night before the builders would start, St. Amīr Tādrus appeared to her with a stick in his hand. He woke her up and said to her: "Take this stick with you." She asked "why, oh martyr for the Lord, since we are children of the King of Peace, we don't know quarrels or strife." But he repeated his words and disappeared. . . . The following morning, while Martha was doing her usual work, some of the nuns suddenly came rushing in and screamed: "Come quickly oh Umminā, the whole neighborhood of al-Bāṭnīya has gathered together to prevent the construction of the church." Suddenly, to the great surprise of the nuns who thought she hadn't understood them, Umminā Marthā smiled. She looked at the icon of St. Amīr Tādrus and mumbled: "So, oh hero, that's why you gave me that stick. . . . I am not afraid, Our God is strong and you are a hero, oh martyr. . . . And as long as God is over us and you are with us, I don't fear anybody." She immediately got up and walked ahead of the nuns who tried to prevent her from going, fearing that the crowd might attack her. She walked to the crowd and asked the troublemakers: "what is the matter my boys? . . . Do you think that a few girls [the nuns] will be afraid of you and run away? . . . No! . . . Our God is strong and able to protect us and our guards are courageous heroes." Then she turned to the workers and yelled at them: "You, get to work; . . . I'll deal with anybody who dares to come close." One by one the agitators slunk off, ashamed.[27]

The records also add that Umminā Marthā used the words "my boys" to address the hooligans because, as she said: "the Amīr made them look to me as if they were all toddlers in a nursery school."[28] In addition to picturing the special relationship between Umminā Marthā and St. Amīr Tādrus, this story is an illustration of her total confidence in his protection and the role of the other nuns in the convent. Their fear is understandable when one imagines the environment of the convent situated in a blind alley in the midst of the nearly all-Muslim quarter called al-Baṭnīyah.[29] This area is known for drug-dealing—a place where one might find a millionaire who owns a laundry and a place where policemen dare not stroll about alone. The alleys are so narrow that it is almost impossible for a car to reach the place. A mob of angry men could easily crush a handful of nuns and construction workers.

From this story it seems that the other nuns do not have any contact with St. Amīr Tādrus. According to interviews with them, the nuns say that this is not true. Each of the nuns works on her relationship with the patron saint and once in a while even sees him. But the nuns would never talk about such an experience, because it is taboo to mention apparitions to anybody except the confessional father. Furthermore, according to the nuns, because Martha was the superior, the Amīr dealt more with her because she was the decision-maker of the convent. But the nuns were always instrumental as Umminā Marthā's helpers in her contacts with the saint; they lit the candles in front of his icon, told people about him, and asked for his intercession.

The stories about her close contact with the saints were revealed only after Martha's death. When she was alive, the stories were known and spread among the community but never openly admitted. The stories were later woven into a hagiography.

THE MAKING OF A SAINT: THE CASE OF ABŪ SAIFEIN

The mechanisms behind the making of a saint can still be witnessed in some of the contemporary convents. At present, the Convent of Abū Saifein is extremely active in promoting its patron saint and the myriad miraculous events that are said to take place through his intercession. The mother superior, Umminā Irīnī, is instrumental in interceding for people with the saint, who regularly appears to her. The role of Irīnī can only be heard about in oral stories, because everything the convent publishes about St. Abū Saifein is strictly presented as the sole action of the saint with no mention ever of the name or intercessory prayers of Umminā Irīnī.

As we have already mentioned, St. Abū Saifein, or St. Mercurius, is a military saint. According to the tradition, he served as a commander in the military forces of Decius, who had published the edict against the

Christians in 250. Abū Saifein was extremely successful in the battlefield but was denounced as a Christian in front of the emperor. Decius requested that he make a sacrifice to Artemis, something which Abū Saifein refused. This refusal led to his being tortured and eventually martyred in Caesarea, Cappadocia. His Arabic name (meaning "father of two swords") is derived from the fact that an angel is said to have appeared to him and handed him a (second) sword. According to the legend, after his martyrdom in 363, St. Abū Saifein killed the emperor Julian the Apostate with this sword. Abū Saifein is often portrayed iconographically sitting on his horse brandishing the two swords over his head while he is in the process of killing Julian.[30]

His relics came for the first time from Caesarea to Egypt sometime during the reign of Patriarch Yoannis XIII (1484–1524). Although when the convent received the relics is not clear, by the time the abbey was renovated in 1912, during the reign of Patriarch Kyrillos V (1874–1927), the relics were already in a reliquary in the convent.[31] Furthermore, the convent possesses an ancient icon of the saint which purportedly causes miracles.

Although St. Abū Saifein was already a popular saint in Egypt, it was not until Mother Irīnī became the superior of the convent in 1962 that a clear link was established between the saint's activities, his relics, and the convent. First, in 1963, the room with the reliquary was transformed into a church. Before that, the nuns had to leave the convent and walk to the church of Abū Saifein through an adjoining alley outside the convent. The rationale for the establishment of a church was that one of the nuns, Mother Theodora, could not go to the outside church because of her advanced age and her blindness. So Irīnī decided that the nuns needed their own church inside the convent.[32] The story is told that during the first mass celebrated in the church, a miracle and an apparition occurred. The blind nun Theodora regained her sight and another nun saw the long-deceased Patriarch Kyrillos V concelebrating the mass.[33] In the years to come, many other similar events followed.

In the meantime, Ummină Irīnī undertook the organization of the cult of St. Abū Saifein. The nuns sing his *madīḥ* and *tamgīd* (praises and glorifications), print those praises, and distribute them among the guests. His feasts are celebrated and Irīnī has made it a point of inviting bishops to attend and celebrate the mass. After the celebrations in the church, among which praises and glorifications for the saint are sung by the nuns, there is a *zaffa* (festive procession). The procession starts in the church and makes several rounds through the convent. The bishops and priests who hold the relics of St. Abū Saifein walk at the head, followed by deacons and men carrying banners with the saint's picture. Behind them come all the nuns with candles in their hands. The nuns walk in the order of their seniority, with the postulants at the end. Ummină Irīnī does not participate since she has withdrawn until after the procession. Later in the evening she will sit on a special platform, together with the church officials, and recount the latest miracles that have happened through the intercession of St. Abū Saifein. One can follow the events on monitors that are placed in and outside the convent. Only the back of Irīnī's veil is visible, as she hides her face from the camera. (Nuns are never supposed to appear in public.)

The atmosphere is electric and full of expectations of miraculous events that can happen any time. Since the crowd is so dense, just being able to touch the cylinder with the relics is considered a special blessing—nearly a miracle. In the meantime boxes are handed out filled with sweets, fruits, a small bottle of holy oil, and a picture of the saint with a spot of *ḥanūṭ* on the back. The boxes are called *baraka* and people consider them as special gifts from the saint and believe that Abū Saifein has commissioned Irīnī to hand them out on his behalf. The sweets are supposedly laden with blessings. The holy oil is used to rub on afflicted body parts in hopes of a cure. Through *ḥanūṭ*, one has a direct contact with the saint since it contains ingredients that were in contact with his relics.

The nuns, with the help of several female volunteers, have spent many days and nights preparing the sweets and other items in the boxes. On their farm, the nuns have grown and dried the flowers that are necessary to prepare the *ḥanūṭ*. All this work and preparation for the feast has become an important part of the nuns' work "for the saint." In addition to this work, the nuns embroider covers for the cylinder with the relics, embroider altar curtains with the saint's picture, and produce painted and woodworked icons. Every miracle connected with St. Abū Saifein is meticulously recorded by the nuns—including supporting evidence for the validity of the miracle. This evidence resulted in the publication of two books: *Sīrat-al-Shahīd al-ʿAẓīm Fīlubātīr Marqūrīyūs "Abī Saifein" wa Tārīkh Dairihi* (The Biography of the Great Martyr Philopater Mercurius "Abū Saifein" and the History of His Convent) (Cairo, 1989) and *Allāh Yuḥibbnī. Muʿjizāt al-Shahīd al-ʿAẓīm Fīlubātīr Marqūrīyūs "Abī Saifein"* (God Loves Me. The Miracles of the Great Martyr Philopater Mercurius "Abū Saifein") (Cairo, 1990).

The biography the nuns wrote about St. Abū Saifein provides in detail any information that is known about the saint: his life, family, martyrdom, when and how the relics were discovered, the number of churches bearing his name inside Egypt, and where in Egypt his relics are to be found (thirteen places).[34] Other information about the present-day cult of the saint includes how he is depicted on icons, the full texts where the saint is mentioned in the Psalmodia, commemorative texts for the saint for special days and occasions, and praises and glorifications. These texts of praises take up a good part of the book—more than one hundred pages.[35] The book closes with some information about the history of the convent, mostly connected with the working of the saint.

The book about the miracles deals with innumerable miraculous events that happened through the intercession of St. Abū Saifein. The miracles are not necessarily directly connected to the convent but took place all over Egypt. The saint appeared in Fayoum to cure the tumors of Mrs. Nabīla Fahmī. He made a brain tumor in Samīḥa Dhakī in Sohaj nearly vanish by means of holy oil and *ḥanūṭ* that she had rubbed on her head while she held a shred from the reliquary cover. The saint rescued the pilot Nabīl Nabīh Mīkhā'īl who had fallen into choppy seas near Alexandria. And Abū Saifein also came to remind the veterinarian Dr. ʿAṭīya ʿAbd al-Bāqī that he had promised the nuns help with their livestock. In none of the stories is Umminā Irīnī mentioned, although people agree that through her intercessions the saint is active today.

Umminā Irīnī

Irīnī herself is careful never to speak to outsiders about her contacts with St. Abū Saifein. Her nuns are the bearers of the news about her latest visions. This information comes either from her or from the witnessing of some extraordinary phenomenon (a bright light shines from Irīnī's cell or a nun who hears Irīnī talking to an invisible visitor). When Irīnī has received a message from the saint that is useful for the community at large, she briefs her nuns about what she has heard or seen. If the message is meant for other Coptic believers or for people in general, she speaks about it during a feast for Abū Saifein or her nuns pass on the message to visitors of the convent. Umminā Irīnī carefully observes the old rule from the desert fathers that one does not speak about one's visions—unless they have a social function or are meant to lead to faith and self-improvement.[36] But when one comes to the convent to thank the nuns for saying prayers that have been answered, the nuns insist on returning the thanks with the remark: "Tamauf has prayed." The prayers of the superior are considered to be more efficacious than their own, and thus one acknowledges her high spiritual level. The nuns are her helpers, and they care for guests, speak with them, and counsel them. The nuns are the keepers and guarders of the saint's relics—

always watching that no disorder or harm occurs in his church. Every day the nuns remember St. Abū Saifein in special songs of praise and encourage visitors to develop a relationship with the saint. The nuns confirm for the laypeople that, in spite of modern times, the saints are tirelessly active on behalf of the believers. Through the saints, the nuns gain this authority to counsel people. By constant reference to the hope one should have in the workings of St. Abū Saifein—and the symbolism of holy oil, water, and *ḥanūṭ*—the nuns can safely give advice without trespassing the borders of their authority.

LEGITIMATION OF THE NUNS' RELATIONSHIP WITH THE SAINTS

The nuns' actions are more or less authorized by their superior, Umminā Irīnī. Her visions and contacts with St. Abū Saifein guarantee an important and credible role for her convent in the Coptic Church. The image is carefully built on tradition, certain models, cultural congruence, charisma, and the authority derived from the words and deeds of St. Mary or, in this case, the martyr saint Abū Saifein.

As far as tradition is concerned, from the time of the desert fathers stories of the saints and visions have been "as much a feature of ascetic conversation as the sayings of the fathers, and were handed on in the same way to future generations."[37] For example, in the biography of Shenute (ca. 348–466), one can read stories of the monks hearing Shenute talking with somebody, but upon entering the room they found it was empty. When asked with whom the holy father was having a conversation, he answered: "It was the Lord Jesus Christ who was with me just now, speaking mysteries to me."[38] And as already observed, the monastic tradition is the basis for the spiritual authority and charisma held by members of the official church hierarchy. I have also mentioned that apparitions of saints and visions are seen as the result of, or perhaps the reward for, an ascetic lifestyle. Both these components provide links with the Coptic origins and place persons like Kyrillos VI, Martha, and Irīnī squarely within the Coptic tradition.

In the last forty years there have been some models to emulate. For instance, Umminā Irīnī started her ministry during this period. When she became the superior, Kyrillos VI was the patriarch and already famous as thaumaturge, or miracle worker. Through his contacts with Māri Mīnā, Kyrillos also set an example in developing relationships with the saints. Irīnī and Kyrillos were on good terms, and Kyrillos was favorable toward the new projects Irīnī proposed. Once, when she asked his permission for a new building and he had not found time to answer her, he appeared to her in a dream to give his consent.[39] With Umminā Marthā, Irīnī seems to have had close contacts, although she refuses to talk about this subject. Martha started her active ministry of building, drawing the attention of the Copts to St. Amīr Tādrus and renovating the convent in 1958. Through the success of her enterprises, Martha was not only a powerful model for superiors to come, but she also gained respect for the efforts of women and paved the way for them. Another mentor of Umminā Irīnī was Abūnā Yusṭus al-Anṭūnī. During stays in the Monastery of St. Antonius, Irīnī seemed to have been encouraged to follow his example of holiness and asceticism. When looking at the people who inspired Irīnī, in view of the scarcity of female models, the importance of the influence of male models becomes clear.

The Cultural Environment

I have already described the Coptic universe that is full of angels and saints. For the Coptic society, saints and the ideals of sainthood reflect the collective mentality. In the Muslim environment, the phenomenon of saints and intercession is widely accepted. Coptic saints are regularly instrumental in Muslim miracles. Furthermore, this Coptic presence reflects the concept of mediation that is normal in Egyptian society: when one wants to obtain a job, a favor, or some permission from a legal authority, the quickest way is to find a person who is close to that authority and willing to put in a good word.[40] Saints have achieved their superior state by the love they had for God while they were alive. Now, in heaven, God rewards them by granting their requests on behalf of human beings. Just as saints have become "friends of God," so people can befriend the saints. The intensity of this relationship depends on how much people are willing to invest in it.

Charisma

The concept of charisma is often defined as "a gift of grace . . . a certain quality of an individual personality by which he is set apart from ordinary man and treated as endowed with supernatural, superhuman, or at least specifically exceptional powers or qualities."[41] In the case of the Copts, the way Peter Brown explains the charisma of the holy person during the Roman Empire is preferable. Brown sees charisma as "less in terms of the extraordinary, set aside from society, so much as the convincing concentration in an event, in an institution, in a discipline or in a person of lingering senses of order and higher purpose."[42] Clifford Geertz explains this as "a sign, not of popular appeal or inventive craziness, but of being near the heart of things."[43]

The Copts consider people like Kyrillos or Martha to have reached "the heart of things," to use Geertz's term. These people are furthermore qualified to be defined as "endowed with supernatural, superhuman . . . powers" because, while they were alive, they could hold conversations with the saints. But in order to use these powers and transform them into innovative activities, other qualities are required as well. The holy person has to convey the message to the believers that what he or he stands for indeed carries a sense of order and higher purpose. The lives of holy men like Yusṭus al-Anṭūnī indicate the different ways in which such a person can deliver this message, whether or not he or she uses the close contacts with the saints.

In the different categories of holy persons, women who would behave like Yusṭus would never become known in Egyptian society. Women like Umminā Marthā and Irīnī need a public position such as mother superior to act out their ministries. Only then do they have access to sufficient authority to make their visions instrumental. Moreover, these women need extraordinarily strong personalities in order to be decisive about projects and to withstand pressure from the social and physical environment. In that way their holiness can become an instrument of change and innovation and these women can serve as models for others.

In Irīnī's case as role model she has become quite visible in less than two decades, while she herself is still alive. Three of the present mother superiors of the other convents in Cairo were chosen from the Convent of Abū Saifein and are spiritual daughters of Umminā Irīnī. All three try to follow in her footsteps and apply the strategies Irīnī has used to expand and renovate her convent.

Martha and Irīnī used the authority received from the office of mother superior, their relationships with the saints, and their charismatic qualities to participate in the revival of the Coptic Church. These women made the existence of contemplative nuns legitimate again; no longer are they seen as "old and disabled maidens." Becoming a contemplative nun nowadays is an alternative to a career or having a family. The presence of the saint's relics in a convent guarantees many activities and a source of income. In all, Irīnī built four new churches inside her convent and a farm. In deciding on projects of this nature, the patron saint is of great help. He or she protects, provides the plot of land and the necessary funds, and causes any lawsuits against the nuns to fail. In fact, some of the superiors and their nuns have moved into the spiritual cosmology where the saints take sides with them.

There are many stories concerning saints taking sides. In one of them, the saint sides with the mother superior and overrules a decision of the patriarch. The story is about St. Mary, who ordered the building of a second church on the grounds of the convent. One of the interesting aspects of the story is that it has both a published and an oral version. I will give the outline of the story with material from the oral version between brackets:

On the south side of the garden stood a house to bake the *qurbān* for the churches in Old Cairo. It had been there for over a hundred years. It had already collapsed during the time of the Mother Superior Kīrīye (1928–1962). . . . Around the year 1964, one morning, one of the nuns [Mother Irīnī] was walking around in the garden of the convent, reciting Psalms, until she reached the dilapidated house. There she noticed the smell of very pure frankincense, she looked up and suddenly saw the Virgin, the Mother of the Savior, sitting on one of the big rocks that were scattered around, and the Virgin said to the nun: "On this place I want an altar to be erected in my name, because I rested in this place during my flight to Egypt with my beloved son." Then the vision disappeared.

. . . During the following visit of the convent's mother superior to Pope Kyrillos VI she informed him of this apparition. But he was in the midst of a long affair that involved important matters and many special requirements for the convent. And because of the many other important affairs, the patriarch and the superior forgot about the instruction of the vision. [But the patriarch was reluctant to give his permission for the building of a new church because he had recently given his consent for the construction of several new churches.] After sometime, the convent decided to build a large guest house to receive groups and it was decided to use the dilapidated part of the garden for this purpose.

Indeed the workers started to build the reception area, and before the construction had finished, in the beginning of February 1968, His Holiness Patriarch Kyrillos VI made a telephone call to Mother Irīnī at four in the morning. . . . He said to her: "Hurry to finish the church for the Virgin in the convent because this night I saw her in a vision and the Mother of God said to me: 'hurry and consecrate an altar in my name for me in the convent of the Martyr Abū Saifein on the place were I rested with my beloved son during my flight in Egypt.' " Then the patriarch finished the conversation and said: "Next week, God willing, I will be present to consecrate that church."

Suddenly the work changed from the construction of a hall for groups to a church . . . and the work was carried out real quick . . . during one week the construction finished and the special fresco of the Virgin was painted.[44]

The story reveals various elements of the power structure and hierarchy the nuns had to manipulate in order to achieve their ultimate goal: transformation of the baking house into a church. The official version carefully abides by the rules of respecting the head of the church hierarchy. Since his decisions are supposed to be infallible, revealing a mistake he made in judging the urgency of the Virgin's request is impossible. The official version molds the patriarch's refusal to grant permission for the construction into an absence of mind. The patriarch and the superior are so swallowed up by day-to-day business that they forget about the apparition. One might argue that this attitude merely indicates the normality, or rather the casual way, of dealing with saints that develops among people who regularly see them. But because of the fact that St. Mary's position is above those of the angels and the prophets, amnesia to the extent that one totally forgets her apparition is unlikely. From a political point of view, the patriarch's refusal to give permission for yet another church at a time he had just ratified the construction of several others is understandable. The reality of the Egyptian Muslim environment is that it is not possible to build an unlimited number of new churches. Regardless of the government's consent, one has to respect popular religious feelings. So for several reasons the superior respects the patriarch's wish and opts for a guest house on the place designated for the church. Because it is within her own domain, the superior has the authority to do this. Obviously the structure of the guest house was multi-applicable—it could be transformed into a church within a week. The strategy of constructing a guest house first is not unknown. Often this is the only way to realize a church—as, for example, at the farms outside Cairo. The building project takes about four years and by the time the guest house is nearly completed the patriarch receives a vision about its final purpose: it is to be a church. The saint has sided with the nuns, the wish of the patriarch is thwarted, and the hierarchic relations have gone topsy turvy. The church's construction gets a final seal of approval by means of a direct, powerful link with tradition: the Lord Jesus rested in that place during his exile in Egypt.

Another dimension of the story is its illustration of the role of the convent for the Coptic community. The convent is a place where saints walk and talk freely, where churches can be built, and tradition is present. This is a place where a Copt can feel truly at home away from the surrounding Muslim world. A Copt knows that he or she is directly protected by the saints through the powerful prayers of the nuns and their superior. This protection is regularly emphasized by occurrences of the impossible—for instance, the story that is told about the Bedouin on the Mediterranean coast who swore that as long as he was alive the nuns would not be allowed to build a farm on the estate adjoining his. (Shortly after that, he died in an accident with a taxi.) In another story, a

Bedouin who tried to prevent the same construction put up his tent on the premises and started to build a house. The day he moved in, the minivan with his furniture toppled and several of his children who were sitting in the trunk of the van fell off and were killed.

Clearly the convent is an institution that guards the Coptic symbols. Peter Brown calls the convent's hosting of saints and holy persons "a little drop of the 'central value system' of Christianity."[45] The "central value system" is a term Brown borrows from Edward Shils who defines it as "the values which are pursued and affirmed by the elites of the constituent sub-systems of a society."[46] Coptic society with its monasteries and convents is one of those "little islands of 'centrality' " in a Muslim world.[47] The importance of the convent with its holy women lies in the fact that they represent Christianity. As the holy man in the Roman Empire "simply was Christianity," in present-day Egypt the human exemplar is still one of the ways to show a Copt how to be a Christian, and to inspire him or her to practice the Christian values.[48]

Maybe that is how one can explain the sudden increase in holy men and women during the twentieth century—concurrent with the revival of the Coptic Church: "The saint is a gift of God to his or her age and region."[49] Kyrillos VI knew the sensitivity of his people and the importance of the holy exemplar, and exploited this situation by pointing back to St. Mary, St. Māri Mīnā, the martyrs, and other saints who served as exemplars of suffering, endurance, and Christian life. These people emphasized the role the Coptic Church could have as a witness to a truly Christlike life. Kyrillos' initiative was soon to be followed by other Coptic Church or monastic leaders, women included.

THE SAINTS AND THE ACTIVE COMMUNITY

The members of the active community of sisters do not fit the system of the contemplative nuns which leans heavily on the intercession of the saints. With respect to interaction with the saints, the active sisters belong to the laypeople. Like all the Copts, the sisters venerate the saints, and several of them have witnessed miraculous events. Sister Hannah's words of consolation for people who faced severe problems were: "Don't be afraid; the Virgin did not leave [you] and Māri Girgis will not remain silent."[50] Of course, like all Copts, the sisters appeal to the saints for intercession and prayers. But the sisters stress that their trust in the saints is combined with solid prayers to God. For example, when the nuns wanted to buy a new mother house and did not have money or land, they relied on regular prayer meetings to find an answer. When a suitable building was found, the sisters were unfortunately still penniless. The sisters decided to say the "Our Father" every time they walked by the place. After two years, the house and its premises were put up for sale and an unexpected gift came in from Germany that equalled the exact amount needed. Indeed, this was seen as a miracle.

Because they work in active service, the sisters are not in a position to live up to high ascetic standards and to devote their time to activities for the saints. Furthermore, the mother house and its annexes are not historical places, and there is no patron saint connected with the site by means of relics. The building is too new to demonstrate any established link with tradition.

But the work of the active community can be seen as exemplary as well. The two hagiographies about Tāsūnī Ḥannah, published immediately after her death, testify to that point.[51] In themselves, these hagiographies show that a certain group of Copts do consider her as holy. According to her biographers, Ḥannah was an exemplar of deep-rooted faith and unselfish love for human beings. Furthermore, her biography revealed after her death that her short marriage before she became a nun had never been consummated. Forced to marry by her in-laws, she and her husband had lived a celibate life until the death of her husband at a young age.[52] This could place Tasūnī Ḥannah in the genre of saints like Amoun (295–353), who lived with his wife in celibacy for eighteen years before he retired to Nitria where he became one of the founders of Egyptian monasticism. Or perhaps one should classify her and the other sisters in the category of laypeople who somehow served as the monk's alter egos in the world. Even St. Antony knew that "there was one who was his equal in the city. He was a doctor by profession and whatever he had beyond his needs he gave to the poor, and every day he sang the Sanctus with the angels."[53]

The example of Sister Hannah indicates that the different religious groups within the Coptic community produce their own types of models. In this context the personality of Abūnā Bishoy Kāmil (1931–1979) deserves mention. He was a contemporary of Hannah and a married priest who started his career in the Coptic Church as a Sunday school teacher. After his ordination, he devoted his life to organizing new churches (in the United States, among other places) to prevent wavering Copts from lapsing and to win new members.[54] Abunā Bishoy Kamīl also lived a celibate life while he was married to his wife for almost twenty years. Bishoy Kamil's hagiography testifies to several miracles that took place during and after his life. Among others, Jesus Christ appeared to him.[55] Kamil was a model for future priests, and nine of his spiritual sons followed in his footsteps and became priests.[56] Like Sister

Hannah, he bore witness to his faith until the end when he died of cancer. After his death hagiographies and booklets were published with his sayings.[57]

SUMMARY

With regard to the cult of the saints, the contemplative nuns have developed a role in the Coptic Church that, for most of the members of the official clergy and lay Copts, is unquestioned. The most visible representative of the community is the mother superior. Through careful coordination of the Coptic tradition and its recognizable models, and at the same time making use of her charisma with its concurrent authority and her office as superior, she can reach a level of holiness comparable to that of holy men. This reputed holiness insures the superior and all her nuns a position within the Coptic cosmology of angels, martyrs, prophets, and saints.

In certain aspects, her gender prevents her full equality. At least to laypeople, though, her gender is a negligible factor. For the most part, all that matters is the holy woman who represents a powerful religious symbol for the Coptic community. During the last forty years two of these exemplary superiors, Umminā Marthā and Irīnī, were sufficient to make the female monastic life more attractive. By drawing more candidates to their convents, the parameters were set for an active participation of contemplative women in the revival of the Coptic Church.

The fact that women lack ecclesiastical power might even be an advantage, because it amplifies their unique position in the church. All too often, authority derived from charisma is confused with authority derived from office or with institutional authority, which often creates confusion among Coptic believers with regard to male clergy who belong to the clerical hierarchy. Because it is impossible to elevate a clergyman with a high office like patriarch or bishop too much, his actions are breeding grounds for the invention of miracles. Because women lack the credentials that automatically come with the office, their holiness is considered more pure and authentic.

Furthermore, there are ordinary people who lead holy lives. These people serve as reminders for the believers that a state of holiness can be reached by anyone who lives a sanctified life. Ordinary laypeople who lead holy lives also indicate that one should not exaggerate the cult of saints and holy men and women. There is always the dormant danger that a community of believers stretches its involvement in the cult of the saints and fabricates its own stories. The greatest danger is that belief and faith in God are replaced by superstitions. Circumstances and details from a story in the Synaxarion are regularly used to reinvent a new miracle. Creating miracles is especially rife in groups that visit the monasteries. Consequently, the Coptic Church meticulously investigates the circumstances of any miraculous event.

Also for contemplative nuns there is a dormant danger in paying too much attention to the supernatural. Although their main work consists of endless prayers, people might burden the nuns with the role of "miracle workers," which would distort their traditional vocation. Nuns who are considered saintly become constant targets for people who seek to gain their blessings. As a result, a daily life with ordinary human interactions becomes quite difficult for such saintly nuns.

The active nuns also play a new role in this setting. Their trademark is serving the poor and the needy, not the saints. Nevertheless, the active community has produced a saintly model as well. The life of Tāsūnī Ḥannah has proven that this way of life does not have to be an obstacle for holiness; it simply shelves those who follow this path to holiness into a different category. By making use of old images, the active nuns are slowly gaining a place for themselves in the Coptic universe. The material for their daily conversation consists of oral tradition with stories about the saints and the miraculous. In this the actives are similar to the contemplative nuns. But while recounting these stories, the sisters focus on "perfect trust in the person of Jesus. Because the perfect nun doesn't expect visions or signs."[58]

The contemplative superiors skillfully exploit the presence of the saints by housing, keeping, and honoring them. The fruits of these actions are work and activities for the whole community. In addition, a byproduct for the superior is that she may well be considered saintly herself. While she has "made the saint," the laypeople have "made her saintly." At the same time the saint provides protection and support, and guarantees the existence—even the expansion—of the convent.

While the nuns serve the saints, the saints serve the nuns. There is direct communication between heaven and earth where heaven is more or less open. As the story of the construction of St. Mary's Church showed, no one can interfere in this mutual relationship—not even the patriarch.

CHAPTER 9

Visitors

The Convent and the World

A nun who has left the world has left behind the secular environment that prevented full development of her devotional life, the Islamic influence over her life, and her family who might want to force her into marriage. Nevertheless, "leaving the world" does not mean that the monastic is fully cut off from the world outside. Monastic life has never been completely isolated from its environment. In this chapter, I will illustrate how and why people visit the convents. Then I will discuss the position of nuns versus Egyptian laywomen—Coptic and Muslim.

VISITORS AND THE CONVENTS

Since the monasteries and convents are centers of Coptic faith and identity, it is not surprising that they receive ample numbers of visitors. Copts want to visit their favorite saints and acquire blessings and profits from the examples and words of their monastic models.[1] To a lesser degree, some of the monastic places also have Muslim visitors.

The monasteries are so well visited that they are often "invaded" by groups. Most of these groups consist of Coptic pilgrims who come for one to three days. On the whole, visitors to the monasteries are frequent, in particular on holidays and feasts. The priest Yūsuf As'ad complains about the phenomenon: "it is unusual to find a quiet group that has a spiritual program and a roster to divide tasks. Three visitors is enough. Too many take the *baraka* away."[2] There are monasteries who face over one thousand guests daily. In order to regulate this stream of visitors, there is a strict protocol for receiving them. First, the guest father, the monk in charge of receiving the guests, gives the group a tour around the churches, reliquaries, and antiquities of the monastery. The father gives a brief account of the history, saintly monks, and the relics and bodies that are buried in the monastery. The people then get time for prayer, for lighting candles, and writing supplications to the saint on a pieces of paper that are wedged behind the saint's icon or deposited in the casket. After the tour has finished, guests are led to the monastery's kiosk where they can purchase pamphlets which contain details on the lives of the saints, spiritual lectures, and small pictures of the saints or saintly monks. After that, in most of the monasteries, the group is then directed outside the walls again.

The convents, less famous than the monasteries, lack accommodations. Consequently, the convents are spared large numbers of religious tourists. In general, the convents receive guests on Fridays and Sundays, although the schedule may differ from convent to convent. During official periods of fasting, most of the convents are closed. Monks, priests, and bishops also like to visit the convents, although the majority of the guests are female.

The world behind the heavy bolted door with the brass knocker seems quite mysterious when a visitor nervously knocks. One visitor remarked, "you have no idea what the nuns are doing. Maybe you disturb them in something important." Standing before the imposing door, the visitor waits for the rustle of the *bawwāba*'s, or doorkeeper's, habit and stands as the doorkeeper inspects the visitor. Once convinced of the guest's respectability, the nun opens wide the door, and the visitor is welcomed. The door is again firmly locked behind with a large brass key and the *bawwāba* rushes off to inform the superior about the visitor. One is always surprised to see the number of people who are present in the churches or in the guest rooms. The large and heavy door to the convent seems to give each visitor the impression that he or she is the first.

People come for manifold reasons, depending on the convent. Most, though, seek to connect with the patron saints or the mother superior. These visitors come for counseling, blessing of the saints, exorcism, or, on some occasions, because they have had a vision of the saint who instructed them to visit the convent. For example, in the book about Umminā Marthā, one finds the account of a man to whom St. Amīr Tādrus appeared, holding a sheep and a knife in his hand. The saint told the astonished man that his wife was going to give birth to a son and that he should donate one sheep to the saint's convent. The woman indeed gave birth to a son, and the father did as he was told. The only problem was that he had no idea where the convent was exactly located. Fortunately the sheep started to walk ahead of him and stopped right at the convent's entrance.[3]

THE POPULAR IMAGE OF THE CONVENTS

What the visitors seek in a convent depends on that convent's popular image among the Copts, who rate its importance on the basis of factors such as its patron saint(s) and the reputation of the superior. Coptic laypeople seem to have constructed a "top five list" of Cairene convents. Some studies on Coptic monasticism that are based on written material, or on oral information provided by some well-informed Copts, simply do not mention certain convents when listing the "convents for Coptic nuns."[4] It is not clear whether certain convents were not deemed important or representative enough to be mentioned in written sources or whether people simply are not aware of their existence. For example, a Coptic woman commented once regarding the Convent of Māri Girgis in Ḥārat Zuweilah by saying "that is not a convent." When pressed about what this institution should be properly called, she answered, "It's just a bunch of women, sitting together and living the life of nuns." Upon further inquiry, the deciding factor in this person's denunciation of the convent was the fact that the nuns are allowed to visit their families once every two years for a day or, if the families are far away, for a week. Older nuns could go outside the convent to visit their families alone, while the younger ones could leave if they were accompanied by an elder nun.

The Coptic Church does not judge the popularity of a convent according to the same standards the laypeople use. The patriarch and the bishops know about all the convents in Cairo and visit them regularly on special occasions and to celebrate the Eucharist. Priests or monks who visit the convents have their own reasons for doing so. For example, maybe a member of their family lives there as a nun, or perhaps the spiritual atmosphere is pleasing. About the same Convent of Māri Girgis, one of the monks at St. Antony's said "Oh, that is my favorite convent. I love to go there because of the pure atmosphere."

In order to find out how the images that exist in the minds of laypeople about the convents in Cairo have been formed, I will describe the way visitors are received in three of the present convents: Deir Abū Saifein and the two convents of Māri Girgis, in Ḥārat Zuweilah and in Old Cairo. In a previous chapter, I have already mentioned the superior of Deir Abū Saifein, Umminā Irīnī. The superior of Deir Māri Girgis in Ḥārat Zuweilah, Umminā Aghāpi, is the only superior left in Cairo who does not originate from the Convent of Abū Saifein. She is considerably older than the other superiors and was not appointed by the patriarch but was chosen by her community. The superior of Deir Māri Girgis in

Old Cairo, Ummināa Yoʾannā, is a pupil of Irīnī. The story goes that the choice of her as superior became clear after a dream she had. Shortly after that the patriarch came, and it was decided she was to be the new superior of Deir Māri Girgis.

Deir Abū Saifein

Deir Abū Saifein is the most frequented of all the convents for women. As we have indicated earlier, this convent's popularity is a recent phenomenon and can be ascribed to the personality of Umminā Irīnī and her promotion of St. Abū Saifein. During the fasting periods the convent is officially closed, but exceptions are made to allow certain visitors. As a result, during a period of closure one can observe groups of people negotiating with the *bawwāba* to enter. When one of these guests is lucky enough to convince the doorkeeper of the necessity of a visit, the guest is often seen crying "*min al-farḥa*" (of joy) to be allowed in. The purpose of such a visit does not have to be a serious or urgent matter. For example, people sometimes come simply to buy goods to have blessings from the convent that members of their family might want to take on a journey.

During the times the convent is officially open (from 9:00 A.M. until 5:00 P.M.), it tends to be filled with church groups and others. As in the monasteries, a standard procedure is applied: there is no conducted tour because convents are much smaller than monasteries, but guests are immediately directed to one of the three churches. Unless the guests are relatives of one of the nuns, the nuns limit their communication to stories about the convent. Groups are met by one of the nuns who has a small discussion with them. At the end of the visit a snack is served as *baraka*, or the convent's special blessing. For example, I once observed the following visit of a group from a retirement home.

While the people were waiting for a nun in one of the churches, the deacon who was their leader told stories about the early monks—how they lived in the desert and combatted the devil. The female volunteers who came to help rushed to answer questions, explain what the deacon said. When the deacon had finished talking, the group started to sing hymns. The visit was a major event for the elderly people. Some of them hoped to take holy oil home to relieve the aches and pains of old age. They also wished to buy scarves with Abū Saifein's picture on it. There were whispers that a miracle might occur. Numerous stories were told and retold about the saint's working of miracles. Somebody suggested that there might be a chance to see Umminā Irīnī because there was the rumor that she had "come down." Finally, one of the nuns arrived and, after greeting the guests, she sat down in front of them on the steps which went up to the altar. In a comfortable squatting position, the nun started to detail the latest miracles wrought by the convent's patron saint. After the third miracle story, she stood up and encouraged the group: "Know that the saints are still living among us and actively involved in our lives as long as we are ready to believe in them and trust them." An approving buzz moved through the group. Some people spontaneously called upon the saint: *"Ishfī rigleeyā yā Abū Saifein!"* (Heal my leg, St. Mercurius!); *"Yā ʿAdhrāʾ, yā Māri Girgis, yā Abū Saifein!"* (Oh Blessed Virgin, Oh St. George, Oh St. Mercurius!). By the time the buzzing quieted down, the nun had already left the church and hastened to another group of guests. After another hymn-sing, the people slowly moved to the exit of the convent. They didn't have the luck to see Irīnī. The whole visit took about two hours.

This story shows that meeting the superior is considered equally as lucky as experiencing a miracle of St. Abū Saifein. When asked why exactly visitors are so intent on meeting Umminā Irīnī, people give answers such as: "After I have met her, I feel much better; I am quiet and feel a great peace." Or "because she is a *qiddīsa* (saint) and *hiyya qurayyib min rabbinā* (close to God)." As observed before, apart from her contacts with the convent's patron saint, some of the virtues people associate with her saintliness are asceticism and an ardent life of prayers. When they are confronted with the remark that all the nuns have this lifestyle and consequently can be equally saintly, people answer: *"humą ḥilwīn, lākin mish qiddīsīn"* (yes, they are good, but not saints). Another proof of Irīnī's saintliness is seen in the fact that she is frequently in retreat. One young woman stated: "of course Umminā Irīnī is a saint; it is very difficult to meet her." Irīnī's nuns indirectly confirm this kind of statement when they tell guests that "it is written in heaven when somebody is destined to meet Irīnī."

When the convent is open to the public, such a number of people ask to see the superior that she has resorted to blessing the visitors during a special audience at the end of the visiting day. After the announcement that Tamauf will start to bless the visitors in half an hour and you can pass by her in the main chapel, the guests queue up to have a successful completion of their visit.

Umminā Irīnī sits on a chair on the left side of the church's altar. For the occasion, nuns have moved the relics of St. Abū Saifein close to the place where she sits, between her and the altar. As the long queue of people shuffle by, Irīnī makes the sign of the cross on the visitors' foreheads and says a few words to some. *"Ez-zayyik?"* (How are you?); *"Entī khaffeetī?"* (Did you recover?); *"Nushkur Rabbinā!* (Thank God!), and *"Zayy al-imtiḥān?* (How is your exam going?). She takes some extra time for parents with a newborn baby. Posted behind her is one of the senior nuns who watches over Irīnī's well–being. If somebody wants to ask too much or talks too long, the mother urges the guest to proceed to the saint's relics and make a prostration at the altar. In her left hand the senior nun holds a bag into which go small gifts, prayer requests, and donations.

Outside the church it is obvious that the people are pleased to merely see and touch Irīnī. These people feel doubly blessed when she has uttered a few words to them. A considerable number of the visitors consists of adolescent girls, women, and couples with young children.[5] Visitors come especially on feast days and prior to important events in the church year, such as the beginning of Lent. In Egypt, visiting holy places on feasts and holidays is a widely practiced custom for both Christians and Muslims.

When the recruitment of novices was discussed previously, I indicated the level of financial and material benefits for a convent when it is popular. Due to its popularity, the Convent of Abū Saifein receives a lot of attention and, as a result, is quite wealthy.

Deir Māri Girgis (Ḥārat Zuweilah)

Between 9:00 A.M. and 5:00 P.M., the door to the Convent of Māri Girgis in Ḥārat Zuweilah is open daily, regardless of fasting periods. After stepping in, one enters a spacious entrance hall. At the end of the hall, a huge mosaic of St. Māri Girgis welcomes the visitor. Next to it sits the nun who is the doorkeeper. After extensive greetings, the guests are directed to the chapel inside the convent and the adjoining room where relics of several saints are displayed. While the guests take blessings from the chapel and the reliquary, the doorkeeper informs the superior, Umminā Aghāpī, about the visitors. Unless she has other obligations, the superior comes to meet the guests. If they happen to come at lunchtime, Umminā Aghāpī joins them for a meal. The guests can stay as long as they wish. Often these guests come to discuss a problem with Aghāpī, who is both deft and quick to observe the needs and problems of the people around her. A story representative of Aghāpī's way of interacting with people follows:

> In the fall of 1990 a young woman came from a village in the Delta to seek Umminā Aghāpī's advice on the man her parents had chosen for her to marry.

The woman was not sure whether or not the man was the right one for her. Aghāpī sat with her and went over the situation. Together, they carefully pored over the couple's ages, education, hobbies, wishes, and dreams. After an hour-long talk, they came to the conclusion that the man was not a bad choice after all, and the woman understood this conclusion. Umminā Aghāpī advised her to go out with the man in order to get to know him better and to put the issue before God who would help to make the final decision. Of course, Aghāpī would remember the woman in her prayers.

Umminā Aghāpī later made a point of following the case up. She phoned the woman regularly until the final decision was made. When the woman happened to visit the convent again one year later, the first question Umminā Aghāpī asked her was, "How do you like married life?"

While Mother Aghāpī meets visitors, nuns drop in and out of the room to ask advice or permission, to remind her that she has forgotten to answer a certain phone call, or to inform her about the arrival of more visitors. From the interaction of Umminā Aghāpī with her nuns, one is aware of the fact that they adore her. Her motherly way of relating to them makes them feel truly like members of a family, which lends a homey atmosphere to the convent. All of the convent's inhabitants are interested in what the guests have to tell and want to learn about the latest political, economic, and social developments. In order to keep in touch with what is happening in the world, and in contrast to the policy in the other convents, these nuns are allowed to read newspapers.

Deir Māri Girgis is financially not as well off as Deir Abū Saifein. The convent is modest and even cramped—sandwiched between buildings. Nevertheless, Umminā Aghāpī managed to renovate the whole abbey and build a bell tower right in the middle of its courtyard. She saved the funds for this tower herself and quietly oversaw its construction. The result is a striking white tower with a cross on top amidst the shabby apartment houses surrounding the convent.

Because the convent's Cairo milieu was quite cramped, Umminā Aghāpī organized a small farm on a detached site on the road to Alexandria. This farm is a pleasant villa with rooms for several nuns or even some visitors, with a spacious garden and a private chapel for daily prayers. The chapel has three altars and Aghāpī herself chose the saints to which each altar is devoted. The convent has a minibus that commutes between Cairo and the annex.

Although St. Māri Girgis is one of the most popular saints in Egypt, people do not come to the convent with great expectations of healings or apparitions. These visitors come, in the words of one, "because it is a peaceful place, filled with prayers all day long. I come here to renew my spiritual strength and enjoy the company of loving people."[6]

The convent has a steady group of visitors and friends who regularly drop in. But not even the feasts of St. Māri Girgis attract large numbers. In spite of the fact that less funds are generated than in the more popular places, Umminā Aghāpī has managed to raise enough for her building projects and to renovate the abbey.

Deir Māri Girgis (Old Cairo)

The system for receiving visitors in Deir Māri Girgis in Old Cairo is very similar to that at Deir Abū Saifein. The convent is closed during fasts and, when it is open, guests are served a refreshment after which they are directed to the convent's churches. As is the case with visitors to Deir Māri Girgis in Ḥārat Zuweilah, people do not come to the convent in Old Cairo expecting miraculous events from the patron saint. Nevertheless, believers say that the power of *baraka* (blessing) pervades the whole place by virtue of its being a convent. Since a few years ago, Umminā Yoʾannā has started to emulate the pattern of celebrating the saint's feasts that is applied in Deir Abū Saifein. For instance, the guests are presented a box with sweets and holy oil that represent the blessings of the saint, there is a *zaffa* (festive procession), and the miracles of St. George are related. Unlike Umminā Irīnī, Yo'annā never tells miracle stories herself, but the people who were healed or had an apparition relate their experiences. As a result the feasts attract more guests than the feasts of the same saint in Umminā Aghāpī's convent, where no miracle stories are told.

During a normal visit people are most interested in the Church of Māri Girgis, where the main attractions are the saint's relics and the so-called chain of martyrs. According to the tradition, this chain was used to torture the early martyrs whose blood gives the chain its beneficial power. The chain is believed to be effective for healings and exorcisms. One can find two of the senior nuns in the church to explain the story of the chain, the saint, and his miracles to the visitors. These two nuns then help visitors who come for healing or special blessing put the chain around the afflicted part.

Because of the area in which it is situated and the feasts that attract quite a number of visitors, this convent is quite well off. But Umminā Yoʾannā has not yet managed to initiate building and renovation projects similar to the ones of Mother Irīnī and Mother Aghāpī. The convent does not have an annex yet. Umminā Yoʾannā lacks the same personal attraction for people as Irīnī or Aghāpī. Consequently, her role in receiving guests and counseling them is more limited.

The way visitors are received and treated again shows the crucial role of the mother superior. If her saintly model fails to draw people, what is left is the general *baraka* of the convent. As observed before, *baraka* prevails in many places and is not a special characteristic of this place alone.

In the three examples described, the personalities of the mother superiors in two—Irīnī and Aghāpī—appeal to people. Both belong to a certain monastic type. This becomes especially clear when other monastic persons, monks and nuns, reveal their reasons for being attracted to the convent. One monk from the Monastery of St. Antony said that the reason he sometimes visited Deir Abū Saifeīn was that Irīnī had known Abūnā Yusṭus. He hoped she would remember things Yusṭus had said or things that had happened. One of the bishops made a special visit to the convent to ask St. Abū Saifein's intercession for the healing of his kidney problem. The rumor goes that Umminā Irīnī offered him a glass of water with a few drops of holy oil. He drank it and the next day he was healed. Another monk from the Monastery of St. Antony likes to frequent Umminā Aghāpī's convent because he feels the more relaxed atmosphere represents monastic life as it "used to be before the general monastic revival." For him the negative side of the revival is that the church hierarchy tries to regulate everything, including daily life in the monasteries and convents. While discussing the implementation of a monastic rule, I have already concluded that there still is not a fixed and firm rule. The attempts of the Holy Synod to create rules are perceived as an intrusion in the lives of the monks. As another reason for his attraction to Umminā Aghāpī, the monk mentioned the fact that she represents the seemingly simple monk or nun. Perhaps these people only pretend to be simple—some seem extremely clever and hide a deep wisdom. Umminā Irīnī represents the type who is in constant communication with the supernatural. So frequent is this, that she cannot hide it; she and her nuns tell the world outside about the messages of the saints.

In observing Umminā Irīnī and Umminā Aghāpī, one notices that both are attentive women—sensitive to the needs of others. During a conversation with them, their eyes are constantly active and they do not miss any details or characteristics, moods or unspoken communications people send out. Both are enterprising and active in making their abbeys worthy places. The difference between them seems to start with their openness to the world and to the Egyptian environment. Umminā Aghāpī's nuns hold normal conversations with people and seem to be more "human" or "normal" than the mostly silent, smiling creatures in Deir Abū Saifein. Everything in Umminā Irīnī's abbey is incredibly clean, relative to the norm in Egyptian society. The nuns themselves dress correctly, with their habits always immaculate—thus conveying the right monastic symbols. At Umminā Aghāpī's abbey, a nun can move around in a plain *gallābīya* (the ordinary Egyptian outfit for manual work).

As observed before, it is exceptional in the Coptic milieu that a monastic like Irīnī talks about her experiences with the spiritual world. When people visit a monastic place, the atmosphere can easily become electric with expectations of saintly interventions. People are willing to declare somebody a saint on the basis of the smallest events. The Coptic hierarchy tries to discourage this kind of behavior in constant public speeches and sermons. Faith should be based on a belief in God, Jesus, and the Bible and not be channeled into excessive veneration of persons—especially when they are still alive. Umminā Irīnī is aware of all this. A cult around her personality would pose a serious challenge to the existing hierarchy. She tries to prevent the building of a cult by her scarce appearances and by seldom talking to people directly about apparitions or her visions. The stories are related to visitors by Irīnī's nuns.[7] Nevertheless, stories are made up, and her absence is seen as a sign of her special gifts. With regard to the church authorities, she is in a situation full of contradictions. On the one hand, members from the church hierarchy respect her and seek her advice precisely because of her spiritual contacts. On the other hand, she is rebuked by the church hierarchy for being public about them and drawing an undue amount of attention to her convent. After all, the patriarch is the convent's official head, not she. The patriarch does not approve of the public independent role Irīnī has started to play in the life of the church.[8] At the same time, there are few sanctions the church hierarchy can impose, because outwardly she does not trespass on any of the written rules. She can always refer to the fact that it is the people who ascribe certain supernatural faculties to her. One could not easily prove whether or not Irīnī encouraged this in any way. Finally, one should not forget that Irīnī lives an austere and ascetic life. Her relationship with the saints is not the only aspect of her holiness. People value her advice because of her spiritual insights. For example, Egyptian Christians from other denominations regularly seek her advice in important matters. In addition, there are mother superiors of other Catholic orders who consult Irīnī concerning important decisions in their orders.[9]

THE ACTIVE SISTERS AND VISITORS

The system of the active community is not centered around one superior. The sisters do not promote a certain saint or strive to emulate a specific lifestyle that is perceived to be traditionally Coptic. The way the sisters deal with visitors differs greatly from the way guests are received in contemplative convents. First of all, people do not come to these convents with high expectations about the supernatural. Second, the sisters are very open to receiving guests—Egyptian or foreign—for discussions and sharing of the communal meal. Finally guests are allowed to speak with any of the sisters. People come to get practical help and advice, to discuss problems, or to discuss spiritual matters or matters of faith. Instead of directing their guests to a reliquary, the members of the community either read the Bible or pray with them about their particular problem.

MUSLIM VISITORS

All the contemplative convents have a certain number of Muslim visitors. Most of the regular visitors are people who work inside the convent or live around it. Some come in time of crises following the advice of Coptic friends. These people seek the blessing of the saint in order to acquire healing or the solution to a problem, or, especially at Deir Amīr Tādrus, they come for exorcism. Around the time of certain feasts one can observe a regular flow of Muslims who seem to be acquainted with one of the convents. Some convents, for example Deir Māri Girgis in Ḥārat Zuweilah, hand out daily packages with food to a number of poor Muslims who live in the vicinity.

Most of the Muslim visitors come for the saint's relics and cannot participate in the sacramental symbols. Muslims will not venerate or kiss the icons, pray the "Our Father," make the sign of cross, or join in with a *tamgīd* (song of glorification) for the saint. Most of the time the Muslims leave the convent before the Copts do. On crowded occasions, such as the saint's feast, one rarely sees a Muslim among the guests. The standard question at the door, before one is allowed to enter during a *ʿeid* (feast) is "which church do you belong to?" This questioning shows that Muslims are not expected to attend such happenings. In addition, due to the small space inside the walled convent, priority is given to Coptic guests.

In a previous chapter, I indicated that this situation is different during the more public and bigger *maulids*. These *maulids* are held in more spacious areas and are composed of activities other than church services. Hence more Muslims come to the convents to seek the saint's blessing. During a feast in a convent, the festivities mainly concentrate on special services in the church.

In the convents, Muslim visitors are treated kindly and are more or less tolerated—but there are limits. For monastics, the Muslim world outside mainly consists of government officials who refuse to issue permissions for buildings or renovations in and around the convent. Additionally, the Bedouins, who were described earlier, come to mind. Whatever the actual situation might have been, this view of the outside, predominantly Muslim world implies an environment that is hostile to the nuns. Thus, the interior of the convent is designed to be purely Coptic—an oasis.

EXORCISM

Each of the Coptic saints has more or less a specialty that draws both Coptic and Muslim visitors. At present, the two outstanding convents and their specialties are St. Abū Saifein for healing and St. Amīr Tādrus for exorcism. This does not mean that miracles occurring through intercession of these saints are limited to these convents. Like St. Mary and St. Māri Girgis, these saints can be called upon for many other reasons. But, as the Copts say, in order to get a prompt response from the saint, one has to have developed a strong relation with him or her.[10] Muslim visitors who lack this strong relation come only in times of serious illness or distress and hence are mostly attracted by the saint's specialty.

Exorcism is an area where Muslims regularly use the services of Copts. Muslims can go to a church that has a renowned priest, to a *maulid,* to a monastery or convent that regularly conducts ceremonies to exorcise spirits.[11] Both Copts and Muslims believe in the existence of *jinn ʿifrīt* (evil spirits), because spirits are mentioned in both the Bible and Qurʾān.[12] Certain priests or monks are well known for exorcism.[13] According to popular belief, spirits can enter a person when he or she is vulnerable—in the dark, having fallen on the floor, in certain houses, or in the toilet. Christians and Muslims do not hold the same views about spirits. Copts see possession as the result of weak faith. In order to get rid of a spirit, the victim's faith has to be restored.[14] This means that a priest or monk, after learning the spirit's name, will first try to cast out the spirit by reciting psalms, making the sign of the cross on the victim's forehead with holy oil, or putting the priest's handcross on the victim's head.[15] Sometimes a picture of a saint will be put on the head of the possessed person so that the saint can give the victim "a feeling of fire." "It burns, it burns," one can hear the person cry out.[16] Sometimes people get this feeling of burning after merely passing by an icon.

The procedure of exorcism involves psalms, the cross, pictures of the saints, and holy oil and is the same for Copts and Muslims.[17] The treatment differs after the spirit has left the person (often through the toe where it is reported that sometimes the sign of the cross appears in blood). A Copt will receive advice on how to become strong in faith—frequent church attendance, prayers, reading the Bible and histories of the saints, and the like. Also, some practical advice is given, such as to stay away from bad places and bad influences. For Muslims this procedure is not applicable. Muslims see spirits in a different light. When a spirit enters a person, it has nothing to do with one's faith. According to the Muslims, during an exorcism a spirit might refuse to leave or the person might need more than one session. When the spirit refuses to leave, a Muslim can placate the spirit. For example, a Muslim may attend a *zār*—a special gathering, mostly for women, during which people dance to appease the spirit. No attempt is made, however, to rid a person of her spirit.[18] This "flirting" with evil spirits and attending a *zār* is absolutely forbidden by the Coptic Church.

When people come to the convent to remove an evil spirit—whether the seekers are Copts or Muslims—the nuns take them to the saint's icon and give them some pictures of the saint, holy oil, or water. Because women are unable to exorcise spirits, the nuns try to find a priest or monk. According to the nuns themselves, one needs the sacrament of priesthood in order to drive out evil spirits—but there is no official explanation for this. In the case of Deir Amīr Tādrus, the powerful presence of Amīr Tādrus, in combination with the sacramental function of a monk or priest, is the key to a successful casting out of the evil spirit.

NUNS AND LAYWOMEN

Coptic women and girls make up the greater part of the visitors to the convents. In a previous chapter, the role of nuns as models for Coptic women in a changing society is discussed. The presence of nuns proves that valid options are available to women apart from the traditional role of wife and mother. However, with other Egyptian women nuns share the expectations and limitations society imposes on them. Furthermore, as role models, nuns belong to a religious/social system in which importance and influence are governed by the popular interpretation of laity on the basis of the nun's charismatic appeal: zeal, sacrifice, and so on.

One item to evaluate in this study is the nuns' position with regard to laypeople. In order to assess this, one should compare the nuns against other women by studying certain aspects of the lives of Egyptian women in general. This also provides some hints concerning the nuns' position in the social hierarchy.

Although Coptic women have their own networks and support systems, their situation is closely linked to the condition of Egyptian women in general. For example, when Mervat Hatem argues that during the 1970s and 1980s the economic and political prospects for women in Egypt have diminished, this observation concerns women from both groups.[19] However, because of the difference in religion, there are aspects of this situation that are specifically Coptic and others that are Muslim; several of these are determinant in evaluating the position of Coptic nuns. Religion dominates Egyptian culture, and many values, morals, and superstitions concerning women follow from this circumstance.

Recently, much research has been done on the topic of women in the Arab world. But the subject of most studies is Muslim women; only a few studies focus on Coptic women.[20] More extensive research is needed to discuss the social, cultural, economic, and legal differences between the position of a Coptic and of a Muslim woman in Egypt.[21] For the present context, I will limit the comparison to the following points: a woman's role in the family and in society and the topic of segregation and modesty.

A Woman's Role in the Family

Based on the text of Ephesians 5:22–6:3, "For the husband is the head of the wife as Christ is the head of the church" (5:23), the Coptic man is considered the head of the household. But the Coptic Church constantly admonishes men to treat their wives with respect and love because the two are interdependent and because each is equal according to Christ.[22] Muslim authors equally have emphasized complementary sex roles.[23] Riffat Hassan argues that "in spite of the Qurʾanic affirmation of man-woman equality, Muslim societies in general have never regarded men and women as equal, particularly in the context of marriage."[24]

Since divorce is forbidden in principle by the Coptic Church, a Coptic woman's position within the family is far more secure than that of a Muslim woman. This security is connected with the fact that "Muslim personal-status law does not support the family as a unit to the extent that Christian law and custom does."[25] One result of this situation is that Coptic husbands and wives share their property, while in Muslim households possessions are carefully distinguished.[26]

A nun has left her natural family to become a member of the monastic family. In the natural family, there is almost always a man who is in charge. In case the husband is missing, a father, brother, uncle, or cousin will see to the protection of the woman. The great majority of Egyptian women depend on male protectors. Women are perceived by men in the society as weak and thus needing to be protected from danger. Nuns face the same situation as many other women in Egypt. Not only does their cloistered life keep them inside the convent, but also nuns are thought to be in danger when they are away from the protective structure of the convent. The nuns are considered vulnerable because they are women and because they fear that their monastic garb might arouse adverse reactions from non-Christians. As far as male protection for nuns is concerned, two aspects show the nuns' dependence on the ecclesiastical hierarchy: first, the patriarch is the official head of the convent, and, second, the nuns depend on a man for the central spiritual moment—the Eucharist. The difference between nuns and laywomen is that men can never interfere with the business inside the convents.

Women's Role in Society

Despite opportunities for women to work outside the home and to assume new responsibilities, the middle-class ideal that the husband should earn enough for the woman to stay at home still prevails in Egypt.[27] For both the Copts and the Muslims, a woman's role as wife and mother should not be jeopardized by employment.[28] Islamic society sees the role of women as sustaining, nurturing, and raising children in the Islamic faith.[29] The Copts agree that a woman's main concern should be "the bearing and nursing of a healthy child." By doing this, she helps to build "the city of God."[30]

By taking the veil, a nun has moved into circles where different rules reign concerning one's career. Successful professional women in Egypt, as Earl Sullivan has found, often come from a privileged social and economic background and have a higher degree of education. Almost all of these women comply with the expectations of their environment and combine a career with marriage and raising a family.[31] In these respects, nuns—contemplative and active—are not subject to the general cultural climate. Once inside the convent, nuns can attain privileged positions regardless of their backgrounds or education. For active nuns, monastic life often creates possibilities for work and study that would never occur otherwise.

Segregation and Modesty

Islamic society and Coptic society both seem to prefer that women accomplish certain tasks among and for women as teachers, social workers, and medical personnel.[32] Of course, there are women who pursue different careers. In church work, the active nuns and the consecrated women tend to be mainly involved in nurturing and sustaining activities among women. Actually, the category of consecrated women was specially developed to serve this purpose.

Segregation is also maintained in many religious activities; for example in Coptic churches women sit on one side and the men on the other. For both Copts and Muslims, leaders of official gatherings are always men. In the discussion about hierarchy, I have already mentioned reasons for this phenomenon among the Copts. In Islam, male leaders are also perceived as knowing more about their religion than women.[33] The Coptic Church nevertheless encourages women to pursue studies at the Coptic seminary. The degree they earn will not lead to priesthood but equips the women to be leaders within their own groups. Several have become professors at the seminary where most of the students are male. In unofficial Muslim gatherings, for example, among the Sufis, one can also find women in religious roles.[34] For the Copts, segregation is limited to the public realm. At home with the family, men and women are never separated. This is also the case for many social and cultural activities (including church activities).

A burning issue in Islamic society is that, for reasons of modesty, women should clad their bodies in garments that only display face and hands. As Valerie Hoffman-Ladd has concluded: "The entire body of a woman (except her face and hands) is to be treated as pudenda; it is a vulnerable, weak object that must be covered to avoid embarrassment and shame—even the voice of a women should not be heard.[35] From the Coptic side one hears that "a woman is female, and as such a point of attraction and a serious form of temptation, by her voice, her face and the form of her body, indeed by every movement and action. Therefore, as long as we live in the body we must avoid exposing the body to temptation, especially in church."[36] However, urban Coptic women never dress in long garments and wear mainly Western, always modest (knees and elbows are covered), styles. Only during the time of Communion in church is a woman required to cover her head with a scarf or even simply with a napkin.[37] As a woman, a nun can be a source of temptation. During her life, she will not raise her voice or dress in provocative garments. In fact, all the rules concerning segregation and modesty are equally applicable to nuns.

So how does a nun who is "dead to the world" fit into the Egyptian social system? Strictly speaking, she has no part in society. As noted above, there are many similarities between nuns and laywomen. As laywomen are not equal to men in the society, nuns are not considered equal to monks or other members of the clergy. An illustration of this point was inadvertently given by Patriarch Shenouda III when he was asked during an interview how many monastic communities there were in Egypt. He answered that there were twelve communities, failing to mention the convents.[38]

A nun derives her social status from her spiritual work. Her unusual choice of celibacy has made her sui generis. Within Coptic circles, and among Muslims who know about the monastic lifestyle, a nun is considered a person who prays for the good of all people. Her virginal state represents the "New Eve"—one who has overcome the barrier of sex and reached the state where there is "neither male nor female" (Gal. 3:28).[39] A nun is what Mary Douglas calls "a virgin source of redemption crushing evil underfoot."[40] Thus, by her profession and in spite of the fact that strictly speaking she does not belong to society, a nun is placed on a different level of the social hierarchy than a laywoman—Coptic or Muslim.

Laypeople's Attitudes Toward the Nuns

The reactions of laypeople toward the nuns show that they consider nuns on a higher level than ordinary believers. Copts regard their monastics as creatures who have left this world, but who have not yet entered heaven. By their choice to become monastics, these people have sacrificed individual lives for the good of the whole Coptic community for whom they pray and intercede relentlessly. Active nuns are always ready to care for believers in times of distress. And as for contemplative nuns, laygirls or laywomen are heartened by just seeing them from a distance.

According to the nuns, many women wish to join this perfect company but few succeed. The result of strong admiration for contemplative nuns, in particular, is that some laywomen perceive themselves as inferior because of their ordinary married life. This perception can lead to exaggerations such as: "Oh, I am going to marry; now I'll go to hell."

The young woman who made this remark felt that marriage would take her away from God. Nuns try to discuss these feelings with women, especially by pointing out to them that several saints were married; that without the prayers of women like Monica, the mother of Augustine, this great church father would never have converted; and, of course, they stress the importance of St. Mary, the mother of Christ.

The situation remains nevertheless ambiguous. In spite of their encouraging talks with laywomen, the nuns' behavior often produces the admiration of outsiders. The nuns are extremely secretive about their lives. For example, in the Convent of St. Dimyānah, visitors never see any of the nuns except for the superior and the nuns in charge of the guest house and the kiosk (with religious paraphernalia for sale). As a result, when visitors spot a nun on the roof of the convent they become nearly ecstatic. As we have mentioned, several of the convents do not volunteer the exact number of nuns. All the nuns in Upper Egypt will say is that the number of nuns is *baraka*. In most of the convents, the nuns just smile politely and hardly speak a word with outsiders. When laypeople ask questions about the nuns' lives, they seldom get a straightforward answer—even when the questions concern topics described in published material. Once, during a talk about monastic life to a group of adolescent girls, the presenting nun was asked whether nuns cut their hair or not. She answered that this information was the *sirr al-rāhibāt* (secret of the nuns). But, in any book about the initiation rites, one can find this information—cutting the hair belongs to the earliest monastic traditions for women.

This secrecy can be seen as a protective mechanism. The less that is known about the conditions inside a convent, the less the outside world (clergy, government) can interfere. At the same time, the effect of withholding information from outsiders can only create mysterious images of the convents and their inhabitants. In this way the nuns can also uphold their image as "angels on earth" and prevent the world from seeing their humanity. The nuns of Deir Māri Girgis in Ḥārat Zuweilah are exceptional because they are more approachable as human beings. The active sisters insist that people see how human and fallible they are and at the same time how they try to live in mutual love and harmony.

The reactions of contemplative nuns to women who express the wish to become nuns are further reasons for outsiders to view monastics as "special beings." Contemplative nuns seldom react enthusiastically to potential candidates or even say that theirs is a wonderful life. Words such as *ṣaʿb* (hard, difficult) and *taʿab* (trouble, tiring) are used to describe the monastic life. All these factors contribute to the molding of the image of contemplative nuns and their convents.

SUMMARY

Contemplative and active convents play an important role for members of the Coptic community—more for women than for men. Convents serve as places where one can get blessings, intercessions, miraculous cures, counseling, and encouragement. In fact, contemplative convents are not cut off from the world.

The public uses different criteria to assess a convent's effectiveness with regard to different areas in life that need problems solved. But the convents that have charismatic superiors are esteemed the most. This seems to appeal to the need of laypeople for miraculous events, close contact with the saints, and a certain holy "otherness" from which one can derive blessing. For the majority, just being in a place of prayer does not seem to be sufficient.

From their side, some contemplatives create a shroud of mystery around their lives in order to protect themselves and uphold the image of "angels on earth." This kind of behavior may lend itself at times to the cult of personality. The active community is more human—thus, less distant and not idolized.

Compared to other women, nuns hold a special position, and their careers are shaped according to different parameters. Nonetheless, their lives are equally governed by the current cultural and social attitudes. In the social and spiritual hierarchy the contemplative nuns obviously rank highest.

Muslim visitors play a marginal role in the system of regular visits to convents. These visitors come with specific needs and seldom entertain a special relation with the convent.

Conclusion

One of the major questions guiding this study has been: Who are the contemporary Coptic nuns and how did they manage to carve out a place within the hierarchic framework of the Coptic Church? All of the actors discussed—the contemplative and active nuns, and sometimes the consecrated women and the monks—operate within the Coptic Church and their position is inextricably bound up with the position, state, and beliefs of the Coptic community and Coptic Church. The revitalization of this church actually prompted the development of a role for Coptic religious women. What one should try to understand is what the nuns did to develop their role in the Coptic Church, and from what points of reference in social and religious life these actions emerged.[1]

The Coptic revival started at the end of the nineteenth century and was influenced by several internal and external factors. Inspired by the example of other churches, concerned lay Copts and clergy tried to revive the church from within. Trends of Egyptian re-Islamization also induced the Coptic community to defend its interests.[2] Several trends that emerged from this revival are still current. In analyzing and describing the present Coptic monastic landscape, the key words for the situation of female monastics seem to be *transition* and *redefinition*. Experiments are still taking place which create new positions and possibilities for women who want to live religious lives.

Traditionally, the Coptic Church with the patriarch at its head, has been the structure defending the welfare of the Coptic community. In spite of countless efforts by laypeople, this structure alone proved able to develop strategies which revived the Coptic Church and equipped it to face the new religious and social challenges produced by modern society. The most prominent Coptic figure who initiated this revival was the "holy man" Patriarch Kyrillos VI (1959–1971). Through his efforts, lives of prayer and intercession of saints received renewed attention. This kind of devotional life had been practiced by the Copts for centuries but had grown lax.

Kyrillos' example drew many well-educated, young laypeople who had been active in the church's projects. These people became aware of the importance of the monastic heritage and the role of the clergy and formed the generation that is governing and reforming the Coptic Church at present: Patriarch Shenouda III, Bishop Athanasius, Father Mattā al-Meskīn, and the late Bishop Samuel, among others. Shenouda complemented Kyrillos' charismatic attraction by structuring and organizing Coptic groups and projects.[3]

Kyrillos also encouraged women to participate in church work. He granted contemplative nuns the freedom to pursue their projects. For example, when Umminā Marthā wanted to build a church next to her convent, he sent her a letter with his approval and encouragement.[4] Supposedly, he granted Umminā Irīnī special executive powers to purchase land and sign contracts herself which encouraged her to undertake projects for her convent.

In this revival, the contemplative nuns followed Kyrillos' monastic pattern. Umminā Marthā was their first known exponent and little is known about the women who were her models. Through her sayings and actions she fashioned a style that was solidly anchored in the Coptic tradition. She set the example for the "true monastic life" through her continuous practice of monastic prayers, her reverence for the Eucharist, her strengthening of the Coptic religious heritage, and her direct connection with the sacred.[5] Mother Martha's sayings underlined the role of the Coptic Church as a witness to the Christian faith in times of troubles and decline. She was one of the inspirations for Umminā Irīnī, who continued the trends and expanded the realm of action for contemplative nuns.

For their part, the active nuns have pursued vocations that were also inspired by Kyrillos. He gave the active community his special blessings when it started as a pilot project in Beni Suef. Changing conditions in society demanded the development of social programs. By ordaining a special bishop for ecumenical and social affairs, Kyrillos showed his concern for the agenda of social development and saw the importance of creating a place for active nuns in the structure of the church. During the time that he was the patriarch, the theological rationale for this type of work was developed. To give this work recognition and to incorporate it into church activities, a clericalization of lay activities took place which had profound consequences for women who sought church work as a career. The active community in Beni Suef was founded as a result of these new programs and was later followed by the experiments with the *mukarrasāt*.

In finding new lifestyles, contemplative and active nuns tried to create, maintain, and reinforce links with the Coptic heritage. Through these links, the nuns tried to legitimize different aspects of their vocations. For directing a convent, one noted that there was no clear rule available comparable to a Catholic monastic rule. The pivot of the governing system is the spiritual guide who sets individual rules for each nun. The pattern of the contemplatives brings to mind St. Dimyānah and her forty virgins. The mother superior is the visible face of the community and interacts with the world outside the convent on behalf of the nuns. The rest, like so many women in the Middle East, remain invisible. This provides the mother superior with a high degree of independence and authority within her convent. She has the final say in everything. This system is based on personal relationships. When personalities clash, or a mother superior becomes despotic, the result can be oppression for the nuns. Nobody from the outside can interfere when the superior becomes despotic, not even the patriarch. In case of a conflict, the only solution for the individual nun is to leave the convent. Outside the convent she is left without a support system to fall back on. She can neither leave the monastic vocation nor return to her family. The lack of any provisions for this kind of situation reflects the Coptic attitude toward monastics: they are supposed to be perfect creatures who never run into conflict within the churchly order. This type of situation also reveals some of the birth pangs of the revival process.

In the active community the superior lacks the authoritarian power a contemplative superior possesses. This provides a safeguard against a tyrannical abbess. The bishop is the spiritual guide, but his guidance leaves personal freedom for his disciples. A picture on the cover of one of the actives' publications illustrates the sisters' strategy of identification: a group of nuns each holding a burning candle. This picture refers to the parable of the wise virgins and conveys the message that they feel equal to the contemplative nuns.

The *mukarrasāt* lack these recognizable structures and connections with the Coptic tradition. These women do not have female superiors but work for bishops or priests. They do not identify themselves as holy women. Of course, the diaconal vocation is mentioned in the Bible but has been somehow forgotten among the Copts. Hence *mukarrasāt* are respected for their work, but the Coptic mind has not yet managed to classify them.

The prominence of monasticism in the Coptic Church probably explains why nearly every young Coptic woman dreams of becoming a contemplative nun. Through the improved Coptic system of religious education, young women are drawn to the monastic life. The active community and the *mukarrasāt* draw many candidates who were rejected in one of the contemplative convents. Some of the candidates had a confessor who encouraged them to then pursue an active vocation. By trying to follow a certain theme from tradition, the active community is creating a recognizable image. As a result, the active nuns have become more accepted as a respectable alternative to the contemplative convent.

After initiation, the nuns become "dead to the world" and are perceived as "angels on earth." Monastics are more or less suspended between heaven and earth. Their clothes and their cells symbolize this state. Contemplative nuns are set apart to pray for humanity—they are the intercessional backbone of the church and as such combat the demons of this world. This is the contemplatives' version of being "warriors for Christ." Instead of feeling hampered by the limitations of their gender, the nuns feel lucky because it enables them to devote their lives solely to prayer. This work of prayer reflects the Coptic ideal that all Christians can achieve holiness while they are still on earth. Contemplative nuns excel in achieving this common goal on behalf of the whole community. The nuns' work is to befriend what one mother called: "the three friends of humanity: asceticism, holiness, and love." She explained that "asceticism brings us half-way up the road. Holiness, or a holy life, leads us to the end of the road where we find the door to heaven. Love gives us guidance and strength to stand in front of God and our Lord Jesus." Active nuns undergo the same initiation rites as contemplative nuns and, strictly speaking, should be considered "angels on earth" as well. Their lifestyle, cells, and clothes, however, prevent this image from materializing.

Contemplative nuns feel a spiritual responsibility for and solidarity with the Coptic believers for whom they pray. The active vocations realize this responsibility and show solidarity through their work. The actives strive to imitate Christ's earthly mission of turning to the poor, the needy, and the oppressed. A female Coptic scholar expressed the way the Copts see the relation between active and contemplative nuns: "The holy mothers [contemplatives] are the source of spiritual powers. This means that their main role consists of prayers through which they create a direct contact with God. The serving sisters [active nuns] receive their spiritual resources from these prayers and transform them into actions. Through their social work, the active nuns indirectly pass the spiritual resources on to the Coptic community."[6]

Each type of vocation explains its activities using examples from the early fathers or highlights special connections with a saint. Work enables them to gain a certain degree of financial independence from (male) benefactors, or, in case of the active nuns, from the Coptic Church.

Among the contemplative nuns Umminā Marthā and Ummināa Irīnī, in particular, managed to achieve a high degree of autonomy. Next to her convent Martha built a church dedicated to St. Amīr Tādrus. Laypeople who attended the services visited the convent afterward and became acquainted with its patron saint. Consequently St. Amīr Tādrus, Martha, and her nuns became more prominent in the Coptic community. Irīnī took the step of building farms in the desert—the place where women had been banned due to their supposed weakness. Because Irīnī's activities were originally given imprimatur by Patriarch Kyrillos VI, in effect nobody can curtail her works. This situation forms a potential source of friction within the highest levels of Coptic male hierarchy who, on the basis of their interpretation of scripture, tradition, and culture, cannot tolerate self-reliant women.

Apart from their devotional work and the manual activities undertaken for income, the contemplatives took upon themselves the role of mediators—a familiar role for women in the Middle East. Instead of being matchmakers for weddings, the nuns mediate between heaven and earth. In all of their activities, the nuns enhance the Coptic heritage and provide the Coptic community with a wellspring of Coptic culture.

The active nuns have undertaken the traditional female tasks of nursing and education. These nuns refer to biblical figures and early fathers such as St. Shenute as legitimization for their activities. Concomitant with traditional activities, active nuns stretch the realm of responsibilities for women within the Coptic Church. Along with their work, the nuns lead Bible studies and provide pastoral care and religious guidance for women and men. For both contemplative and active nuns, segregation in work prevails—women mainly serve women.

The male initiators of the revival served as models for the contemplative and active nuns as well. Few female models were available. The prime model of Christian life for Kyrillos had been the virtually unknown desert hermit ʿAbd-al-Masīḥ al-Ḥabashī. Living in the desert, and spending his days in praise of God, al-Ḥabashī showed Kyrillos how the Christian keeps him or herself unpolluted in a world filled with disturbances. This pattern was a vivid reminder of the lives of the desert fathers. The desert fathers functioned as prototypes and continue to do so. According to the needs of the times, the lives of the desert fathers began to be replayed in modern life. The lives of the desert fathers helped shape the tradition which is an anchor for the Copts. The themes of the stories of the desert fathers and mothers are kept alive by the monastics.

Other models, both male and female, came from the era of the martyrs. These martyrs had been heroic in clinging to their faith and, according to the hagiographic material, had frequently received support of the angels, St. Mary, or Jesus Christ who came to console, encourage, or heal them. For the Copts, what occurred yesterday is re-enacted today.

The contemplative nuns also participated in this living tradition. These nuns seek to imitate the way the desert fathers and mothers dressed, prayed, fasted, read the Bible, and had access to the sacred. Thus, they have become female models of Coptic life and truly Coptic resources for the laypeople.

Within the framework of the same spiritual and devotional life, the active sisters follow another line of the tradition—they do not withdraw from the world to keep themselves undefiled but face it by trying to alleviate its woes in a practical way. Their models are not well known among the Copts. Thus, the actives had to create other references within the tradition. These nuns point out that there are other models besides the unmarried contemplative desert fathers and mothers. For instance, Sister Hannah served as a prototype for the new tradition of active sisters.

For the Coptic public, the role of the active sisters is somehow not traditional and as such not truly Coptic. Many consider it a foreign phenomenon that was imported by the Latin Catholics. Through their work, the active sisters serve as models for Coptic laywomen, much as the contemplatives do. But in Coptic piety the ideal still is the purely contemplative life, hence the active nuns find themselves not as highly regarded as the contemplatives. One can conclude however, that both Coptic contemplative and active nuns play a significant role in the revival of their church by their activities and position as models, especially for Coptic women.

From the material presented, one can also conclude that the reformation of the Coptic Church was brought about by a deliberate and conscious reconstruction of the Coptic system of tradition, asceticism, holiness, and saints.[7] Patriarch Kyrillos VI provided the necessary holy model while the present patriarch, Shenouda III, has built a more efficient system to manage the Coptic Church. Shenouda's weekly public Bible study, in combination with the manifold religious publications produced by him and several of the bishops and priests, educate the community concerning correct Coptic theology and tradition. Judging by their activities, one can observe that contemplative as well as active nuns all participate in this process of reconstructing and reviving Coptic culture.

In this Coptic universe there is, strictly speaking, no place for Muslims who entered Egypt after the time of the heroic Coptic age. The Copts prefer to stress their pre-Islamic tradition that has not been contaminated by the Muslim environment. However, common beliefs and customs between Copts and Muslims attract some Muslims to the convents. These Muslims venerate the Christian saints, in particular St. Mary, the Mother of Christ, and come with expectations of miracles or exorcism. Muslim visitors respect the nuns and ask for their prayers and intercessions. But the main role Muslims play for the Coptic convents is indirect. The Muslim environment has created a need for truly Coptic places. Whether or not there is interreligious strife, Copts have to live with the reality of "the abiding instinct of Islam to conscious superiority and dominance."[8] This reality may have contributed to an antiworldly attitude in the Coptic consciousness. Islam has become equated with the evil of the world that Copts prefer to avoid. Muslims embody the challenge of the worldly evils that can be utilized as a means to "earn a crown" in the life to come on the basis of suffering, patience, and endurance. Convents and monasteries, by virtue of their Copticness, whether or not intentionally, probably contribute to the ambiguous attitude of Copts with regard to the world.

Summing up the position of contemplative nuns in the three levels of hierarchy, from the outset it has been clear that women have no place in the ecclesiastical hierarchy. As initiated monastics, the nuns participate in the unofficial side of this hierarchy. This does not provide them with any ecclesiastical power but does grant a certain spiritual authority. The mother superior can become a spiritual guide, and all the nuns can act as religious advisers for laypeople. People will ask nuns for prayers and blessings, gifts which are regarded with the same importance as a monk's prayers or blessings.

A monk only becomes a member of the ecclesiastical hierarchy when he is ordained a priest. Likewise, the bestowal of the great skema was used to grant an official recognition of spiritual authority. The abolition of this degree contains a veiled statement that contemporary superiors of convents and monasteries are considered to be managers of some sort and not official holy women. Inadvertently, the abolition of the great skema deprived women of their only possible "spiritual ordination." Some of the superiors did become more manager types, but the most successful superiors combine this managing position with the old model of holy woman.

The authority of active nuns is enhanced by the fact that they are allowed to speak about religious topics in public meetings. On account of their active vocation, these nuns could never be candidates for the great skema. Hence, they lack the spiritual authority associated with that state. For these same reasons, *mukarrasāt* lack a strong spiritual authority.

On the whole, Copts consider contemplative nuns, active nuns, and *mukarrasāt* to be of higher status than laywomen (or laymen). The monastics' choice of celibacy is considered virtuous. The nuns represent the "New Eve" and thus surpass in status Coptic laywomen who are married. However, as is true on the ecclesiastical level, nuns remain subordinate to comparable males.

The level of the spiritual or divine hierarchy is where the contemplative nuns excel in spiritual exercises and relate to the saints, a situation which causes them to surpass all the social conventions governing women. In principle, anyone can attain a high position in the spiritual hierarchy. But, because of their lifestyle, monastics are more prone to achieve higher levels than laypeople. The more time devoted to worship and prayers, the better equipped nuns become to develop contacts with the saints. Through these contacts and a holy life, nuns gain spiritual authority and find a rank in the spiritual hierarchy. Contact with the holy makes the nuns into holy beings who are removed from outsiders, lay and clerical, and grants them a place in the spiritual cosmology.

There are certain differences between saintly women and men. There are no pictures available of saintly women, as there are of saintly men, in particular clergy like Patriarch Kyrillos VI. Because nuns do not hold hand crosses, they can not use this powerful symbol in a process of healing or blessing. Nevertheless, Mother Martha and Mother Irīnī do bless people by making the sign of the cross on their foreheads, often combined with the use of holy oil. Supposedly, Patriarch Kyrillos invested Irīnī with a special power to anoint the sick with holy oil. This type of unction belongs, strictly speaking, to the priestly office. The case of Umminā Irīnī shows that a high rank in the spiritual hierarchy can provoke frictions within the hierarchy of her church. She has broken through the regular conventions concerning power of authority over her milieu.

Once the holy nun dies and joins the community of saints in heaven, her spiritual authority can be openly acknowledged. While the final resting place of most monks and nuns is not known, Martha's grave can be found in the church she built—situated in an alcove of the sanctuary, next to the altar dedicated to St. Amīr Tādrus. Believers come to touch it for *baraka* and to ask for Martha's intercessions.

In the spiritual hierarchy, the active nuns do not hold a special position parallel to the contemplatives—they simply serve people's needs within the social hierarchy. Based on their lives of prayer, the active nuns provide religious counseling. Their connections with the saints belong more to the realm of private piety and are not a public trademark. In the monastic spectrum, appreciation by the Coptic community is closely connected with whether a monastic type is readily recognizable or not. Thus the active nuns pointed at other models in the tradition. For them, Sister Hannah was a gift of God sent to serve their specific needs and circumstances. In their capacity as active nuns, they show that everyone can lead a holy life. Indirectly, these actives point to the dangers of a system where veneration of saints receives too much attention. Their way of working silently points to the question of how one can appreciate a worldview that considers the supernatural as natural.

The activities of the active nuns and the *mukarrasāt* can be considered a means to strengthen the Coptic community in a pastoral and social way. The sisters in Beni Suef also attempt to create a bridge between the Copts and the Muslims by providing equal care for both. In areas where there is a large Christian population, this can work as a stabilizing factor.

The importance of the contemplative nuns is first and foremost to the Coptic community. In the contemplative convents, nuns achieve holiness on behalf of the Coptic community—they have their (warrior) saints to protect them. Through the mothers' intercessions, the rest of the Coptic population shares in this protection. As the hagiographies recount the heroic deeds of St. George and St. Theodore killing dragons, these warrior saints still intervene on behalf of the community and crush evil underfoot.

The leading women among the contemplative nuns have made it part of their vocation to remind the Coptic believers of the fact that God has not forgotten them. According to the nuns themselves, God keeps sending his saintly envoys to the Copts to prove that, regardless of the external circumstances, "Heaven is yet open."[9]

NOTES

INTRODUCTION

1. In this study I will use the word *Coptic* when referring to Coptic Orthodox. In the case of speaking of Coptic Catholics or Coptic Protestants, I will specify the denomination. Coptic is synonymous with Egyptian. The word *Copt* is derived from the Greek *Aigyptos/Aigyptioi,* which was used to refer to the native inhabitants of Egypt. After the Arab conquest of Egypt in 640 A.D., the Arabs reduced the word to root consonants: *kpt* from which the word *Qibt* was formed. Originally the word had no religious connotation but was used in a geographic and ethnic sense.

2. Veilleux, *Pachomian Koinonia,* vol. 1, 49, 50. Lucot, *Palladius,* 225.

3. St. Mary, the Mother of Jesus, is considered to have been the first nun, because, as the nuns themselves say, "the Virgin, after Jesus had left the world, dwelt with other women on the Mount of Olives and led a life of seclusion."

4. *Fī Ṣaḥrā᾿ al-ʿArab wa al-Adyīra al-Sharqīya* (In the Desert of the Bedouins and the Eastern Monasteries) (Cairo, 1939).

5. Ibid., 32, 34.

6. Strothmann, *Die Koptische Kirche,* 124.

7. Atiya, *A History,* 126.

8. Although it is generally recognized that the revival of the Coptic Church started with lay activities, there was also a number of charismatic clergy to whose activities the revival can be ascribed.

9. Giamberardini, "Le Suore Copte Ortodosse," *La Voce del Nilo* 14, no. 12 (1955): 3–23.

10. Ibid., 3–23; Habib al-Masri, "A Historical Survey," *BSAC* 14 (1950–1957): 63–111; Stegeman, "Contrasting Philosophies," *BSAC* 20 (1971): 159–65; "Several Philosophies," *BSAC* 23 (1981): 33–42; Meinardus, "Zur Renaissance," *OK* 37 (1988): 123–30; Chaillot, "Vie de Moniales," *MC* 16 (1989): 60–65; and "Comment Vit la Femme," *MC* 16 (1989): 66–74.

11. Vansleb, *The Present State;* Butler, *Coptic Churches of Egypt;* Jullien, *L'Égypte.*

12. Vansleb, *The Present State,* 146.

13. Butler, *Coptic Churches,* 128.

14. Coquin, *Édifices Chrétiens,* lists the historical sources mentioning the convents, 57–59; Deir Abū Saifein, 147–51; Deir Māri Girgis in Old Cairo.

15. Jullien, *L'Égypte, Souvenirs,* 232, 233.

16. Of the general works very few mention the nunneries: Jamʿīya Mār Mīnā, *Al-Rahbana,* 81–84 and ʿAbd al-Mesīḥ Ṣalīb al-Masʿūdī al-Baramūsī, *Kitāb Tuḥfa al-Sā'ilīn,* 116, 117. Coquin, *Édifices Chrétiens,* vol. 1, gives further Arabic sources that mention the convents from an architectural point of view. From the convents themselves there are: Dair al-Amīr Tādrus, *Al-Umm Marthā,* and the Convent of Abū Saifein: *Sīrat-al-Shahīd* and *Allāh yuḥibbunī.* From the Banāt Maryam: *Al-Batūlīya wa al-Khidma, Al-Tarahhub wa al-Khidma,* and *Tāsūnī Ḥannah.*

17. Anbā Matāʾus, *Sumūw al-Rahbana;* Y. Asʿad, *Al-Rahbana;* Meinardus, *Monks and Monasteries* (1961, 1989); Gruber, "Sacrifice." In the spring of 1993 a special issue appeared of *Le Monde Copte* 21–22 that was dedicated to Coptic monasticism.

18. The names of these convents and the names of the mother superiors are the real names I have used. When I quote one of the contemplative nuns or monks, I have changed the names in order to safeguard their anonymity. Nuns from the active community are quoted under their own names.

19. Butler, *Coptic Churches,* vol. 1, ix.

20. For illustrations on this topic see Carter, "On Spreading the Gospel," 18–36.

21. Of the contemplatives, eight nuns regularly furnished information. In total I interviewed thirty contemplative nuns and all their superiors. In the active community, I regularly interviewed six sisters and their bishop. I spoke at least once to nearly all the other sisters. The interviews were not conducted according to a certain set structure. In some cases I had to submit a list with questions in advance and received the prepared answers during the interview. Most interviews took place in Arabic. Often note-taking was inappropriate or forbidden, so I was forced to write notes after the meetings. This means that the material is less a verbatim report and often a paraphrase of what the nuns I interviewed said. Notes were taken in Dutch and Arabic and then translated into English.

22. Donlon, "Hierarchy."

23. Lutfi al-Sayyid Marsot, "Revolutionary Gentlewomen"; Jansen, *Women Without Men;* Abu Lughod, *Veiled Sentiments.* Also see Abu Lughod's article "Zones of Theory."

24. See the discussion of Coleman about Louis Dumont's book, *Homo Hierarchicus* in "Conclusion: After Sainthood," Hawley, *Saints and Virtues,* 209.

25. Ibid.

26. The seven Holy Orders in the Coptic Church are: Reader, Subdeacon, Deacon, Archdeacon, Priest, Hegoumenos, and Bishop.

27. Shenouda III, interview by C. Chaillot, 21 February 1988.

28. Mattā al-Meskīn, *Women,* 38.

29. Ibid.

30. 1 Tim. 2:13,14.

31. Mattā al-Meskīn, *Women,* 39.

32. The Coptic Church still practices the "churching" of women, the purification of a woman forty days after the birth of a boy and eighty days after the birth of a girl (Lev. 12). During this time the new mother is not allowed to take communion. At the ritual concluding this time, the "Holy Spirit is invoked to renew her inwards parts and to cleanse her from her impurities." Burmester, *The Egyptian or Coptic Church*, 113. 33. Riffat Hassan, "An Islamic Perspective," 107. Also see N. Al-Saadawi, *The Hidden Face of Eve.*

34. See Abu Lughod *Veiled Sentiments*, 130ff.

35. However, menstruating women are always prohibited contact with the holy chrism (*mairūn*), the sacred oil used in anointing and in ceremonies of consecration.

36. For the theories about "clean" and "unclean" I am indebted to Douglas, *Purity and Danger*, and Jansen, *Women without Men.*

37. In this context Dumont's observation holds true that "each social subsystem is governed in the first place by the system to which it belongs." Dumont, *Homo Hierarchicus*, 245.

38. Eickelman, *The Middle East*, 229.

39. Droogers and Siebers, *Popular Power in Latin American Religions*, 2, stress the "dynamic and actor oriented character of religion" and see religion as "a dialectical process of (re)production of religious representations and practices, in which the actor (re)produces his or her natural and social surroundings as well as himself as herself."

40. Droogers, *Macht in Zin*, 14.

41. Dumont, *Homo Hierarchicus*, 244, 249.

CHAPTER 1: THE COPTS IN EGYPTIAN SOCIETY

1. Wallace, "Revitalization Movements," 422.

2. Pearson, "Earliest Christianity in Egypt," 137–45. Habib al-Masri, *Story of the Copts*, 13ff, even gives the story about St. Mark's childhood, personality, and how he operated in Egypt.

3. For more information about early Christianity in Egypt see Griggs, *Early Egyptian Christianity*, 13–43.

4. For more details on the calendar systems see Meinardus, *Christian Egypt*, 70ff.

5. Atiya, *A History*, 69. Frend gives the following definition in the article "Monophysitism," in *The Coptic Encyclopedia:* "The incarnate Christ is one Person and has one divine nature as opposed to the orthodox doctrine that he is one person and has two natures, one human and one divine." In fact, this definition does not reflect the Coptic belief.

6. For a concise overview of the different Christologies that caused debates and controversies in the early Christian centuries: Assfalg and Kruger, *Kleines Wörterbuch.*

7. Frend, *Monophysite Movement*, 125.

8. Ibid., 137.

9. Johnson, "Anti-Chalcedonian Polemics," 220, 221. Nestorius denied the teaching of Cyril I (412–444) that St. Mary was the *Theotokos,* the God-bearer and taught that she was only the Mother of Jesus. This eventually led to the doctrine of the two natures of Christ (see Roncaglia, "Nestorians and Copts").

10. Frend, *Monophysite Movement,* 104, 123.

11. Ibid., 323.

12. Ibid., 143–83. The "Henotikon" of Zeno, drafted in 482, is the most prominent of these attempts.

13. Ibid., 79.

14. Ibid., 180. It is difficult to determine at what point the Chalcedonians in Alexandria became consciously "Melkites."

15. Ibid., 351.

16. For a reconstruction of how Egypt was conquered by the Arabs, see Butler, *The Arab Conquest,* 320–27. Also see Den Heijer, "Kerk en Staat," 33–35.

17. Butler, *The Arab Conquest,* 275–90, 293–98, 312; Den Heijer, "Kerk en Staat," 34.

18. Entry "*Dhimma*" in Kramers and Kramers, *Shorter Encyclopaedia of Islam.* Also see Bat Ye'or, *The Dhimmi.*

19. Cragg, *The Arab Christian,* 181.

20. Khalil Samir, "Arabic Sources," 82–97.

21. Atiya, *A History,* 17–19.

22. Ibid., 13, 79, and further for the Copts under Arab rule.

23. Ibid., 101–3.

24. Seikaly, "Coptic Communal Reform," 268. Also Pennington, "The Copts," 160. According to Pennington, by the end of the nineteenth century the Copts provided 45 percent of all civil servants.

25. Cragg, *The Arab Christian,* 187.

26. Ibid., 187. Cragg also points out that the elements of challenge for the Coptic Church to reorganize can be traced to the Mamluk period (184).

27. Seikaly, "Coptic Communal Reform," 247.

28. Ibid., 248–50; Atiya, *A History,* 104–6.

29. Carter, *The Copts,* 8, 9. According to Carter, the Protestant missionaries started in the mid-nineteenth century and, by 1878, had opened more than thirty-five schools.

30. Ibid., 7, 8.

31. Seikaly, "Coptic Communal Reform," 252.

32. Ibid., 261, 262.

33. Ibid., 261.

34. Ibid., 252–65. This gives a detailed account of the interactions between the laity, clergy, and the patriarch during the reign of Kyrillos V (1874–1927). Seikaly also points out the socioeconomic dimension of the struggle: clergy and monks were mostly from low origins, while the reformers belonged to the rich upper class.

35. Cragg, *The Arab Christian,* 189, 190.

36. Carter, *The Copts,* 12, 13.

37. Ibid., 12.

38. Ibid., 14, the statement was read by Luṭfī al-Sayyid.

39. Bowie, *The Copts,* 113. Bowie remarks that choosing two Copts "was a break with the past when only one Copt had been appointed to any cabinet." Until the 1952 revolution Copts participated in the cabinet of every government.

40. Pennington, "The Copts," 161. For more information about the *Wafd* see Carter, *The Copts,* 60–79.

41. Pennington, "The Copts," 163.

42. For more information see "Migration, Coptic," *Coptic Encyclopedia* and Atiya, *A History,* 166ff. According to Patriarch Shenouda III, at present the number of Coptic churches abroad is: United States, 50; Canada, 12; Australia, 17; Europe, 38 (interview on 23 January 1992).

43. Atiya, *A History,* 165. Also Waterbury, *Egypt,* 360.

44. Chitham, *The Coptic Community,* 105, 106, gives a chronological list of events between 1978 and 1981. Clashes are also described in (among others): Vogt, "Religious Revival," 59–61; Farah, *Religious Strife;* Schlicht, "Muslime und Kopten," 23–35.

45. M. Martin, "The Coptic-Muslim Conflict," 38.

46. Ibid., 35.

47. Waterbury, *Egypt,* 361, 362.

48. Martin, "The Coptic-Muslim Conflict," 38.

49. Esposito, "Trailblazers," 40, 41.

50. Pennington, "The Copts," 168.

51. Ibid., 176.

52. About this period also Wakin, *A Lonely Minority;* Samaan and Sukkary, "The Copts and Muslims," 128–55; Heikal, *Autumn.*

53. Esposito, "Trailblazers," 45.

54. Pennington, "The Copts," 162.

55. Martin, "The Coptic-Muslim Conflict," 41.

56. Ibid., 42.

57. Meinardus, *Monks and Monasteries,* (1961), 154–57. Also "Zeitgenössische Gottesnarren," 302ff.

58. Atiya, *A History,* 122.

59. Meinardus, *Monks and Monasteries,* (1961), 279–81; Meinardus, "The Hermits of Wadi Rayān," 294–317.

60. Victor Turner actually uses the term *liminars* for "persons undergoing ritualized transitions," *Ritual Process,* 143. According to Turner, this state of transition of living "betwixt and between" can become itself institutionalized (107).

61. Assad, "Ägyptisches Mönchtum," 54. Also the present Patriarch Shenouda III is a prolific writer; to date he has published over seventy titles.

62. Martin, "The Coptic-Muslim Conflict," 42.

63. F. Sidarouss, (Beirut, 1978) 195.

64. Ibid., 197.

65. El-Khawaga, "Le Renouveau Copte Actuel," 126.

66. Martin, "The Coptic-Muslim Conflict," 49.

67. Pennington, "The Copts," 158.

68. C.A.P.M.A.S., *General Census,* (Cairo, 1986); Courbage and Fargues, *Chrétiens et Juifs,* 328. At present the Egyptian population numbers approximately sixty million.

69. Betts, *Christians,* 65; Chitham, *The Coptic Community,* 32.

70. Chitham, *The Coptic Community,* 83. The table on p. 84 shows that of the Christians 19 percent had completed secondary education, against 10.8 percent of the Muslims, and 4.8 percent of the Christians held a completed university first degree, against 1.8 percent of the Muslims.

71. Vogt, "Religious Revival," 58.

72. Chitham, *The Coptic Community,* 82–87; Pennington, "The Copts," 159.

73. Pennington, "The Copts," 177; Meinardus, *Christian Egypt,* 219. Also Viaud *Magie.* For the saints see chapter 8.

74. Pennington, "The Copts," 177, 178. About apparitions of St. Mary, see Nelson, "Stress," 48–57; Anba Athanasius, "Die Koptische Kirche Heute," 85.

75. Cragg, *The Arab Christian,* 196, 197.

76. See Viaud, *Magie.*

77. See Alt, *Ägyptischen Kopten.*

78. Viaud, *Magie,* 35–38, 69–89, 133–48.

79. Martin, "Sur Quelques Comportements," 138.

80. For fasting, see Wissa Wassef, *Pratiques Rituelles;* Viaud, *Les Coptes,* 32–69. For the calendar, see Wassef, *Pratiques Rituelles;* Viaud, *Les Coptes d'Egypte,* 25–30; O. Meinardus, *Christian Egypt,* 70–74.

81. Kopp, *Glaube,* 74–215; Viaud, *Les Coptes,* 77–103.

82. See chapter 7 on spiritual life (paragraph about fasting).

83. Sidarouss, *Eglise Copte,* 240.

84. Martin, "Sur Quelques Comportements," 135.

85. This liturgy is not originally Coptic. See S. Khalīl, "Arabic sources," 85; Atiya, *A History,* 127–30. The other liturgies that are sometimes used are the Liturgy of St. Gregory of Nazianzen (Christmas, Epiphany, and Easter) and St. Mark (or St. Cyril, rarely used, mainly in monasteries). The liturgies of St. Basil and St. Gregory are not of Coptic origin.

86. A similar observation was also made around 1918 by Leeder: "The devil is largely ignored, with all his works; the martyrs are pictured untroubled and serene." *Modern Sons,* 218.

87. Matthew 19:21. Bible translation according to the Revised Standard Version (RSV). The RSV will be used throughout this study. Gregg, *Athanasius,* 31.

88. Chitty, *The Desert a City,* 2.

89. Ibid., 2.

90. Rubenson, *The Letters,* 9.

91. Chitty, *The Desert a City,* 9.

92. That is why the Copts call Pachomius *Āb al-Sharika* (the father of the communal life). See Rousseau, *Pachomius;* Veilleux, *Pachomian Koinonia,* vol. 1; Goehring, "New Frontiers in Pachomian Studies," 236–58.

93. Regnault, *La Vie Quotidienne*, 179–85.

94. See Leipoldt, *Schenute von Atripe*, Timbie; "The State," 258–70, Van Cauwenbergh, *Étude;* and Bell, *The Life of Shenoute.*

95. Lucot, *Palladius;* Meyer, *Palladius;* Russell, *The Lives;* Ward, *The Sayings.*

96. Chitty, *The Desert*, 2.

97. Veilleux, *Pachomian Koinonia*, vol. 1, 49, 50; Lucot, *Palladius*, 225.

98. Lucot, *Palladius*, 42, 51, 208, 348, 358. Pp. 358–60 mention Ammā Talis. She was the superior of a convent with sixty nuns and impressed Palladius by her intense spirituality and loving care for her nuns. Olympias was a rich widow who became a deaconess and assisted John Chrysostom in his ministry.

99. Ward, *Sayings*, 229–35.

100. For Mary of Egypt, see Ward, *Harlots*, 26–57; For Hilaria, see Van Esbroeck, "Hilaria, St."; For Theodora, see Pezin, "Les 'Mères,' " 57–59.

101. De Lacy O'Leary, *The Saints of Egypt*, 187, 188. O'Leary also treats the saints mentioned above. With the revival several booklets have been produced in Arabic with detailed hagiographies of these saints, even when little historic material is available. For a compilation about monastic women in the first centuries of Christianity, also see R. Albrecht, *Das Leben . . . Makrina.*

102. Ibid., 123.

103. A. Rouselle, *Porneia*, 235, 236.

104. Timbie, "The State," 265, Van Cauwenbergh, *Étude*, 145–48.

105. Patriarch Shenouda III, *Taʾammulāt*, 56.

106. Gruber, "Sacrifice," 92.

107. Den Heijer, "History."

108. Gruber, "Sacrifice," 108.

109. Strothmann, *Die Koptische Kirche*, 128.

110. Bishop Athanasius, Metropolitan of Beni Suef and Bahnasa, interview January 1992.

111. "Christ is God" was "the spontaneous cry of the Egyptian bishops at Chalcedon." Frend, *Monophysite Movement*, 137.

CHAPTER 2: THE MONASTIC LANDSCAPE

1. Megally, "Synod, Holy."

2. The convents in the heart of Cairo are located in a quarter of the city called Ḥārat Zuweilah. The Convent of St. Theodore Stratelates is located in Ḥārat al-Rūm (the alley of the Greeks in a district called Al-Darb al Aḥmar (the red road). The quarters of Ḥārat Zuweilah and Ḥarat al-Rūm are probably the oldest in Cairo that were inhabited by a Coptic community. Wissa, "Ḥārit Zuweylah," does not give the exact year but writes: "The concentration of Copts in this area during the Middle Ages led to the foundation of some of the most ancient churches in Cairo (in Ḥarat Zuweilah)." Ḥārat al-Rūm was the area where Coptic clerks and officials lived. They left the area at the beginning of the nine-

teenth century and moved to Claude Bey. Ḥārat Zuweilah was the center for the Coptic merchants.

3. The term *reinhabitation* means that an old but deserted monastic site or the site of a pilgrimage is repopulated with monks or nuns. This can entail building a whole new abbey, as was the case in Deir Sitt Dimyānah, or restoring old buildings.

4. Meinardus, *Monks and Monasteries* (1961), 339–48. Coquin and Martin, "Dayr Sitt Dimyānah"; Leeder, *Modern Sons*, 141–45.

5. For the names and location of these monastic sites, see Van Doorn, "Les Vierges Sages," 117, 118.

6. For "contemplative" the word *mu'takif* is used, which stems from the verb *i'takaf* (to retire, seclude oneself, go into seclusion). Also used is the word *maḥbūs* (shut-off from the outside world, isolated, or secluded).

7. Information provided by Bishop Athanasius, January 1992. ʾAnbā Athanasius, "Die Koptische Kirche," 76.

8. This active community was not the very first group of its kind. In January 1960 a group of women had started a home in Giza (Cairo South). They were guided by the local priest, Salīb Suryāl. Though the home never developed into a blooming community like the community of the active nuns, it still exists.

9. Unpublished pamphlet by the Banāt Maryam, (n.d.), 2.

10. Interview with Sister Hannah, 15 July 1989.

11. The information about the consecrated women is derived from an unpublished interview in English that Christine Chaillot had with Pope Shenouda III on 21 February 1988. The French translation of the interview was published by Chaillot as "Comment vit la Femme," 66–74.

12. The consecration of the Coptic women harkens to the consecration as it is known from the fourth century, being the vow of virginity, accompanied by the liturgical blessing. N. Lohkamp, "Consecration."

13. The two other major projects where consecrated women are involved are in Deir Drunka, near Assiyut (started 1968), and on the premises of the convent of St. Dimyānah.

14. Shenouda III, interview by C. Chaillot, 21 February 1988.

15. English Kiraza 1/1, 1992.

16. Shenouda III, interview by C. Chaillot, 21 February 1988.

17. Information from Bishop Arsanius of Minya, interview 2 January 1989.

18. In an interview on 23 January 1992, Patriarch Shenouda III also could not answer the question as to how many *mukarrasāt* are active in the Coptic Church.

19. The estimation is given by Bishop Ruweis (January 1992) who states the *mukarrasāt* are active in more than forty dioceses, between ten and twenty *mukarrasāt* each diocese.

20. Meinardus, *Monks and Monasteries* (Cairo, 1989), x. By 1986 Meinardus had counted 630 monks in 11 monasteries.

21. Meinardus, *The Holy Family*, 40. The route the Holy Family took was allegedly revealed in a dream to Theophilus, the patriarch from 384–412. See Iris Habib al-Masri, *Story of the Copts*, 185.

22. A. Naṣr, *Al-Qiddīsa Dimyānah,* 88, 89.
23. ʿAbd al-Masīḥ Ṣalīb al-Masʿūdī al-Baramūsī, *Kitāb Tuḥfa al-Sā'ilīn,* 117.
24. Ibid.
25. Hinds and Badawi, *Dictionary of Egyptian Arabic.*
26. Giamberardini, "Le Suore," 21.
27. Ibid.
28. Lane, *Manners and Customs,* 30.
29. Meinardus, *Monks and Monasteries* (1989) 16.
30. The saying is from St. Moses the Black, *Bustān al-Ruhbān,* 75.
31. Hall, *The Silent Language,* 187.
32. Gruber, "Sacrifice," 168.
33. Also see Naṣr Rizq, *Al-Qiddīsa Anāsīmūn,* 33.
34. See De Lacy O'Leary, *The Saints of Egypt,* 210, 219, 262–66.
35. A jar with this oil has been put in the altar during the mass on the night of Holy Saturday (*sabt al-faraḥ* or *ṣabt al-nūr*). During that night the entire book of the Apocalypse is read. The name "Abā Ghalamsīs oil" is a corruption of "Apocalypse."
36. Dair Rāhibāt al-Amīr Tādrus, *Al-Amīr Tādrus,* 107, 108.
37. Also see Meinardus, *Monks and Monasteries* (1961), 339ff.

CHAPTER 3: THE RULING MOTHERS AND FATHERS

1. Guillaumont, "Nitria," and "Kellia," *Aux Origines;* Cody, "Scetis." For the spiritual guide's role see Rousseau, *Ascetics.*
2. Veilleux, "Pachomius, Saint."
3. Veilleux, *Pachomian Koinonia,* vol. 2, 127.
4. Rousseau, *Pachomius,* 100.
5. Ibid., 101, 106.
6. Goehring, "New Frontiers," 236–57.
7. Rousseau, *Ascetics,* 23; Goehring, "New Frontiers," 240ff.
8. Bishop Athanasius, foreword to *Al-Tarahhub wa al-Khidma* (Monasticism and Service) by Banāt Maryam, 9ff.
9. Meinardus, *Monks and Monasteries* (1989), 189.
10. Patriarch Shenouda III, *Taʾammulāt,* 55.
11. Also see Chaillot, "Vie de Moniales Coptes," 60–65.
12. See Veilleux, *Pachomian Koinonia,* vol. 2, 7: "These rules were certainly not a set text. They developed with the evolutions of the *Koinonia* during Pachomius' lifetime as well as under his successors."
13. The sources can be found in the *Bustān al-Ruhbān,* 5.
14. Ibid., 6, 7, 8.
15. Meeus, "Herleving," 8–14 gives several illustrations of how Mattā al-Meskīn guides his monks.
16. Bishop Athanasius, interview of 20 February 1989.
17. Viaud, *Qawānīn al-Anbā Bākhūmīyūs—Āb al-Sharika.*

18. The section Umminā Alexandra showed me was Al-Āb Yūsuf Maḥfūẓ, *Qawānīn al-Rahbānīyah al-Lubnānīya* (The Lebanese Monastic Rules).

19. Rāhibāt Dair Banāt Maryam, *Qānūn*, 6.

20. Andrāʾus ʿAbd al-Masīḥ, *Kitāb*, 13.

21. ʾAsʿad, *Al-Rahbana*, 60–64.

22. Ibid., 74. Also see Andrāʾus ʿAbd al-Masīḥ, *Kitāb*.

23. ʿAbd al-Masīḥ, *Kitāb*, 15. Bishop Abraam, the saintly bishop of Fayoum (canonized in 1963), was in 1870 removed from his position as abbot of Deir al-Muḥarraq after being accused of being too generous and wasting the monastery's money. Malaty, *Anba Abraam*, 49.

24. Interview with Patriarch Shenouda III, 12 May 1989.

25. Veilleux, *Pachomian Koinonia*, vol. 1, 50.

26. For the abbess as spiritual guide, see chapter 7.

27. That is "eskīm"; see the section in this chapter entitled "Unofficial Positions in the Hierarchy."

28. Dair Rāhibāt al-Amīr Tādrus, *al-Umm Marthā*, 55.

29. Patriarch Shenouda III, *Ta'ammulāt*, 55.

30. Banāt Maryam, *Qānūn*, 20.

31. Ibid.

32. Ibid., 21; Banāt Maryam, *Al-Batūlīya wa al-Khidma*, 132.

33. Dair Abī Saifein, *Sīrat-al-Shahīd*, 321, 322.

34. "Reader" is the lowest of the seven ecclesiastical Holy Orders.

35. Maksīmūs al-Anṭūnī, *Al-Qiddīs*, 23. Meinardus, *Monks and Monasteries* (1961), 75, 76.

36. Maksīmūs al-Anṭūnī, *Al-Qiddīs*, 11.

37. Abnāʾ al-Bābā Kīrillus al-Sādis, *Sīrat*, 9.

38. Ibid., 16.

39. For more about the history and development of the megaloskema, see Innemee, *Ecclesiastical Vestments*, 90ff.

40. Burmester, *The Egyptian or Coptic Church*, 189.

41. Mattā al-Meskīn, *Al-Rahbana*, 353.

42. This liturgy will be discussed in chapter 5. For its text see Burmester, *The Egyptian or Coptic Church*, 194–96.

43. Anbā Matāʾus, *Sumūw*, 150.

44. Ibid., 111. See Meinardus, *Monks and Monasteries* (1989), 195.

45. Anbā Matāʾus, *Sumūw*, 112.

46. Strothmann, *Die Koptische Kirche*, 128.

47. Rugh, *Family*, 44.

CHAPTER 4: LEAVING THE WORLD: THE NOVITIATE

1. Patriarch Shenouda III during a public Bible study (10 May 1989). This practice is also recommended when the candidate is the child of Coptic immigrants and lives abroad.

2. Patriarch Shenouda III, public Bible study on 30 May 1990.

3. Mother Irīnī, as quoted by Mother Aghāpī of Deir Abū Saifein, during several interviews.

4. M. Gruber, "Sacrifice," 139.

5. Ibid., 139.

6. Asʿad, *Al-Rahbana*, 89.

7. Also see Atiya, *A History*, 123.

8. Asʿad, *Al-Rahbana*, 87. The story is also quoted in Banāt Maryam, *Al-Tarahhub*, 29.

9. Rugh has pointed out in *Family* that "the rigidity of sex roles within the family [has] often been underemphasized by writers focusing on the increasing number of Egyptian women receiving extended educations or engaged in full-time employment outside the home" (72).

10. Anbā Matāʾus, *Sumūw*, 70.

11. Gruber, "Sacrifice," 141.

12. Ibid., 147, shows that most of the young monks who entered after the 1960s were college educated.

13. Turner, *The Ritual Process*, 170.

14. Anbā Matāʾus, *Sumūw*, 16, 17.

15. The motives presented here to become a nun coincide with the findings of Weinstein and Bell, *Saints and Society*, 17–48.

16. Campbell-Jones, *In Habit*, 75.

17. An expression that shows the maternal position the Coptic Church strives to achieve in the lives of the young members is that they are gathered in "*ḥoḍn al-kenīsa*" (the arms, or the bosom, of the Church).

18. The 1978 dissertation by Fadel Sidarouss called *Église Copte et Monde Moderne* provides a study in depth about the Coptic youth programs. An abstract of the study under the same title can be found in *Proche-Orient Chrétien* 30 (1980): 211–65.

19. About fifteen child saints belong to the Coptic tradition and are known by name. In addition to these there are some thirty children whose ages and names are unknown. Most of them were martyrs and died together with their families. I am indebted for this information to Ms. Nora Stene, University of Oslo.

20. An observation courtesy of Nora Stene.

21. Stegeman, "Contrasting Philosophies," 163.

22. Gruber, "Sacrifice," 139.

23. This topic will be elaborated in chapter 6 (about work).

24. Rugh, *Family*, 156, quoting from G. L. Fox, "Nice Girl: Social Control of Women through a Value Construct," *Signs* 4 (1977): 805–17.

25. Ibid., 156.

26. Gruber, "Sacrifice," 56ff.

27. Anbā Matāʾus, *Sumūw*, 49.

28. See Rugh, *Family*, 73.

29. Anbā Matāʾus, *Sumūw*, 50, 53.

30. For example, Asʿad, *Al-Rahbana,* clearly warns against family members visiting the monastic.

31. Mother Martha became a nun after a vision of her aunt who was an abbess. Dair al-Amīr Tādrus, *Al-Umm Marthā,* 14.

32. Exceptions can be made if the leave is temporary or if there are special circumstances.

33. Hausherr, *Spiritual Direction,* 297, quotes St. Theodore Studites on this subject: "Studite canon law admitted only two kinds of leave from the convent: one for the perfect religious who had been duly elected superior of another house, the other for the imperfect religious who, after long . . . care, chose to go over to another 'fraternity.' "

34. Coquin, "Canon Law." What is more or less considered the official canon manual of the Coptic Church was compiled in the thirteenth century by Al-Ṣāfī ibn al-ʿAssāl.

35. At the time of this writing, she had been waiting for more than one year and her situation had not yet changed.

36. Some nuns said they felt that they had been assigned too many duties, so that there was not enough time left for devotions. Others wanted to prevent a personality clash with the superior.

37. Rugh, *Family,* 158.

38. Thorbjørnsrud, "Messias Piker," 129, 130.

39. Ibid., 203, 204. Mervat Hatem found this same kind of frustration with parents' sense of religiosity among young upper-middle-class Muslim women who had started to wear the veil. "Demise," 235.

40. Thorbjørnsrud, "Messias Piker," 208.

41. Ibid., 203.

42. N. Atiya, *Khul-Khaal,* 53.

CHAPTER 5: DEAD TO THE WORLD

1. For example, Patriarch Shenouda III initiated the new nuns in Deir Māri Girgis in Ḥārat Zuweilah in May 1989, and the nuns of the convent with the same name in Old Cairo in October 1992.

2. Several of the facts about the initiation of monks I drew from Mark Gruber, "Sacrifice," 142, 143.

3. Anbā Mataʾus, *Sumūw,* 87.

4. Gruber, "Sacrifice," 143.

5. Ibid.

6. Burmester bases his critical text on Tūkhī's as well as on unpublished manuscripts from the fifteenth and eighteenth centuries. Burmester, *The Egyptian or Coptic Church,* 188ff.

7. ʾAnbā Mataʾus describes a version that is slightly different as far as the Bible readings are concerned and which is used in the monastery of Anbā Bishoy. Anbā Matā'us, *Sumūw,* 86–91.

8. Ibid., 91.

9. Anbā Mataʾus, *Sumūw*, 154. Also see Dair al-Suryān, *Al-Zayy al-Rahbānī* (The Monastic Attire), 1990.

10. Anbā Matā'us, *Sumūw*, 90; Burmester, *The Egyptian or Coptic Church*, 193, 194, 198. The images are taken from Eph 6:10–17.

11. When a monk becomes a bishop and hence has to return to the world, the crosses on his *qalansūwa* are embroidered higher up so that he can cover them with his *ʿimma* (turban) in order not to give offense to Muslims by showing the crosses.

12. Asʿad, *Al-Rahbana*, 96.

13. 2 Kgs 2:9.

14. Innemee, *Ecclesiastical Vestments*, 89.

15. Meinardus, "The Hermits of Wadi Rayān," 307.

16. The vows are dealt with under the section about *tadbīr al-irāda*, "directing or controlling the will," 157–222.

17. Banāt Maryam, *Qānūn*, 8.

18. Burmester, *The Egyptian or Coptic Church*, 198–200.

19. The daily requirements for the great skema bearer are: (1) recite all the 150 psalms; (2) recite the entire *tesbiḥa*; (3) make five hundred prostrations; (4) do not speak more than seven words; (5) study the Bible and the sayings and lives of the desert fathers continuously; (6) fast until sunset; and (7) take a minimum of food and drink. See Zakhāriyās al-Anṭūnī, *ṭaqs Siyāmat*, 288.

20. The quotations are my translations from the text as published in *al-Kiraza* (September 1990), 24.

21. Gruber, "Sacrifice," 144, 145, estimates that at least 80 percent of the monks will be ordained priests.

22. Anbā Mataʾus, *Sumūw*, 111.

23. Veilleux, *Pachomian Koinonia*, vol. 1, 51.

24. Asʿad, *Al-Rahbana*, 180.

25. See Gruber, "Sacrifice," 157.

26. Ibid., 159.

27. Ibid., 157. The term is coined by Gruber.

28. Maria Shenouda, undated, unpublished paper in the library of the mother house of the Banāt Maryam about the position of women in the early church.

29. Ibid.

30. Ibid.

31. About the desert fathers and the demonic, see Regnault, "Anges et Démons," in *La Vie Quotidienne*, 189–209; Van der Vliet, "Demons," 135–55.

32. Gregg, *Athanasius: The Life of Antony*, 69.

33. Ibid., 79.

34. For more about this topic, see Guillaumont, *Aux Origines*, 69–87.

35. Anbā Mataʾus, *Sumūw*, 274, quotes the story as well. The translation here is taken from Ward, *The Wisdom*, 20.

36. Dair Abī Saifein, *Sīrat al-Shahīd,* 324.
37. *ʿInd al-Ghurūb* (Monastery of Baramus, n.d.), 24–28.

CHAPTER 6: WORK AND INCOME

1. In Modern Standard Arabic the word is pronounced *khidma.*
2. For example, see the articles of Lutfi al-Sayyid Marsot ("The Revolutionary Gentlewomen") and Philipp ("Feminism").
3. Carter, *The Copts,* 48.
4. Al-Anbā Ṣamū'īl, *Al-Khidma,* 8. These are his teachings published after he died in 1981.
5. Meinardus, *Monks and Monasteries* (1961), 31.
6. De Sa, "De situatie van de Kopten in Egypte," 23–35.
7. Assad, "Prägung," 87–117.
8. Interview with Sister Hannah, 15 July 1989.
9. Also see Bānūb, *Namūdhaj,* 8.
10. Al-Anbā Ṣamūʾīl, *Al-Khidma,* 28.
11. Ibid., 28.
12. Ibid., 12, 13.
13. Ibid., 24.
14. Banāt Maryam, *Al-Batūlīya wa al-Khidma* (Beni Suef, 1971), 45; Al-Anbā Ṣamūʾīl, *Al-Khidma,* 25.
15. Al-Anbā Ṣamūʾīl, *Al-Khidma,* 26–28.
16. Ibid., 55, 53.
17. Mattā al-Meskīn, *Al-Khidma,* 19.
18. Also Sidarouss, *Église Copte.*
19. From the Old Testament the following women are mentioned: Miryam, the sister of Moses and Aaron (Ex 15:21); Deborah (Jgs 4, 5); Hulda (2 Kgs 22:14–20); and the women who ministered at the door of the sanctuary (Ex 38:8). From the New Testament: St. Mary, Mary Magdalene (Mark 16:9); Mary the sister of Lazarus; Phoebe (Rom 16:1); the women who followed Jesus (Luke 8:1–3); the four unmarried daughters of Philip the evangelist (Acts 21:9); and the New Testament mentions widows who devote their lives to God (1 Tim, 5:3–11).
20. Luke 10:42.
21. Banāt Maryam, *Al-Tarahhub,* 31. The quote is from "an old man," *Bustān,* 206, 207.
22. St. Antony left his cave a few times for trips to Alexandria where he visited persecuted Christians in prison and defended the orthodox faith against Arius. And St. Shenute's monastery gave shelter to thousands of people who were fleeing raids of the barbarians. *Al-Batūlīya wa al-Khidma,* 48–67.
23. The core of the information for the following description is based on interviews. The latest were held in the fall of 1990. Also see Bānūb, *Namūdhaj;* Dair Banāt Maryam, *Tāsūnī Ḥannah.*
24. *Al-Tarahhub,* 31, 32.
25. About how this contact started, see Bānūb, *Namūdhaj,* 20–28.

26. *Bustān*, 205.

27. Waddell, *The Desert Fathers*, 229. The first saying of St. Antony concerns this topic. Ward, *The Sayings*, 1, 2.

28. *Bustān*, 205. The active community speaks of "attacks of the enemy" (the devil), *Al-Tarahhub*, 32. Asʿad in *Al-Rahbana* (Monasticism) calls it "evil thoughts" and adds "thoughts about matters concerning the body," ("al-tafkīr fī al-jasadīyāt"), 27.

29. Ward, *The Sayings*, 1, 2. Also Anbā Matāʾus, *Sumūw*, 94–111.

30. Ibid., 41; in a saying of Bessarion we find an exception.

31. Also see Asʿad, *Al-Rahbana*, 83.

32. A special issue of *Le Monde Copte* 19 (July 1991) is devoted to Coptic iconography, 5–53.

33. Gruber, "Sacrifice," 128, 129.

34. Giamberardini, "Le Suore," 13, 14. He refers to Y. Butrus, *Al-Baḥth al-awwal fī al-Rahbana baina al-Sharq wa al-Gharb* (The First Research on Monasticism between East and West) (1953), 80.

35. Giamberardini, "Le Suore," 13, 14; Butrus, *Al-Baḥth*, 80.

36. In an average year, two sisters study in a North American or European country. Funds and scholarships come from different sources including church and developmental organizations.

CHAPTER 7: THE SPIRITUAL LIFE

1. Some people choose a bishop as their spiritual guide.

2. Anbā Matāʾus, *Sumūw*, 266.

3. *Bustān al-Ruhbān*, 248ff.

4. Gregg, *St. Athanasius: The Life of Anthony*, 46.

5. Ward, "Spiritual Direction," 3.

6. Ibid., 8.

7. Ibid. Also Rousseau, *Ascetics*.

8. See 2 Kgs 2:10–12.

9. *ʿInd al-Ghurūb* (Dair Baramūs, n.d.), 33–64. The story is reminiscent of the one mentioned by Palladius in the *Lausiac History* about the monk Valens who became arrogant. Lucot, *Palladius*, 188–94.

10. Hausherr, *Spiritual Direction*, 272, 273.

11. Three ammās are mentioned among 130 abbās.

12. The French version is by Sister Bernard, *Vie de Sainte Synclétique*. In 1990 an English translation was published by Elizabeth Castelli, "Syncletica," 265–312.

13. Castelli, "Syncletica," 275.

14. Ibid.

15. Naṣr Rizq, *Al-Qiddīsa Anāsīmūn (Efrūsīnā)*, 29.

16. Dair al-Amīr Tādrus, *Al-Umm Marthā*, 14.

17. Naṣr Rizq, *Efrūsīnā*, 30.

18. Ibid., 31.
19. Dair al-Amīr Tādrus, *Marthā,* 14.
20. Ibid., 15.
21. Ibid., 58.
22. It is impossible for an outsider to check whether this rumor is true or not.
23. Naṣr Rizq, *Efrūsīnā,* 32.
24. Dair al-Amīr Tādrus, *Marthā,* 52.
25. Naṣr Rizq, *Efrūsīnā,* 33.
26. Dair al-Amīr Tādrus, *Marthā,* 38.
27. Ibid., 56, 70.
28. Naṣr Rizq, *Efrūsīnā,* 33.
29. Dair al-Amīr Tādrus, *Marthā,* 52, 54, 75, 86, 88.
30. Anbā Matāʾus, *Sumūw,* 218.
31. Dair al-Amīr Tādrus, *Marthā,* 59.
32. Ibid., 21.
33. Dair Abī Saifein, *Sīrat al-Shahīd,* 321, 323.
34. Ibid., 322, 323.
35. Dair al-Amīr Tādrus, *Marthā,* 55.
36. Ibid., 39.
37. Naṣr Rizq, *Efrūsīnā,* 33.
38. Dair al-Amīr Tādrus, *Marthā,* 63.
39. Ibid., 54–58; Dair Abī Saifein, *Al-Shahīd,* 323.
40. B. Stegeman, "Contrasting Philosophies," 37.
41. Bat Ye'or, *The Dhimmi,* 71.
42. Ibid., 193.
43. Interview with Patriarch Shenouda III, 12 May 1989.
44. Ward, *The Sayings,* 6. The same theme is found in the apocryphal book of 2 Esdras 5:51–56.
45. M. Gruber, "Sacrifice," 151.
46. Interview 20 February 1989.
47. Interview 10 January 1991.
48. Dair Banāt Maryam, *Tāsūnī Ḥannah,* 5.
49. Ibid., 12.
50. Ibid., 11.
51. Ibid., 15.
52. Ibid., 13.
53. Ibid., 13, 14.
54. Ibid., 14.
55. Anbā Matāʾus, *Sumūw,* 166, 192, 233, 234.
56. Gruber, "Sacrifice," 207.
57. Ibid.
58. Muslims traditionally respect St. Mary. This respect is based on the Qurʾān, which mentions St. Mary several times (Sūras 3:35–37, 42–51, 4:156, 19:16–33, 21:91, 66:12). Sūra 19, Sūrat Maryam bears her name.

59. Malaty, *St. Mary*, 75. Copts always stress the point that commemorating and invoking St. Mary does not mean that they worship her.

60. Ibid., 94–96.

61. Ibid., 13.

62. Ibid., 28. This belief is based on apocryphal documents such as the "Odes of Salomo" and "The Protoevangelium of James." See Goodspeed, *Christian Literature*, 57–59.

63. Malaty, *St. Mary*, 45.

64. Dair al-Amīr Tādrus, *Marthā*, 41.

65. Taft, *The Liturgy of the Hours*, 250.

66. Gruber, "Sacrifice," 172.

67. *Bustān al-Ruhbān*, 142.

68. Quecke, *Untersuchungen*, 35.

69. Taft, *Liturgy*, 253.

70. Ibid., 253ff.

71. Gruber, "Sacrifice," 166.

72. About the *Agbīya*, also see Viaud, *Les Coptes*, 92–103, and Leeder, *Modern Sons*, 529.

73. For the Psalmodia see Quecke, *Untersuchungen*, 52–90.

74. Interview 31 January 1992.

75. Gruber, "Sacrifice," 201, expresses a similar thought.

76. For the first part of the observation, about quick digestion and the pure stomach, I am indebted to Nora Stene; the second part I heard in a class taught by a *mukarrasa* for village children in Luxor.

77. Gruber, "Sacrifice," 182.

78. Ibid., 201.

79. Some convents adjoin a public church where the nuns can attend the Eucharist in a special enclosed section.

80. Gruber, "Sacrifice," 167, 201.

81. Interview with Bishop Athanasius, 24 April 1993.

82. See Guillaumont, "The Jesus Prayer among the Monks," 66–71.

83. *Bustān al-Ruhbān*, 126.

84. See Gruber, "Sacrifice," 168, 169. According to Gruber, this is especially true of male monastics for whom the night is a dangerous time for maintaining the purity of the monk's imagination and body.

85. The fasting days are forty-three days during Advent (until the eve of 6 January), on the vigil for Epiphany (19 January), the fast of Jonah (three days, ten weeks before Easter), Lent (fifty-five days before Easter), the fast for the Apostles (from the day after Pentecost until 12 July; depending on the date of Pentecost this fast can endure from fifteen to forty-nine days), and the fast for St. Mary (fifteen days until 22 August).

86. For a detailed study about this topic, see Wissa Wassef, *Pratiques Rituelles;* Viaud, *Les Coptes*, 44.

87. Viaud, *Les Coptes*, 69, 70.

88. Also see El-Khawaga, "Le Renouveau Copte Actuel," 128, 129.
89. Regnault, *La Vie Quotidienne,* 84, 85.

CHAPTER 8: THE SAINTS

1. Although Julian the Apostate ruled later, the official end of the so-called "era of the martyrs" is in 313.

2. Maktabat al-Maḥabba, *Kitāb al-Synaksār,* 2 vol. Also De Lacy O'Leary, *The Saints.*

3. Abnāʾ al-Bābā Kīrillus al-Sādis, *Muʿjizāt al-Bābā Kīrillus,* vols. 1–12.

4. Leeder, *Modern Sons,* 265–304, gives an eyewitness account of a visit to the bishop made around 1913.

5. Biegman, *Moulids,* 92. Abūnā Fānūs was still alive in January 1992.

6. Meinardus, *Christian Egypt,* 143.

7. The personality of St. Theodore Stratelates can actually be divided between two characters: Theodore Stratelates and Theodore the Eastern, or the Syrian. According to De Lacy O'Leary in *The Saints,* 262–66, the Copts made Theodore Stratelates into an Egyptian, although he was a Greek. In order to carry on the original Stratelates tradition, the Copts invented Theodore the Eastern. Also see Delahaye, *Les Légendes,* 11–43.

8. See Delahaye, *Les Légendes,* 51–55, for the passion of St. Georges and 91–101 for St. Mercurius.

9. Anṭūnīyūs, G., *Sīrat Mārīnā,* 31–69; Naṣr, A., *Al-Qiddīsa Dimyānah,* 33–74. Also De Lacy O'Leary, *The Saints,* 123, 187.

10. Leeder, *Modern Sons,* 297.

11. Meinardus, *Christian Egypt,* 154. A *maulid* is a feast that lasts several days to commemorate the day that a saint was born or died—death being considered a second birth, into eternal life. The *maulid* differs from the *ʿeid,* which is a one-day feast to commemorate, for example, the translation of the saint's relics or the dedication of a new church that bears the saint's name. (Confusingly, the last day of a *maulid* is also called *ʿeid*). The celebration of a feast tends to be smaller and few Muslims attend. The official church approves of the feasts, but because of the amount of folk religion involved, *maulids* are considered unorthodox happenings.

12. See Viaud, *Les Pélerinages,* 20.

13. The relics are in Ḥārat al-Rūm in the church of the Holy Virgin, which is next to the convent of Amīr Tadrūs.

14. Also see Biegman, *Moulids,* 91.

15. T. Baumeister, *Martyr Invictus,* 52.

16. Ibid., 62; Gregg, *Athanasius: The Life of Antony,* 96, 97.

17. The categories are derived from Weinstein and Bell, "Perceptions of Sanctity," in *Saints and Society,* 139ff. These elements of sainthood are seen as universal and not only applicable to the Copts.

18. For a Coptic definition of saintly virtues, see Anbā Matāʾus, *Sumūw,* 204–8.

19. Rousseau, *Ascetics*, 22–24.
20. Ibrahim, *Das wunderbare Wirken*, 15.
21. Ibid., 16.
22. Ibid., 54, 55. From the Arabic miracles, vol. 1, 97.
23. Ibid., 111, 112. From the Arabic miracles, vol. 1, 65.
24. Dair al-Amīr Tādrus, *Al-Umm Marthā*, 75.
25. Ibid., 70.
26. Ibid., 25. According to her biographers, this happened 5 April 1959.
27. Ibid., 49, 50.
28. Ibid., 50.
29. The percentage of Christians in al-Baṭnīyah is 2.7, while in Cairo as a whole it is 10.2 percent. Chitham, *The Coptic Community*, 90–91.
30. De Lacy O'Leary, *The Saints*, 201; Delahaye, *Légendes Grecques*, 91–101.
31. Dair Abī Safein, *Sīrat-al-Shahīd*, 310.
32. Ibid., 311.
33. Ibid., 312.
34. Ibid., 159–68.
35. Ibid., 193–295.
36. Rousseau, *Ascetics*, 28, 29.
37. Ibid., 28.
38. Bell, *Besa: The Life of Shenoute*, 50.
39. Ibrahim, *Das Wunderbare Wirken*, 52. The Arabic miracles, vol. 1, 92.
40. Eickelman discusses this concept with regards to *marabouts* (Muslim holy men) and North African Jewish holy men in Morocco in *The Middle East*, 228–35.
41. Weber, *The Theory of Social and Economic Organization*, 358.
42. Brown, "The Saint as Exemplar," 9. Brown builds his definition on the theory of Edward Shils, *Center and Periphery: Essays in Macrosociology* (Chicago, 1975), 130.
43. Geertz, *Local Knowledge*, 123.
44. Dair Abī Saifein, *Sīrat-al-Shahīd*, 312, 313. The church was consecrated 9 March 1968.
45. Brown, "Saint as Exemplar," 10.
46. Ibid., 8, quoting Shils, *Center and Periphery*, 4.
47. Brown, "Saint as Exemplar," 9.
48. Ibid., 9, 10.
49. Ibid., 6.
50. Dair Banāt Maryam, *Tāsūnī Ḥannah*, 18. Concerning the Virgin, the literal translation would be: "where did the Virgin go?"
51. Dair Banāt Maryam, *Tāsūnī Ḥannah*, and Hedī Banūb, *Namūdhaj*.
52. Dair Banāt Maryam, *Tāsūnī Ḥannah*, 4.
53. Ward, *The Sayings*, 6.
54. See Iris Habib al-Masri, *The Story of Father Pishoy Kamel*.
55. Ibid., 11.
56. Ibid., 17.

57. Kanīsat al-Shahīd al-ʿAẓīm Mār Girgis bi-Sbūrting, *Min ʾAthmār al-Firdaus.*
58. Banāt Maryam, *Al-Batūlīya wa al-Khidma,* 12.

CHAPTER 9: VISITORS

1. Also see Martin, "Sur Quelques Comportements," 135–38.
2. Asʿad, *Al-Rahbana,* 80, 81.
3. Dair al-Amīr Tādrus, *Al-Umm Marthā,* 84.
4. Watterson's *Coptic Egypt* is an example of this phenomenon. On page 98 one reads that "the three major convents for Coptic nuns are all in Cairo." Chaillot, "Vies Moniales Coptes," 61, leaves out the convent of St. Amīr Tādrus in Ḥārat al-Rūm.
5. Statistics on this subject are not available. Convents themselves only estimate how many people come and do not divide them into categories based on age and gender. For reliable numbers, further research is needed.
6. Interview with this visitor, June 1988.
7. People do wonder why Irīnī relates her contacts with the saints to the nuns. The current explanation is that St. Abū Saifein has commissioned her to do so in order to spread the fame of the saints and their miracles.
8. Patriarch Shenouda III first expressed his opinion in an interview on 12 May 1989. The question was whether Umminā Irīnī would be allowed to start a convent outside Egypt. His answer was abrupt and sharp: "She has nothing to say in these matters since they are decided by the Holy Synod."
9. The information about the Catholic orders is courtesy of Christiaan van Nispen tot Sevenaar, S.J.
10. van Doorn, "The Importance," 101–18.
11. For the church see Rugh, *Family,* 215.
12. In the Bible, see Matt 8:28–34 (Jesus meets two demoniacs at the country of the Gadarenes) and Mark 5:1–10 (Jesus casts out the spirit called Legion). From the Qurʿān, Sura 72:11 is often mentioned to indicate that people can be possessed by either of two types of spirits—righteous or contrary.
13. For a brief note on famous exorcists in Coptic history see Meinardus, *Christian Egypt,* 225, 226.
14. Also see Rugh, *Family,* 213.
15. Psalm 91 is the main psalm for exorcism. It is about God's protection. Viaud quotes the following as other powerful psalms: 7, 22, 31, 36, 50, 81, 92, and 123 (against evil spirits); 127, 7, 27, 40, and 46 (against spells). Viaud, *Magie,* 71.
16. Leeder, *Modern Sons,* 288, describes an exorcism where the possessed person cried out "Take away this fire. Oh! I am going to burn!," when the saintly Bishop Abraam stepped into the room.
17. Rugh, *Family,* 215, describes the Muslims who go to Christian exorcists.
18. Ibid., 214. Also Nelson, "Self, Spirit Possession," 194–209.
19. Mervat Hatem, "Demise," 231–51.

20. A study devoted to adolescent Coptic girls is B. Thorbjørnsrūd, "Messias Piker"; *MC* 16 (June 1989) devoted a special issue to Coptic women, and *Die Frau bei den Kopten und Moslems in Ägypten* [Frau Hamra] compares the position of Muslim and Coptic women in Egypt. Studies produced by the Copts themselves are more concerned with family life than with women as such: Al-Anbā Ghrīghūriyūs, *Al-Dars al-Awwal lil-Marʾa.* Father Mattā al-Meskīn's *Women* mainly deals with the Bible and the writings of the early fathers. Here and there the work refers to the position of women in the contemporary church.

21. To my knowledge, few publications about this topic are available. See [Hamra], *Die Frau bei den Kopten und Moslems;* and Rugh, *Family,* has a chapter on religious differences.

22. Mattā al-Meskīn, *Women,* 21.

23. Hoffman-Ladd, "Polemics," 36.

24. R. Hassan, "An Islamic Perspective," 109. Mervat Hatem, "Demise," expresses the same argument (referring to the Association of Young Muslim Women): "men were the leaders of both the women and the children within and outside the family. The complementary Islamic ideal does not allow women to aspire to leadership roles even in their own separate domain" (247).

25. Rugh, *Family,* 209.

26. Ibid., 210.

27. Ibid., 263; also see Hatem, "Demise," 236, 239.

28. Rugh, *Family,* 262–71.

29. Haddad, "The Revivalist Literature," 12. Also Hoffman-Ladd, "Polemics," 27, 28.

30. Mattā al-Meskīn, *Women,* 14, 15.

31. Sullivan, *Women,* 153–58.

32. For the Muslims, see Sullivan, *Women,* 156–58 and Haddad, "Revivalist Literature," 12.

33. Hatem, "Demise," 246.

34. For example, see Fernea and Fernea, "Variation," 385–401. Also Hoffman-Ladd, "Vitality, Leadership."

35. Hoffman-Ladd, "Polemics," 43.

36. Mattā al-Meskīn, *Women,* 37.

37. During a public Bible study (15 January 1992) in St. Mark's cathedral, Cairo, one of the questions posed was why Coptic women wear scarfs. Patriarch Shenouda III answered that this was not obligatory but a convention suggested by the Muslim environment.

38. The interview took place 1 October 1992.

39. Douglas, *Purity and Danger,* 157, 158.

40. Ibid., 158.

CONCLUSION

1. Ortner, *High Religion,* 12. The reference is taken from Ortner's discussion around the theory of "practice."

2. Carter, *The Copts,* 303.

3. For more about the current conflicts within the Coptic power structures, see El-Khawaga, "Le Renouveau Copte Actuel," 115–34.

4. Dair al-Amīr Tādrus, *Al-Umm Marthā,* 23, 24.

5. Ibid., 39.

6. Interview with Amani Barsoum, December 1990.

7. Wallace, "Revitalization Movements," 422.

8. Cragg, *The Arab Christian,* 280.

9. The expression "heaven is yet open" was coined by Bishop Gregorios (for higher education and research) and refers to the Coptic beliefs in saints, miracles, and supernatural events, in contrast to Protestantism where these beliefs are generally lacking. The expression is regularly used by Maurice Martin, S.J., in his articles about the Copts. The whole expression is: "For you Protestants, heaven is closed, but for us Copts it is still open."

GLOSSARY

āb al-sharika: the father of the communal way of life; title used to refer to St. Pachomius.
abbā: spiritual father.
abūnā: "our father"; title used to address a priest or monk.
afkār: "thoughts" sent by the devil in order to disturb a monastic.
agbīya: book with the Coptic prayers of the hours.
aghābī: 1. blessed bread, 2. a meal of hospitality, or "love meal," served in a monastery, convent, or after the Eucharist.
ᶜahd al-irtibāṭ: vow of affiliation or promise of commitment for novices in the active community.
ākh: "brother," title used for a male novice.
al-ᶜamal: "work," one of the seven promises taken by members of the active community.
amīn al-deir: prior in a monks' monastery.
al-amīna al-ᶜāma: title of the mother superior of the active community for nuns in Beni Suef.
ammā: spiritual mother.
anbā: title of a bishop or a male saint.
baraka: power of blessing.
bawwāb (fem. **bawwāba**): the monk or nun who is the doorkeeper at a monastery or convent.
biṭāla: accidie; idleness or inactivity due to listlessness, depression without any specific reason.
dair/deir: monastery; convent.
ᶜeid: 1. feast to commemorate an event related to a saint. For example, the translation of relics or the consecration of a church. 2. The last day of a *maulid*.
al-eskīm: great skema or megaloskema; the highest degree that can be bestowed on a contemplative monastic.
al-fardīya al-mutarābiṭa: the idiorythmic system.
gallābīya: long caftanlike garment of Egyptian workers. In the monastic context, the floor-length black garment worn by an initiated monk or nun.
haikal: the altar or sanctuary in a Coptic Church.

ḥanūṭ: a mix of fragrant spices that is rubbed on the container with the relics of a saint.
ḥizām: alternative word for *minṭaqa;* the monastic belt.
hudūʾ: quietness (one of the monastic virtues).
hūs: one of the four parts of the Psalmodia.
ʿiffa: chastity (one of the monastic promises).
iḥtimāl: endurance (one of the monastic virtues).
ʿimma: bishop's head cover worn over the qalansūwa.
irshād rūḥī: spiritual guidance.
khādim (fem. **khādima**): man or woman who works in church service.
khalwa: spiritual retreat.
khedma: service, especially service for God.
kilma manfiʿa: "a word" or "saying" from a nun or monk.
lābis al-eskīm: monk or nun who has received the degree of the great skema.
majmaʿ al-deir (majmaʿ al-ruhbān, majmaʿ al-rāhibāt): the assembly of monks or nuns without the novices.
mandīl: part of the contemplative nun's dress; a triangular scarf that is fastened at the back of the head.
maqarr: house of a monastery in the city (mostly Cairo) where monks can stay and where the monastery's business can be attended to.
mār/māri: "saint"; for example, Māri Girgis.
maulid: feast to commemorate the death or birth of a saint.
meṭānīyā: metanoia; prostrations to express repentence.
minṭaqa: monastic belt a monk or nun wears after consecration.
muʿallim: Coptic liturgical singer.
makers (fem. **mukarrasa**): consecrated or dedicated man (or woman).
murshid rūhī: spiritual guide.
nusk: asceticism.
qalansūwa (qalaswa): monastic cowl for monks and nuns.
qallāya (qillāya): cell of a monk or nun.
qiddīs (fem. **qiddīsa**): saint.
quddās: Eucharist.
qurbān: communion bread or blessed bread.
rāhib (fem. **rāhiba**) (pl. **ruhbān, rāhibāt**): monk or nun (contemplative and active).
raʾīs (fem. **raʾīsa) al-deir**: abbot or abbess.
rubeitah: prior or a monastery.
ṣalāt: prayer.
al-ṣalāt al-dāʾima or **ṣalāt yasūʿ**: the "Jesus Prayer"; continuous prayer.
al-ṣaum: fasting.
shafāfīya: Godly enlightenment, transparency, clairvoyance.
shahīd (pl. **shuhadāʾ**): martyr.
shammās (fem. **shammāsa**): deacon, deaconess.
al-sharika: monastic community.
synaksār: Synaxarium, Synaxarion; the official list of Coptic saints.

ṭāʿa: obedience (one of the monastic promises).

taḥlīl: the absolution after confession.

taḥt al-ikhtibār: "under examination"; precandidacy period in a convent or monastery.

tajarrud: poverty (one of the monastic vows).

ṭālibāt rahbana: female novices.

taltīma: part of a contemplative nun's dress; a square scarf that is folded into the shape of a wimple.

tamauf: (Coptic) title used to address a contemplative nun, in some convents used to address the mother superior only.

tamgīd: song of glorification especially written for a saint.

ṭaqs al-risāma or **ṭaqs al-siyāma**: initiation rite for monastics and consecration rite into one of the seven ecclesiastical orders.

ṭarḥa: veil of a contemplative nun.

tāsūnī: (Coptic) "my sister," title used to address an active nun or a consecrated woman.

tasbiḥa: daily office of the Psalmodia.

umminā: "our mother," title used to address a contemplative nun.

umminā raʾīsa, al-umm al-raʾīsa: the mother superior of a convent.

wakīla: an nun who is assistant to the mother superior.

waqf (pl. **awqāf**): religious endowment.

zaʿabūṭ: a garment made of coarse wool a nun wears during her initiation ceremony and that will serve as her shroud.

zaffa: a festive procession made after a nun's initiation and on the feast of a saint.

zār: special (Muslim) gathering to appease an evil spirit.

ziyāra: "visit," used for a visit to a monastic place, the shrine of a saint, or the regular visit of a monastic candidate to the monastery or convent.

SELECTED BIBLIOGRAPHY

ARABIC LITERATURE

ʿAbd al-Masīḥ Ṣalīb Al-Masʿūdī al-Baramūsī. *Kitāb Tuḥfa al-Sāʾilīn* (The Book of the Gem for Seekers). Cairo: Maṭbaʿat al-Shams, 1932.

Abnāʾ al Bābā Kīrillus al-Sādis, ed. and publ. *Muʿjizāt al-Bābā Kīrillus al-Sādis* (The Miracles of Pope Kyrillos VI). 12 vols. Cairo, [1973]–1988.

———. *Sīrat-al-Qiddīs Yusṭus al-Anṭūnī* (The Life of the St. Yustus from the Monastery of St. Antony). Cairo, 1988.

Amīn, H. *Dirāsāt fī Tārīkh al-Rahbānīya wa al-Dairīya al-Maṣrīya* (Studies about the History of Monasticism and the Egyptian Monasteries). Cairo, 1963.

Andrāʾus ʿAbd al-Masīḥ, *Kitāb. Ḥayāt al-Rahbana al-Ḥaqīqīya* (A Book: The True Monastic Life). 2d ed. Cairo, 1985.

Anṭūnīyūs, Girgis. *Sīrat al-Qiddīsa al-Shahīda al-Mukhtāra Mārīnā* (Life of the Chosen Martyr St. Marina). 3d ed. Cairo, 1988.

Asʿad, Y. *Al-Rahbana* (Monasticism). Cairo: Dār al-ʿĀlam al-ʿArabī, 1988.

Banāt Maryam, Rāhibāt Dair. *Al-Batūlīya wa al-Khidma* (Celibacy and Service). Beni Suef: Muṭrānīya Beni Suef, 1971.

———. "Qānūn Dair Rāhibāt Banāt Maryam lil-Aqbāṭ al-Urthūdhuks." Beni Suef, n.d.

———. *Al-Tarahhub wa al-Khidma: Nidāʾ al-ʿAṣr* (Monasticism and Service: The Call of the Time). Cairo: Al-Anbā Ruways, 1988.

———. *Tāsūnī Ḥannah, al-Salām al-ʿAmīq wa al-Imān al-Basīṭ* (Sister Hannah, Profound Peace and Simple Faith). Beni Suef: Banāt Maryam, 1991.

Baramūs, Dair, ed. and publ. *ʿInd al-Ghurūb* (At Sunset). N.d.

———. *Ujarāʾ we Abnāʾ* (Servants and Sons). N.d.

———. *Fuqarāʾ wa lakin* (Poor, but . . .). N.d.

———. *Ḥaithumā tadhabu!* (Wherever you go). N.d.

Dair Rāhibāt al-Amīr Tādrus bi Ḥārat al-Rūm. *Al-Amīr Tādrus al-Shuṭbī* (St. Tadrus al Shuṭbī). Cairo: Dair al-Amīr Tādrus, 1989.

———. *Al-Umm Marthā* (Mother Martha). Cairo: Vīktūr Kīrillus, 1989.

———. *Dhikrā al-ʾArbaʿīn lil-Umm al-Qiddīsa Marthā Raʾisa al-Dair* (Pamphlet on the Occasion of the Commemoration of the 40th Day [after the Passing Away] of the Saint Martha, Superior of the Convent). Cairo, 1989.

_____. *The Monastery of Saint Theodore for Nuns*. Cairo: Dair al-Amīr Tādrus, n.d. In Arabic and English.

Dair al-Shahīd Abī Saifein lil-Rāhibāt bi Maṣr al-Qadīma, ed. *Allāh Yuḥibbunī. Muʿjizāt al-Shahīd al-ʿAẓīm Fīlubātīr Marqūrīyūs Abī Saifein* (God Loves Me. The Miracles of the Great Martyr Philopater Mercurius "Abu Saifein"). Cairo: Al-Shirka al-ʿArabīya lil-ṭibāʿa, 1990.

_____. *Sīrat-al-Shahīd al-ʿAẓīm Fīlubātīr Marqūrīyūs "Abī Saifein" wa Tārīkh Dairihi* (The Biography of the Great Martyr Philopater Mercurius "Abī Saifein" and the History of His Convent). Cairo: Al-Anbā Ruways, 1989.

Ghrīghūriyūs, Al-Anbā. *Al-Dars al-Awwal lil-Marʾa* (The First Lesson for Women). Cairo: Usqufīyat al-Dirāsāt al-ʿUlīya al-Lāhūtīya, 1983.

Ḥabashī, Labīb, and Zakī Tāwuḍrūs. *Fī Ṣaḥrāʾ al-ʿArab wa al-ʾAdyira al-Sharqīya* (In the Desert of the Bedouins and the Eastern Monasteries). Cairo: Egyptian Archeological Society, 1939.

Ḥabīb, Raʾūf. *Tārīkh al-Rahbana wa al-Dairiah fī Maṣr wa Āthārhumā al-Insānīya ʿala al-ʿĀlam* (The History of Monasticism and Monasteries in Egypt and their Human Influences on the World). Cairo: Maktabat al-Maḥabba, 1978.

Haydī Bānūb. *Namūdhaj al-Riʿāyat al-Fitāh. Tāsūnī Ḥannah kamā ʿariftuhā* (A Model of Caring for Young Girls. How I Knew Sister Hannah). Beni Suef: Muṭrānīya Beni Suef, n.d.

Jamʿīya Mār Mīnā, ed. and publ. *Al-Rahbana al-Qibṭīya* (Coptic Monasticism). Cairo, 1984.

Kanīsat al-Shahīd al-ʿAẓīm Mār Girgis bi-Sbūrting, ed. and publ. *Min ʾAthmār al-Firdaus. Aqwāl Maʾthūra lil-Qummuṣ Bishoy Kāmil* (From the Fruits of Paradise. Sayings Transmitted from the Priest Bishoy Kāmil). 5 vols. Alexandria: Sporting, n.d.

Maksīmūs al-Anṭūnī. *Al-Qiddīs al-Rāhib Yusṭus al-Anṭūnī* (The Saintly Monk Yusṭus al-Anṭūnī). Cairo: Dar al-ʿĀlam al-ʿArabī lil-ṭibāʿa, 1987.

Maktabat al-Maḥabba, ed. and publ. *Kitāb al-Synaksār* (Synaxarion). 2 vols. Cairo, 1978–79.

Matāʾus, Anbā. *Rūḥānīyet al-Tasbiḥa* (The Spirituality of the Psalmodia). Beni Suef: Muṭrānīya Beni Suef, 1980.

_____. *Sumūw al-Rahbana* (The Excellence of Monasticism). 2d ed. Cairo: Vīktūr Kīrillus, 1990.

Mattā al-Meskīn, Abūnā. *Ḥayāt al-Ṣalāt al-Urthūdhuksīya* (Orthodox Prayer Life). 5th ed. Monastery of St. Macarius, 1986.

_____. *Al-Khidma* (Service). 4th ed. Monastery of St. Macarius, 1982.

_____. *Al-Rahbana al-Qibṭīya fī ʿaṣr al-Qiddīs Anbā Maqār* (Coptic Monasticism in the Time of St. Macarius). 2d ed. Monastery of St. Macarius, 1984.

Muṭrānīya Beni Suef, ed. and publ. *Bustān al-Ruhbān* (The Garden of the Monks). Beni Suef, 1968.

Naṣr, Amir. *Al-Qiddīsa Dimyānah al-Shahīda* (St. Dimyanah the Martyr). Cairo, 1983.

Naṣr Rizq, N. *Al-Qiddīsa Anāsīmūn, al-Qiddīsa Efrūsīnā, al-Āb Babnūda, al-Qiddīsa Tha'ūghnusṭa* (St. Anasimun, St. Efrusina, Father Babnuda, St. Theognosta). Cairo: Maktaba Mār Girgis, 1983.

Samū'īl, Al-Anbā. *Al-Khidma wa al-ʿAmal al-Jamāʿī* (Godly Service and Community Work). Cairo: Maktabat al-Tarbīyat al-Kanasīya bī al-Gīzah, 1987.

Samū'īl al-Suryānī and Badīʿ Ḥābīb. *Al-Dalīl ilā al-Kanā'is wa al-Adyīra al-Qadīma min al-Gizah ilā Aswān* (Guide to the Ancient Churches and Monasteries from Gizah to Aswan). Cairo: Al-Anbā Ruways, n.d.

Shenouda III, Patriarch. *Ta'ammulāt fī Ḥayāt al-Qiddīs Anṭūnīyūs* (Meditations on the Life of St. Anthony). 4th ed. Cairo: Al-Anbā Ruways, 1985.

Dair al-Suryān, ed. and publ. *Al-Zayy al-Rahbānī* (The Monastic Attire). 1990.

Viaud, G. *Qawānīn al-Anbā Bākhūmīyūs—Āb al-Sharika* (The Rules of Anbā Pachomius, Father of the Community). Cairo, 1972.

Zakhāriyās al-Anṭūni. *Taqs Sīyāmat al-Ruhbān wa Ḥayāt Kibār Qāda al-Rahbana* (The Consecration Rite of the Monks and the Life of the Great Leaders of Monasticism). Cairo: Al-Anbā Ruways, 1988.

WORKS IN OTHER LANGUAGES

Abu-Lughod, L. *Veiled Sentiments: Honor and Poetry in a Bedouin Society.* Berkeley: University of California Press, 1988.

———. "Zones of Theory in the Anthropology of the Arab world." *Annual Review of Anthropology* 18 (1989): 267–306.

Albrecht, R. *Das Leben der heiligen Makrina auf dem Hintergrund der Thekla-Traditionen.* Gottingen: Vandenhoeck and Ruprecht, 1986.

Alt, E. *Ägyptischen Kopten—eine einsame Minderheit.* Saarbrücken: Fort Lauerdale, 1980.

Assad, M. "Prägung der koptischen Identität." In *Koptisches Christentum,* edited by P. Verghese, 87–117. Stuttgart: Evangelisches Verlagswerk, 1973.

Assfalg, J., and P. Kruger. *Kleines Wörterbuch des Christlichen Orients.* Wiesbaden: Otto Harrassowitz, 1975.

Athanasius, Bishop Anba. "Die Koptische Kirche Heute." In *Koptisches Christentum,* edited by P. Verghese, 74–87. Stuttgart: Evangelisches Verlagswerk, 1973.

Atiya, A. S., ed. *The Coptic Encyclopedia.* 8 vols. New York: Macmillan, 1991.

———. *A History of Eastern Christianity.* Millwood, N.Y.: Kraus Reprint, 1980.

———. "Kibṭ." In *Encyclopaedia of Islam.* 6 vols. Leiden: E. J. Brill, 1960–.

Atiya, N. *Khul-Khaal.* 7th ed. Cairo: A. U. C. Press, 1989.

Baumeister, T. *Martyr Invictus.* Munster: Verlag Regensberg, 1972.

Becher, J., ed. *Women, Religion and Sexuality: Studies on the Impact of the Religious Teachings on Women.* Geneva: W. C. C. Publications, 1990.

Beck, L., and N. Keddie, eds. *Women in the Muslim World.* Cambridge, Mass.: Harvard University Press, 1978.

Bell, D. N., trans. and ed. *Besa: The Life of Shenoute.* Kalamazoo: Cistercian Publications, 1983.

Bernard, O. B., and J. Bouvet, trans. *Vie de Sainte Synclétique* and Bouvet, *Discours de Salut à une Vierge.* Abbaye Notre Dame de la Bellefontaine, Maine: 1972.

Betts, R. B. *Christians in the Arab East: A Political Study.* Athens: Lycabettus Press, 1975.

Biegman, N. H., trans. *Egypt: Moulids, Saints, Sufis.* London: Kegan Paul International, 1990.

Bourguet, P. du. *Les Coptes.* Paris: PUF, 1988.

Bowie, L. "The Copts, the Wafd and Religious Issues in Egyptian Politics." *The Muslim World* 67 (1977): 106–26.

Brown, P. "The Rise and Function of the Holy Man in Late Antiquity." *Journal of Roman Studies* 61 (1971): 80–101.

_____. "The Saint as Exemplar in Late Antiquity." *Representations* 1, no. 2 (1983): 1–25.

Burmester, O. H. E. *The Egyptian or Coptic Church: A Detailed Description of her Liturgical Services and the Rites and Ceremonies Observed in the Administration of her Sacraments.* Cairo: Société d'Archéologie Copte, 1967.

Butler, A. J. *The Ancient Coptic Churches of Egypt.* 2 vols. Oxford: Clarendon Press, 1884.

_____. *The Arab Conquest of Egypt and the Last Thirty Years of the Roman Dominion.* 2d ed. Edited by P. M. Fraser. Oxford: Clarendon Press, 1978.

Byrne, L., ed. *Traditions of Spiritual Guidance.* Collegeville, Minn.: Liturgical Press, 1990.

Campbell-Jones, S. *In Habit.* London: E. Faber, 1979.

Cannuyer, C. *Les Coptes.* Turnhout: Brepol, Collections de Fils d'Abraham, 1990.

C.A.P.M.A.S. (Central Agency for Public Mobilisation and Statistics). *General Census of Population and Housing, all Egypt.* Cairo, 1986.

Carter, B. L. *The Copts in Egyptian Politics, 1918–1952.* London: Croom Helm, 1986.

_____. "On Spreading the Gospel to Egyptians Sitting in Darkness: The Political Problem of Missionaries in Egypt in the 1930s." *Middle Eastern Studies* 20 (1984): 18–36.

Castelli, E. A. "Pseudo-Athanasius, The Life and Activity of the Holy and Blessed Teacher Syncletica." In *Ascetic Behavior in Greco-Roman Antiquity: A Sourcebook,* edited by V. L. Wimbush, 265–312. Minneapolis: Fortress Press, 1990.

Cauwenberg, P. van. *Étude sur Les Moines d'Égypte depuis le Concile de Chalcédoine (451) jusqu'à l'Invasion Arabe (640).* 2d ed. Milan: Cisalpino-Goliardica, 1973.

CEDEJ, ed. *Modernisation et Mobilisation Sociale: Égypte-Brésil 1970–1989.* Cairo, 1991.

CEMAM Reports 1: Tensions in Middle East Society. Beirut, 1973.

Chaillot, C. "Comment vit la Femme Copte aujourd'hui au sein de l'Église." *Le Monde Copte* 16 (1989): 66–74.

———. "Vies de Moniales Coptes." *Le Monde Copte* 16 (1989): 60–65.

Chitham, E. J. *The Coptic Community in Egypt: Spatial and Social Change.* Durham: Centre for Middle Eastern and Islamic Studies, 1986.

Chitty, D. J. *The Desert a City.* New York: St. Vladimir's Seminary Press, 1966.

Cody, A. "Scetis." In *The Coptic Encyclopedia,* edited by A. S. Atiya. 8 vols. New York: Macmillan, 1991.

Coleman, J. A., S.J. "Conclusion: After Sainthood?" In *Saints and Virtues,* edited by H. J. Stratton. Berkeley: University of California Press, 1987.

Coquin, C. "Canon Law." In *The Coptic Encyclopedia,* edited by A. S. Atiya. 8 vols. New York: Macmillan, 1991.

———. *Les Édifices Chrétiens du Vieux-Caire.* Vol. 1. Cairo: Institut Français d'Archéologie Orientale, 1974.

Coquin, C., and M. Martin. "Dayr Sitt Dimyānah." In *The Coptic Encyclopedia,* edited by A. S. Atiya. 8 vols. New York: Macmillan, 1991.

Courbage, Y., and P. Fargues. *Chrétiens et Juifs dans l'Islam Arabe et Turc.* Paris: Fayard, 1992.

Cragg, K. *The Arab Christian: A History in the Middle East.* Louisville: Westminster/John Knox Press, 1991.

De Lacy O'Leary. *The Saints of Egypt in the Coptic Calendar.* Published for the Church Historical Society. London, New York, 1937. Reprint, Amsterdam: Philo Press, 1974.

Delahaye, H. *Les Légendes Grecques des Saints Militaires.* Paris: Librairie Alphonse Picard et Fils, 1909.

Donlon, S. E. "Hierarchy." In *The New Catholic Encyclopedia.* 17 vols. New York: McGraw-Hill, 1967.

Doorn, N. van. "The Importance of Greeting the Saints; the Appreciation of Coptic Art by Laymen and Clergy." In *Coptic Art and Culture,* edited by H. Hondelink, 101–19. Cairo: Shouhdy Publishing House, 1990.

———. "Les Vierges Sages: le Monachisme Féminin Contemporain dans l'Église Copte Orthodoxe." *Le Monde Copte* 21–22 (April 1993): 115–32.

Douglas, M. *Purity and Danger: An Analysis of Concepts of Pollution and Taboo.* 2d ed. New York: Frederick A. Praeger, 1969.

Droogers, A. F. *Macht in Zin: Een Drieluik van Braziliaanse Religieuze Verbeelding.* Amsterdam: VU uitgeverij, 1990.

Droogers, A., G. Huizer, and H. Siebers, eds. *Popular Power in Latin American Religions.* Saarbrucken: Verlag Breitenbach Publishers, 1991.

Dumont, L. *Homo Hierarchicus.* Paris: Editions Gallimard, 1966.

Eickelman, D. I. *The Middle East: An Anthropological Approach.* Englewood Cliffs, N.J.: Prentice Hall, 1981.

Encyclopaedia of Islam. 6 vols. Leiden: E. J. Brill, 1960–.

Esbroeck, M. van. "Hilaria, St." In *The Coptic Encyclopedia,* edited by A. S. Atiya. 8 vols. New York: Macmillan, 1991.

Esposito, J. L. "Trailblazers of the Islamic Resurgence." In *The Contemporary Islamic Revival,* edited by Y. Y. Haddad, J. O. Voll, and J. L. Esposito. New York: Greenwood Press, 1991.

Farag Rofail Farag. *Sociological and Moral Studies in the Field of Coptic Monasticism.* Leiden: E. J. Brill, 1964.

Farah, N. R. *Religious Strife in Egypt: Crisis and Ideological Conflict in the Seventies.* New York: Gordon and Breach, 1986.

Fernea, E. W., ed. *Women and the Family in the Middle East.* Austin: University of Texas Press, 1985.

Fernea, W. F., and R. A. Fernea. "Variations in Religious Observance among Islamic Women." In *Scholars, Saints and Sufis: Muslim Religious Institutions since 1500,* edited by N. R. Keddie, 385–401. Berkeley: University of California Press, 1978.

Frend, W. H. C. "Monophysitism." In *The Coptic Encyclopedia,* edited by A. S. Atiya. 8 vols. New York: Macmillan, 1991.

_____. *The Rise of the Monophysite Movement.* 2d ed. Cambridge: Cambridge University Press, 1979.

Geertz, C. *Local Knowledge: Further Essays in Interpretive Anthropology.* New York: Basic Books, 1983.

Giamberardini, G. P. "Le Suore Copte Ortodosse." *La Voce del Nilo* (Cairo) 14, no. 12 (1955): 3–23.

Gibb, H. A. R., and J. H. Kramers. *Shorter Encyclopaedia of Islam.* Leiden: E. J. Brill, 1974.

Goehring, J. E. "New Frontiers in Pachomian Studies." In *The Roots of Egyptian Christianity,* edited by B. A. Pearson and J. E. Goehring, 236–58. Philadelphia: Fortress Press, 1986.

Goodspeed, E. J. *A History of Early Christian Literature.* 1942. Revised and enlarged by Robert M. Grant. Chicago: University of Chicago Press, 1966.

Gregg, R. C., trans. and ed. *Athanasius: The Life of Antony and the Letter to Marcellinus.* New York: Paulist Press, 1980.

Gribomont, J. "Monasticism." In *The New Catholic Encyclopedia.* 17 vols. New York: McGraw-Hill, 1967.

Griggs, C. W. *Early Egyptian Christianity From Its Origins To 451 C.E.* Leiden: E.J. Brill, 1990.

Gruber, M. F. X. "Sacrifice in the Desert: An Ethnography of the Coptic Monastery." Ph.D. diss., State University of New York, 1990.

Guillaumont, A. *Aux Origines du Monachisme Chrétien.* Maine: Abbaye de Bellefontaine, 1979.

_____. "The Jesus Prayer among the Monks of Egypt." *Eastern Churches Review* 6 (1974): 66–71.

_____. "Kellia," "Nitria." In *The Coptic Encyclopedia,* edited by A. S. Atiya. 8 vols. New York: Macmillan, 1991.

Habib Al-Masri, I. "A Historical Survey of the Convents for Women in Egypt up to the Present Day." *Bulletin de la Société d'Archéologie Copte* 14 (1958): 63–111.

———. *The Story of Father Pishoy Kamel.* Alexandria: St. George Church Sporting, 1989.

———. *The Story of the Copts.* Cairo: M.E.C.C., 1978.

Haddad, Y. Y. "The Revivalist Literature and the Literature on Revival: An Introduction." In *The Contemporary Islamic Revival,* edited by Y. Y. Haddad, J. O. Voll, and J. L. Esposito. New York: Greenwood Press, 1991.

Haddad, Y. Y., J. O. Voll, and J. L. Esposito, eds. *The Contemporary Islamic Revival: A Critical Survey and Bibliography.* New York: Greenwood Press, 1991.

Hall, E. T. *The Silent Language.* Garden City, N.Y.: Doubleday, 1959.

[Hamra, Frau]. *Die Frau bei den Kopten und Moslems in Ägypten.* Christentum und Islam 13. Wiesbaden: Breklumer Verlag, 1982.

Hassan, R. "An Islamic Perspective." In *Women, Religion and Sexuality,* edited by J. Becher, 93–128. Geneva: W. C. C. Publications, 1990.

Hatem, M. F. "Economic and Political Liberation in Egypt and the Demise of State Feminism." *International Journal of Middle East Studies* 24 (1992): 231–51.

Hausherr, I. *Spiritual Direction in the Early Christian East.* 1955. Translated by A. P. Gythiel. Kalamazoo: Cistercian Publications, 1990.

Heijer, J. den. "The History of the Patriarchs of Alexandria." In *The Coptic Encyclopedia,* edited by A. S. Atiya. 8 vols. New York: Macmillan, 1991.

———. "Kerk en Staat in de Geschiedschrijving van de Kopten." *Sharqiyyāt* 3/3 (1991): 29-51.

Heikal, M. *Autumn of Fury.* London: Andre Deutsch, 1983.

Hinds, M., and Badawi, El-Said. *A Dictionary of Egyptian Arabic.* Beirut: Librairie du Liban, 1986.

Hoffman Ladd, V. J. "Polemics on the Modesty and Segregation of Women in Contemporary Egypt." *International Journal of Middle East Studies* 19 (1987): 23–50.

———. "Vitality, Leadership and Gender: Observations on Sufism in modern Egypt." Paper presented at the annual meeting of the American Academy of Religion, Chicago, Ill., 1988.

Hondelink, H., ed. *Coptic Art and Culture.* Cairo: Shouhdy Publishing House, 1990.

Ibrahim, F. N., trans. and ed. *Das Wunderbare Wirken des koptischen Papstes Kyrillos VI (1902–1971).* Kröffelbach: Koptisch-Orthodoxes Zentrum, St. Antonius Kloster, 1990.

Innemee, K. C. *Ecclesiastical Vestments in Nubia and the Christian Near East.* Leiden: E. J. Brill, 1992.

Jansen, W. *Women Without Men.* Leiden: E.J. Brill, 1987.

Johnson, D. W., S.J. "Anti-Chalcedonian Polemics in Coptic Texts, 451–641." In *The Roots of Egyptian Christianity,* edited by B. A. Pearson and J. E. Goehring, 216–34. Philadelphia: Fortress Press, 1986.

Joseph, S., and B. L. K. Pillsbury, eds. *Muslim-Christian Conflicts: Economic, Political and Social Origins.* Boulder: Westview Press, 1978.

Jullien, R. P. M. *L'Égypte, Souvenirs Bibliques et Chrétiens*. Lille: Société Saint-Augustin, 1889.

Keddie, N. R., ed. *Scholars Saints, and Sufis: Muslim Religious Institutions since 1500*. 2d ed. Berkeley: University of California Press, 1978.

El-Khawaga, D. "Le Renouveau Copte Actuel: Raisons D'Emergence et Modes de Fonctionnement." In *Modernisation et Mobilisation Sociale: Égypte-Brésil 1970–1989*, edited by CEDEJ, 115–134. Dossier du CEDEJ. Cairo, 1991.

Kolta, K. S. *Christentum im Land der Pharaonen*. Munchen: Verlag J. Pfeiffer, 1985.

Kopp, C. *Glaube und Sakramente der Koptischen Kirche*. Rome: Pont. Institutum Orientalium Studiorum, 1932.

Laanatza, Mejdell, Stagh, Vogt, and Wiestrand, eds. *Egypt under Pressure*. Uppsala: Institute for African Studies, 1986.

Lane, E. W. *Manners and Customs of the Modern Egyptians*. 1836. Reprint, London: East-West Publications, 1981.

Leeder, S. H. *Modern Sons of the Pharaohs*. 1919. Reprint, New York: Arno Press, 1973.

Leipoldt, J. *Schenute von Atripe*. Leipzig: Hinrichs, 1903.

Lessa, W., and A. E. Vogt. *Reader in Comparative Religion: An Anthropological Approach*. New York: Harper and Row, 1979.

Lohkamp, N. "Consecration." In *The New Catholic Encyclopedia*. 17 vols. New York: McGraw-Hill, 1967.

Lucot, A. *Palladius Histoire Lausiaque*. Paris: Librairie Alphonse Picard et Fils, 1912.

Lutfi al-Sayyid Marsot, A. "The Revolutionary Gentlewomen in Egypt." In *Women in the Muslim World*, edited by L. Beck and N. Keddie, 261–77. Cambridge, Mass.: Harvard University Press, 1978.

Malaty, T. Y. *Anba Abraam: The Friend of the Poor. 1829–1914*. Alexandria: St. George Coptic Orthodox Church Sporting, 1982.

_____. *St. Mary in the Orthodox Concept*. St. Fitzroy: Palaprint, 1978.

Martin, M. "The Coptic-Muslim Conflict in Egypt: Modernization of Society and Religious Renovation." In *CEMAM Reports 1: Tensions in the Middle East*, 31–51. Beirut, 1973.

_____. "Sur Quelques Comportements Symboliques Specifiques de la Communauté Copte." In *Modernisation et Mobilisation Sociale: Égypte-Brésil 1970–1989*, edited by CEDEJ, 135–38. Dossier du CEDEJ. Cairo, 1991.

Matta El-Meskin, Father. *Women: Their Rights and Obligations in Social and Religious Life in the Early Church*. The Monastery of St. Macarius, 1984.

Meeus, P. "Herleving Kopties Monnikendom." *Benediktijns Tijdschrift* 40 (1979): 2–21.

Megally, F. "Synod, Holy." In *The Coptic Encyclopedia*, edited by A. S. Atiya. 8 vols. New York: Macmillan, 1991.

Meinardus, O. F. A. *Christian Egypt, Ancient and Modern*. Cairo: A. U. C. Press, 1977.

———. *Christian Egypt, Faith and Life.* Cairo: A. U. C. Press, 1970.

———. "The Hermits of the Wādī al-Rayān." *Studia Orientalia Christiana Collectanea* (Cairo) 11 (1966): 294–317.

———. *The Holy Family in Egypt.* 2d ed. Cairo: A. U. C. Press, 1987.

———. *Monks and Monasteries of the Egyptian Deserts.* Cairo: A. U. C. Press, 1961. Rev. ed., Cairo: A. U. C. Press, 1989.

———. "Zeitgenössische Gottesnarren in den Wüsten Ägyptens." *Ostkirchliche Studien* 36 (1987): 301–10.

———. "Zur Renaissance der koptischen Nonnenklöster." *Ostkirchliche Studien* 37 (1988): 123–30.

Meyer, R. T., trans. *Palladius: The Lausiac History.* London: Longmans, Green and Co., 1965.

Nelson, C. "Self, Spirit Possession and World View: an Illustration from Egypt." *The International Journal of Social Psychiatry* 17, no. 3 (1971): 194–209.

———. "Stress, Religious Experience and Mental Health." *Catalyst* 6 (1972): 48–57.

The New Catholic Encyclopedia. 17 vols. New York: McGraw-Hill, 1967.

The New Oxford Annotated Bible with the Apocrypha. Revised Standard Version. Edited by Herbert G. May and Bruce M. Metzger. New York: Oxford University Press, 1977.

Ortner, S. B. *High Religion: A Cultural and Political History of Sherpa Buddhism.* Princeton: Princeton University Press, 1989.

Pearson, B. A. "Earliest Christianity in Egypt: Some Observations." In *The Roots of Egyptian Christianity,* edited by B. A. Pearson and J. E. Goehring, 132–59. Philadelphia: Fortress Press, 1986.

Pearson, B. A., and J. E. Goehring, eds. *The Roots of Egyptian Christianity.* Philadelphia: Fortress Press, 1986.

Pennington, J. D. "The Copts in Modern Egypt." *Middle Eastern Studies* 18, no. 2 (1982): 158–79.

Pezin, M. "Les 'Mères' du Désert." *Le Monde Copte* 16 (1989): 57–59.

Philipp, T. "Feminism and Nationalist Politics in Egypt." In *Women in the Muslim World,* edited by L. Beck and N. Keddie, 277–95. Cambridge, Mass.: Harvard University Press, 1978.

Quecke, H. *Untersuchungen Zum Koptischen Stundengebet.* Louvain: Université Catholique, Institut Orientaliste, 1970.

Regnault, L. *La Vie Quotidienne des Pères du Désert en Égypte au IVe Siècle.* Mesnil-sur-l'Estrée: Hachette, 1990.

Roncaglia, M. *Histoire de l'Église Copte.* 2d ed. 2 vols. Beirut: Librairie St. Paul, 1985–87.

———. "Nestorians and Copts." In *The Coptic Encyclopedia,* edited by A. S. Atiya. 8 vols. New York: Macmillan, 1991.

Rousseau, P. *Ascetics, Authority and the Church: In the Age of Jerome and Cassian.* Oxford: Oxford University Press, 1978.

———. *Pachomius: The Making of a Community in Fourth-Century Egypt.* Berkeley: University of California Press, 1985.

Rouselle, A. *Porneia: De la Maîtrise du Corps à la Privation Sensorielle IIe-IVe Siècles de l'ère Chrétienne*. Paris: P. U. F., 1983.

Rubenson, S. *The Letters of St. Antony: Origenist Theology, Monastic Tradition and the Making of a Saint*. Lund: Lund University Press, 1990.

Rugh, A. *Family in Contemporary Egypt*. Cairo: A. U. C. Press, 1985.

Russell, N., trans. *The Lives of the Desert Fathers: Historia Monachorum in Aegypto*. Kalamazoo: Cistercian Publications, 1981.

Sa, R. de. "De Situatie van de Kopten in Egypte." *Het Christelijke Oosten* 35 (1983): 23–35.

Al-Saadawi, N. *The Hidden Face of Eve: Women in the Arab World*. 3d ed. London: Zed Press, 1982.

Samaan, M., and S. Sukkary. "The Copts and Muslims of Egypt." In *Muslim-Christian Conflicts: Economic, Political and Social Origins*, edited by S. Joseph and B. Pillsbury, 128–55. Boulder: Westview Press, 1978.

Samir, Khalil S. "Arabic Sources for Early Egyptian Christianity." In *The Roots of Egyptian Christianity*, edited by B. A. Pearson and J. E. Goehring, 82–97. Philadelphia: Fortress Press, 1986.

Schlicht, A. "Muslime und Kopten im Heutigen Agypten." *Orient* 2 (1983): 226–34.

Seikaly, S. "Coptic Communal Reform: 1860–1914." *Middle Eastern Studies* 6 (1970): 247–75.

Shenouda III, His Holiness Patriarch. Interview by C. Chaillot. Cairo, 21 February 1988.

Sidarouss, F. "Église Copte et Monde Moderne." Ph.D. diss., Beirut University, 1978.

_____. "Église Copte et Monde Moderne." *Proche Orient Chrétien* 30 (1980).

Stegeman, B. "Contrasting Philosophies of Monasticism in the Modern Coptic Church." *Bulletin de la Société d'Archéologie Copte* 20 (1971): 159–65.

_____. "Several Philosophies of Service within the Modern Coptic Church." *Bulletin de la Société d'Archéologie Copte* 23 (1981): 33–42.

Stratton, H. J., ed. *Saints and Virtues*. Berkeley: University of California Press, 1987.

Strothmann, R. *Die Koptische Kirche in der Neuzeit*. 1930. Reprint, Nendeln, Liechtenstein: Kraus Reprint, 1966.

Sullivan, E. L. *Women in Egyptian Public Life*. 2d ed. Cairo: A. U. C. Press, 1989.

Taft, R. *The Liturgy of the Hours in East and West*. Collegeville, Minn.: Liturgical Press, 1986.

Thorbjørnsrud, B. "Messias Piker. En Analyse an Koptisk-Ortodoks Revitalisering i et Identitets Perspektiv." Ph.D. diss., University of Oslo, 1989.

Timbie, J. "The State of Research on the Career of Shenoute of Atripe." In *The Roots of Egyptian Christianity*, edited by B. A. Pearson and J. E. Goehring, 258–70. Philadelphia: Fortress Press, 1986.

Turner, V. *The Ritual Process: Structure and Anti-Structure.* Ithaca: Cornell University Press, 1977.

Vansleb, J. M. *The Present State of Egypt: Or, a New Relation of a Late Voyage into that Kingdom. Performed in the Years 1672 and 1673.* 1678. Reprint, Westmead: Gregg International Publisher Ltd., 1972.

Veilleux, A., trans. *Pachomian Koinonia.* Vol. 1, *The Life of Saint Pachomius and his Disciples.* Kalamazoo: Cistercian Publications, 1980.

———. *Pachomian Koinonia.* Vol. 2, *Pachomian Chronicles and Rules.* Kalamazoo: Cistercian Publications, 1981.

———. "Pachomius, Saint." In *The Coptic Encyclopedia,* edited by A. S. Atiya, 8 vols. New York: Macmillan, 1991.

Verghese, P., ed. *Koptisches Christentum: Die Orthodoxen Kirchen Ägyptens und Äthiopiens.* Stuttgart: Evangelisches Verlagswerk, 1973.

Viaud, G. *Les Coptes d'Égypte: La Liturgy des Coptes d'Égypte.* Paris: Librairie d'Amérique et d'Orient, 1978.

———. *Magie et Coutumes Populaires chez les Coptes d'Égypte.* Sisteron: Éditions Présence, 1978.

———. *Les Pélerinages Coptes en Égypte (D'après les notes du Qommes Jacob Muyser).* Cairo: Bibliothèque d'études Coptes, 1979.

Vliet, J. van der. "Demons in Early Coptic Monasticism, Image and Reality." In *Coptic Art and Culture,* edited by H. Hondelink, 135–55. Cairo: Shouhdy Publishing House, 1990.

Vogt, K. "Religious Revival and Political Mobilisation: Development of the Coptic Community in Egypt." In *Egypt under Pressure,* edited by Laanatza, Mejdell, Stagh, Vogt, and Wiestrand, 44–62. Uppsala: Institute for African Studies, 1986.

Waddell, H. *The Desert Fathers.* 1936. Reprint, London: Constable and Co. Ltd., 1987.

Wakin, E. *A Lonely Minority: The Modern Story of Egypt's Copts.* New York: W. Morrow and Co., 1963.

Wallace, A. F. C. "Revitalization Movements." In *Reader in Comparative Religion: An Anthropological Approach,* edited by W. Lessa and A. E. Vogt. New York: Harper and Row, 1979.

Ward, B., trans. *Harlots of the Desert: A Study of Repentance in Early Monastic Sources.* Oxford: Mowbray and Co., 1987.

———. *The Sayings of the Desert Fathers: The Alphabetical Collection.* Kalamazoo: Cistercian Publications, 1975.

———. "Spiritual Direction in the Desert Fathers." In *Traditions of Spiritual Guidance,* edited by L. Byrne, 3–16. Collegeville, Minn.: Liturgical Press, 1990.

Waterbury, J. *The Egypt of Nasser and Sadat.* Princeton: Princeton University Press, 1984.

Watterson, B. *Coptic Egypt.* Edinburgh: Scottish Academic Press, 1988.

Weber, M. *The Theory of Social and Economic Organization.* Translated by A. M. Henderson and Talcott Parsons. New York: Oxford University Press, 1947.

Wehr, H. *A Dictionary of Modern Written Arabic*. Edited by J. Milton Cowan. Wiesbaden: Otto Harrassowitz, 1966.

Weinstein, D., and R. M. Bell. *Saints and Society: The Two Worlds of Western Christendom, 1000–1700*. Chicago: University of Chicago Press, 1982.

Wimbush, V. L., ed. *Ascetic Behavior in Greco-Roman Antiquity: A Sourcebook*. Studies in Antiquity and Christianity. Minneapolis: Fortress Press, 1990.

Wissa, M. "Ḥārit Zuweylah." In *The Coptic Encyclopedia*, edited by A. S. Atiya. 8 vols. New York: Macmillan, 1991.

Wissa Wassef, C. *Pratiques Rituelles et Alimentaires des Coptes*. Cairo: Institut Français d'Archéologie Orientale, 1971.

PERIODICALS

Annual Review of Anthropology
Benediktijns Tijdschrift
Bulletin de la Société d'Archéologie Copte (*BSCA*)
Catalyst
Het Christelijke Oosten
Eastern Churches Review
International Journal of Middle East Studies (*IJMES*)
International Journal of Social Psychiatry
Journal of Roman Studies
Magallet Al-Kirāza (Preaching the Gospel)
St. Mark Monthly Review
Middle Eastern Studies
Le Monde Copte (*MC*)
The Muslim World
Orient
Ostkirchliche Studien (*OK*)
Proche Orient Chrétien
Representations
Sharqiyyāt
Studia Orientalia Christiana Collectanea
La Voce Del Nilo

INDEX